The Urban Life and Urban Landscapes Series

The Failure of Planning

Permitting Sprawl in San Diego Suburbs, 1970–1999

RICHARD HOGAN

The Ohio State University Press

Columbus

Library of Congress Cataloging-in-Publication Data

Hogan, Richard.
  The failure of planning : permitting sprawl in San Diego suburbs,
1970–1999 / Richard Hogan.
      p. cm. — (The urban life and urban landscape series)
Includes bibliographical references and index.
  ISBN 0-8142-0923-8 (hardcover : alk. paper) — ISBN 0-8142-5104-8
(pbk. : alk. paper) — ISBN 0-8142-9005-1 (CD-ROM)
  1. City planning—California—San Diego. 2. Suburbs—California—San
Diego. 3. San Diego (Calif.)—Economic policy. 4. San Diego
(Calif.)—Social policy. I. Title. II. Series.
  HT168.S197 H64 2003
  307.1'216'0979498—dc21
                                         2002151548

Cover design by Dan O'Dair
Printed by Thomson-Shore Inc.

9 8 7 6 5 4 3 2 1

Contents

List of Figures

Preface

All research is personal to the extent that the researcher is personally involved in the effort to understand the subject. The nature of personal involvement is, however, quite different when the researcher lives and works in the time and place that is the subject of the research. Quite apart from my relationship with the principle characters, particularly my old and dear friend Tom (not his real name), this story has roots in my experiences, including some that predate my life in San Diego.

My family moved to San Diego in 1962 after one painful year in Glendale, Arizona, which is a suburb of Phoenix. Why we ever moved from suburban New York in the first place is an interesting question—one that I've only recently begun to consider in the context of land-use politics. In the 1950s my parents had a house built in Nanuet, in Rockland County, New York, at the end of a dead-end street that was bordered by woods on two sides. At the time, as I recall, Nanuet was a small suburban community with a modest downtown shopping district that included a bakery, a hotel-restaurant, and a funeral parlor, and with a large Catholic church and its associated elementary and high schools. When I went to elementary school from 1957 to 1961, I would walk to school through the woods behind our house, which were my favorite place to walk and play.

Soon, however, the woods were sold to a developer, who constructed the Grandway Shopping Center, the first of what became a string of strip malls (all on the site of the woods). They chopped down the trees, "paved paradise and put up a parking lot," and thus produced a serious drainage problem.[1] During the construction there was a major rainstorm, and the builder sent bulldozers in to drain the lot. Legend has it that my mother ran out in the storm to stop the bulldozers, which were about to dump the mud in our backyard, draining the runoff from their lot into our basement. Our basement did flood; I remember because my bedroom was in the basement. I also remember my father's anger about what he alleged to be the secretive nature of the zoning board decision to allow the woods to be developed. He claimed that so much neighborhood opposition was expressed at the first meeting that the board rescheduled discussion of the issue for a future meeting. He said that public notice for that second meeting was posted on the backs of signs, where it was hidden from view. At this secret meeting the project was approved.

Aside from this encounter with the conspiracy of the growth-machine coalition, my parents also had some experience with the real estate market.[2] After the woods were destroyed, they sold their home in Nanuet in 1961 in a buyer's market and bought a house in Glendale, Arizona, more or less sight unseen. The development where it was located was already filled with foreclosed and abandoned houses. They sold that house less than a year later, so they lost money on it too. Then, sadder but wiser, they moved to San Diego in 1962. They refused to buy the suburban East County ranch house that we lived in from 1962 to 1970, and in the course of the 1970s they moved to another house, then to a duplex, and finally to an apartment. They remained tenants rather than risking their meager resources on the purchase of another house.

All three of the suburban houses that my parents owned or rented between 1950 and 1970 (in Nanuet, New York; Glendale, Arizona; and Spring Valley, California) must have increased tremendously in value—or, more accurately, in market price—during the speculative frenzy of 1972–1989.[3] It's likely that their old neighbors were among the Reaganites of the 1980s who, after making a killing on local real estate, joined the thousands who said, "I got mine. To hell with the rest of you."[4]

My father's father allegedly used to flaunt his shanty Irish sensibilities by saying, "First they leave the party; then they leave the faith." My father also seemed to be proud of the fact that he was still a wage, or salary, worker when he retired. (He taught special education classes.) He used to talk of his poor judgment in the early days after World War II, when he turned down the opportunity to buy IBM stock. He didn't live long enough to appreciate how poorly he had fared in his real estate investments. Obviously he lacked the extended timeline and deep pockets that characterize enlightened developers.[5]

Beginning in 1969 I left San Diego repeatedly—to find my roots in New York in 1969, to attend college in Santa Cruz in 1972, and to attend graduate school in Michigan in 1975. Before this last, apparently permanent, exodus, I had periodically delivered furniture in San Diego County (in 1969, 1971–1972, and 1974–1975). I remember riding around in the furniture van and watching the new housing developments grow along the new freeways. Our customers were primarily people who lived in tract homes and bought plastic furniture. Sometimes they asked us to haul away old furniture that was made of solid wood and, although scarred, would have been likely to last long after their new furniture was discarded. We thought these new suburbanites were crazy and their new suburbs pathological.

We used to refer to the Highway 15 (previously Highways 163 and 395) Inland Corridor as the "Cancer of L.A." It made an end run around Camp Pendleton and crept into San Diego County from the northeast. Maybe my father was right in refusing to buy San Diego real estate. At least it made it easier to leave and never to return. It is clear to me that San Diego is not good for me now, if it ever was. For one thing, after my years of delivering everything from pizza to refrigerators to Cadillacs, I hate to drive and would rather walk or ride my bike to work.

During my last extended stay in San Diego, however, in the winter of 1992, I was fortunate. With the support of Purdue University and its Department of Sociology and Anthropology, I spent my sabbatical leave in San Diego with a computer and a salary. Andy Scull and his colleagues in the Department of Sociology at the University of California, San Diego (UCSD) were most hospitable, although I'm sure they didn't believe me when I told them that I did not want to apply for a job in San Diego—"been there; done that." They provided me with access to the UCSD library, where Larry Cruse, in the government documents section, was especially helpful. On the days I spent in the library Larry was always there, helping me find information and frequently alerting me to interesting material that I otherwise never would have found.

Most of my time was spent in the field, in my friend Tom's office or at public and private meetings with city, county, and state officials; consultants; concerned citizens; and environmentalists. Because I need to protect the anonymity of my contacts, I can't thank all of the people who were so kind. They welcomed me into their world and took the time to talk with me one-on-one, in a focus group discussion, and in open-ended interviews that I conducted before leaving the field. Still others provided valuable information in telephone or personal interviews conducted in 1994, when I returned briefly during the American Sociological Association meetings in Los Angeles. Tom and some of my other contacts have continued to provide feedback on my published and unpublished papers. Some old respondents and a few new ones provided valuable information by phone or e-mail in my 1999 update interviews. I'm hoping they will see the impact of their critical comments on the final product even if they still disagree with my interpretation.

Among my colleagues, Tom Rudel offered an early and penetrating critique of my first efforts. Max Pfeffer offered a more sympathetic, less critical perspective. Their critical comments and published works were most useful in helping me frame my argument.[6] Here at Purdue, Carolyn and Bob Perrucci continue to offer support and assistance. Bob read some of the early work and has offered valuable advice in the proper response to editorial overtures. Carolyn has encouraged me to finish this project even though she is personally interested in another project on which we are collaborating. Harvey Marshall and particularly John Stahura have provided me with guidance in the general area of urban and suburban studies. Jack Spencer offered helpful advice on participant observation and on using focus group discussions. My colleague Harry Potter, a sociologist at Purdue, has provided a role model of the academic environmentalist and has offered a variety of insights and observations, along with some useful references that have shaped my perspective on environmentalism in a variety of ways.

Undergraduate and graduate students and American studies faculty have suffered through my theory courses and various versions of American studies and sociology courses that were invariably related to local politics, social movements, and social change even if the course title did not suggest so. They deserve special credit for their perseverance in attempting to understand that which was still not terribly clear in my mind at the time that it was presented. Harry Targ and Vernon Williams (in American studies) and Angel Rodriquez and Matt Bahr (in sociology) have been particularly long-suffering in this regard.

Beyond this, old friends who are also colleagues or former teachers, including Steve Rytina and Bob Leibman, Chuck Tilly and Bill Gamson, continued to believe that I was (or eventually would be) doing something worthwhile even as little evidence was forthcoming. To this list I should add Bob May and Dave Caputo, both of whom encouraged me to complete this project. Their support, along with that of my wife and daughter, with or despite the efforts of other family and friends, has sustained me through these trying times that will undoubtedly later be remembered as the good old days.

To this list of other supporters I should add some of my old and new personal friends and acquaintances, including aging hippies and rednecks, musicians, drunks, drug addicts, and other fellow travelers from past and present lives in California, Colorado, Michigan, New Jersey, and Indiana. More sober, focused, and sustained judgment was offered by the series editor, Zane Miller, whose indefatigable efforts have resulted in a much more readable manuscript and a more grounded and well-considered argument. Heather Lee Miller, the acquisitions editor at Ohio State University Press, and two anonymous reviewers also offered valuable suggestions. Tony Faiola produced the illustrations. All such assistance and support notwithstanding, I take full responsibility for what appears in the following chapters and for my successes and failures in my effort to get the facts straight and to maintain my sanity and my optimism regarding human nature, if not the human condition. To Chuck Tilly I credit the following inspirational message:

> Pity deskman's feeble scheming;
> None of them gets paid for dreaming.

Hopefully in my efforts to understand the real world I will never lose the ability to dream of a world that does not really exist and might not ever be achieved. Special thanks is offered to all those who help me keep that dream, or faith.

Rich Hogan
West Lafayette, Indiana
December 2001

The Argument

Beginning around 1974 big-picture—or comprehensive regional—planning developed as the latest progressive response to the problem of uncontrolled growth. This progressive vision was limited to reforming or making changes in the existing U.S. economic and political system; representative government, private ownership of the means of production, and market-based commerce would be maintained. Consequently, big-picture planning failed to resolve the fundamental problems of community interest, legal rationality, and popular participation.

The Implications

First, even in the most progressive planning departments, such as those in the San Diego County suburbs, the quest for community is still plagued by the conflict between the contradictory inclusionary and exclusionary interests that are associated with the alienation of life and work in contemporary U.S. communities. Second, the legal constraints of general plans, coastal plans, and other regulatory programs continue to provide the benefits of overregulation that result from the irrationality of legal rationality, or bureaucracy, and accrue to large-scale corporate development companies. Finally, even in the incredible public relations efforts associated with general plan updates and environmental impact reports, the irony of popular participation is that it creates new problems calling for creative solutions that only large-scale corporate developers have the ability and interest to provide. Progressive grassroots movements for tax reform, environmental regulation, and growth control simply increase local government's dependence on the private sector.

What Can Be Done

Progressive political movements and professional organizations face a strategic choice in deciding which interests are to be accommodated, repressed, and tolerated. The traditional, early-twentieth-century progressive path has been to accommodate liberal and conservative challengers, repress radicals, and tolerate reactionaries, particularly racists. Perhaps it is time to consider some radical alternatives to the progressive vision of the practical reform of republican government and capitalist economy. In the spirit of the French students of 1968, perhaps we should be "practical" and demand the impossible.[1] In the spirit of the international student revolt of that year, and in memory of John Lennon, perhaps we should try to imagine a better world.

Personal and Professional:
The Format of What Follows

More than anything else that I've written, this book represents the contradictions between the possibilities and limits of my professional training and analysis versus my personal experience and opinion. There are, in fact, two voices—the voice of subjective experience and the voice of objective evidence. As yet I've not discovered a synthesis. The scientific, objective, disciplinary approach cannot be abandoned in postmodern whimsy without doing irreparable damage to the historically situated subject. At the same time, the claim to objective "facticity" must be tempered with the admission that all sources are biased. Even the official numbers provided by local, regional, and federal authorities—for example, of new housing units approved—evidence discrepancies despite the fact that they all are supposedly based on the same local government records.

In the chapters that follow I use the historian's convention of endnotes, as opposed to the parenthetical references that sociologists use, to cite sources. As a concession to the social scientists, however, complete citations for the referenced works are also offered in the bibliography so the reader need not search the endnotes for the citations. The nonacademic reader will probably prefer to ignore the endnotes entirely. Some contain only bibliographic references. Others offer long discussions of purely academic points that would bore all but the most interested specialists.

Some of the references are intentionally vague in order to maintain the anonymity of my contacts. After facing many moral and professional dilemmas related to this issue, I have chosen not to identify any of my contacts. If the cities were identified by name, the identities of the actors would be a matter of public record. As it is, the insiders can guess which city is which and who is being quoted. I will not confirm or deny such speculation. Instead, I have invented names for the cities and the major characters that appear in the following chapters. To aid the reader I have listed these names in the "Cast of Characters."

Despite my commitment to professional rules of research—I have triangulated sources wherever possible, using independent accounts, preferably two or more, to confirm information obtained from a single source—I have tried to offer a narrative that is accessible to the general reader. Because I have already published an empirical analysis of the speculative frenzy of 1972—1989 and of growth control and affordable housing in five San Diego suburbs, tables and numbers are not presented here.[1] Here and elsewhere I am torn between my professional commitment to provide documentary evidence and my personal inclination to simply assert what should be obvious to anyone familiar with San Diego County in the years from 1962 to 1992.

The problem of providing too much or too little theory is equally vexing. The rather pedantic presentation of political attitudes (in the notes to chapter 1) and the recurring discussion of political interests and organizations are offered to ground the theoretical and practical debates in clearly defined terms. The radical critique of the progressive coalition of liberals and conservatives is rooted in a dialectical and materialist theoretical perspective that is much more effective when applied in critical analysis of existing institutions than when applied to the practical problem of suggesting alternative institutions or predicting the future. This will undoubtedly frustrate both academic and general readers.

The critique of big-picture planning provides the structure upon which the stories of affordable housing, growth control, and the conservation of habitat and species are constructed. Underlying that critique is a theoretical perspective that is developed to some extent in the endnotes, and is more generally developing as I continue to read, write, teach, and talk about these issues. The fact that the perspective is emergent and that the ultimate solution is likewise emergent is likely to frustrate reformers and to fuel the standard conservative and liberal challenge, "So what country would you rather live in?" (My friend Tom should be credited here for clearly articulating this challenge in personal correspondence).

Toward a response to this question, a sketch of utopia is offered in the closing pages, but only as an illustration of the possibilities. My job is not planning but analysis. The critical analysis of existing institutions and the revolutionary process of mobilizing political challengers and facilitating political change should not be confused with the efforts of hucksters or preachers who attempt to motivate customers or followers with the promise of the money-back guarantee or the eternal reward. We begin with real premises, grounded in material life, in building a critique of what is now in the hope that others who have learned from our mistakes and successes will carry the struggle farther than we might presently anticipate. The promise of, or faith in, a better way must ultimately be rooted in a critique of what exists and a commitment to struggle for something better without the expectation of short-term success, let alone eternal reward.

Cast of Characters

Five Suburban Cities: Belleville, Castleton, Farmington, Paradise, Waterton

Ben: property owner, Citizen Advisory Group, Habitat Protection Plan, Castleton

Bill: Local CEO (Vice President), The Patterson Company (Master Plan Developer), Castleton

Bob: Orange County Natural Community Conservation Planning (NCCP) official and planning consultant

Brigadoon: Local Project, The Peterson Company (Master Plan Developer), Castleton

California Bank: foreclosed on Peterson and took over the undeveloped Brigadoon site, Castleton

Camelot: Local Project, The Patterson Company (Master Plan Developer), Castleton

Carl: Audubon Society representative, Citizen Advisory Group, Habitat Protection Plan, Castleton

Chuck: Planning Director, City Planning Department, Castleton

Dan: Statewide Natural Community Conservation Planning (NCCP) official and environmental biologist

Dave: City Planner (Doug's Associate), City Planning Department, Castleton

Dick: Private-Sector Planning Consultant, Castleton (former Castleton City Planning Department employee)

Doug: Program Director, City Planning Department, Castleton

Emma: concerned citizen, Citizen Advisory Group, Habitat Protection Plan, Castleton

Fred: California Fish and Game official

Harold: City Planning Director, Waterton

Harry: Private-Sector Planning Consultant, Castleton (former Castleton City Planning Department employee)

James: California officer, The Nature Conservancy

John: Head of Construction, The Patterson Company (Master Plan Developer), Castleton

Ken: San Diego Association of Governments (SANDAG) official

Larry: Head Engineer, The Patterson Company (Master Plan Developer), Castleton

Len: Castleton Lagoon Foundation official, Citizen Advisory Group, Habitat Protection Plan, Castleton

Lou: Facilitator, Citizen Advisory Group, Habitat Protection Plan, Castleton

Matt: San Diego officer, The Nature Conservancy

Millie: Marketing Director, The Patterson Company (Master Plan Developer), Castleton

Pat: Planning Assistant, The Patterson Company (Master Plan Developer), Castleton

Paul: Assistant Planning Director, City Planning Department, Castleton

Pete: Local CEO, The Peterson Company (Master Plan Developer), Castleton

Ruby: concerned citizen, Citizen Advisory Group, Habitat Protection Plan, Castleton

Stan: Dick's assistant (Private-Sector Planning Consultant, Castleton)

Steve: Southern California Habitat Defenders leader

Tim: Biological Consultant, Citizen Advisory Group, Habitat Protection Plan, Castleton

Tom: Head Planner, The Patterson Company (Master Plan Developer), Castleton (former Castleton City Planning Department employee)

Tommy: City Planning Director, Farmington

Will: Engineer, City Planning Department, Castleton

The Williams sisters: previous owners of Project Camelot, 1979–1987, Castleton

Overview: The Promise of Planning in Twentieth-Century U.S. Cities

> Make no little plans. They have no magic to stir men's blood. Make big plans; aim high in hope and work.
>
> Daniel Burnham and Edward H. Bennett, 1908

With these words Daniel Burnham and his fellow city planners introduced what may be the most famous municipal plan for urban development in the United States—the plan for the City of Chicago.[1] So inspiring were these words that they were offered again four score and seven years later in the videotaped introduction to the Chicago skyline on the tour of the Sears Tower.[2] Thus Chicago continues to celebrate the progressive planning vision that guided the development of this modern urban metropolis, a city that is, in the eyes of its Chamber of Commerce at least, second to none in the nation.[3]

Chicago was a bastion of progressive planning in the first decade of the twentieth century. It was home to the Chicago School of Sociology at the University of Chicago, which also housed such progressive reformers as George Herbert Mead and John Dewey in its Department of Philosophy. The work of activists such as Jane Addams, in the emerging field of social work, complemented the planning vision of Burnham and his colleagues in the emerging field of city planning. Chicago was and is, however, only the best example of a nationwide trend. Virtually all U.S. cities, from Cincinnati to San Diego, followed a similar pattern of planned development, starting with municipal plans circa 1908 and moving on to more comprehensive general plans circa 1968 and to comprehensive regional plans circa 1988. Some cities were more progressive than others, but the general trend has held.[4]

Most striking, however, is the extent to which these plans have failed. New plans appear to be nothing more than old wine in new bottles. In San Diego County the comprehensive regional plans of 1992 and 1999 sound like a rehash of the first such plan (*Temporary Paradise?*), which was commissioned by the San Diego city planning department and then published in 1974. In some sense, all of these plans offer the same progressive vision as the first municipal plan, commissioned by George Marston and the San Diego Chamber of Commerce in 1907 and then published in 1908. It appears that after ninety years of progressive planning we are still trying to implement the municipal plans of 1908.[5]

Neither academics nor practitioners agree among themselves about the extent to which planning has failed, although most seem to recognize that planning has not (or, at least, has not yet) lived up to its promise. The most protracted debates center on why planning has failed and how it might be more successful in the future.[6] As is frequently the case, the academic debate is characterized by contradictory assertions. Some sociologists and planners argue that local government is held hostage by corporate development interests that dictate policy in planning for continued growth at the expense of the quality of life and the interests of local citizens. These critics argue that grassroots citizen movements (e.g., environmentalist, antinuclear, and growth-control movements) are necessary to counteract the undemocratic nature of municipal government.[7] Other critics, including some urban historians, economists, and planners, argue that the problem is too much democracy. The tradition of local autonomy exacerbates political fragmentation and complicates rational planning as an increasing number of suburban cities oppose centralized regional or metropolitan planning. Compounding the problem of political fragmentation associated with the incorporation of suburban cities is the highly unpredictable and increasingly volatile neighborhood opposition to unwanted land uses. The problem of too much democracy, according to these critics, is that local officials tend to court the interests of their concerned citizens. Consequently, grassroots democracy and local autonomy combine to make comprehensive regional planning all but impossible.[8]

This academic debate on barriers to progressive planning is reproduced in somewhat different terms in land-use disputes. Developers and the private-sector planners who work for them frequently argue that local government caters to the interests of "little old ladies with tennis shoes" who routinely complain at city council and planning commission meetings. Environmentalists, on the other hand, frequently contend that local officials turn a deaf ear to constituents but are always prepared to respond to the demands of developers. Public-sector planners often view both developers and constituents as potential barriers to planning solutions, but they also recognize that planning is inherently political. As government officials, or public servants, they must somehow accommodate the demands of developers, neighbors, and environmentalists.

Ironically, the divergent perspectives of developers, environmentalists, and city planning officials have led the three to a similar conclusion: the more enlightened or progressive developers, planners, and environmentalists have followed different paths to the goal of comprehensive regional planning. Developers seek a more predictable future protected from the whims of local officials and their constituents. Environmentalists seek to overcome the limits of local governments that are committed to growth at any cost. Public-sector planners seek a mechanism for accommodating the competing interests of local residents, developers, and environmentalists, as well as the demands of state and federal authorities.

Comprehensive regional planning is opposed only by extremists on the right and left of the political spectrum. On the right, the no-growth and no-tax interests oppose everything that resembles public service, including public schools. On the left, deep ecologists such as members of Earth First! refuse to accept the sanctity of private property and free enterprise. Clearly, opposition from extremists, including tree spikers and tree house squatters,[9] is a barrier to creative planning solutions. The demands of the extremists compound the complexity of the planning problem. This creates additional incentives, however, for enlightened developers, planners, and environmentalists to embrace comprehensive regional planning as an alternative to project-by-project approvals or denials within the constraints of existing law.

The contradictory interests of no-growth suburban residents and pro-growth urban business boosters both confound and compel efforts to move beyond selfish local interests in hopes that disinterested professionals might find a win-win solution, or at least a compromise that all parties will grudgingly accept. The quest to achieve an optimal solution that can be legally negotiated and sanctioned is plagued, however, by the inherent irrationality of formal legal systems. In fact, part of the inspiration for comprehensive regional planning was the apparent failure of the environmental and Great Society legislation of the 1960s and 1970s. In both cases it appears that the ultimate goals of saving endangered species and alleviating poverty were lost in the narrow-minded pursuit of legal remedies, which produced outcomes that no one was prepared to accept.

Nevertheless, enlightened developers, environmentalists, and planners continue to set the limits of their progressive vision within the institutional constraints of republican capitalism.10 They continue to struggle within the confines of an inefficient political system that sells politicians, parties, and policies like soap. Big-picture planning solutions are sold through the dramatic efforts of "land rapers" (developers) and "tree huggers" (environmentalists) who entice the interested public into enacting a soap opera. This drama may be scripted in the form of a citizen advisory committee created by local government in a public relations effort to secure approval for its general plan for future development. Alternatively the drama may be more extemporaneous, as in the public outcry that surrounds the preparation of an Environmental Impact Report (EIR) under the terms of the National Environmental Policy Act (NEPA) of 1970 or the California Environmental Quality Act (CEQA) of that same year. Regardless of the staging, the tragedy of land-use planning as soap opera is that housing units and land-use policy must be sold like soap, creating an endless variety of products that nobody can do without yet no one can afford to buy.

The drama of land-use politics presents elected officials as the arbitrators in the struggle between local people and outside investors. The contradictory public-versus-private or inclusive-versus-exclusive interests are not, however, products of the battles between the people and the developers. These contradictory community interests are rooted in the alienation of life and work, the two aspects of community that are effectively separated and pitted against each other in the course of economic and political development.[11]

The irrationality of bureaucratic government, with written rules and regulations, is similarly inherent in the institutional structure. The system is not necessarily corrupt. The conflict between means and ends is inherent in a system where experts manipulate means to efficiently produce ends that are immune to expert, or even lay, scrutiny. The law, which was developed as a means to an end, becomes an end in itself. Then experts, particularly lawyers, increase their wealth and power by increasing the complexity of the game of law. The increasing complexity of environmental impact and product liability regulations makes it all but impossible for any business but a multinational corporation to provide commodities that are both legally secure and financially profitable. Thus the benefits of overregulation accrue to the large corporate interests that can afford to hire the best lawyers, engineers, and biological and planning consultants and thus beat the public-sector regulators at their own game.[12]

The people have limited impact on these institutional processes unless they are prepared to attack the institutional order.[13] The irony of popular participation is that it aggravates an already complex planning problem, generating crises that only private-sector planners and developers have the interest and ability to solve. Thus, increased popular participation, particularly neighborhood opposition to suburban development and environmentalists' opposition to rural development, has increased local governments' dependence on the developers who are willing to build. Unless grassroots movements challenge the institutional structure of the capitalist economy and representative government, their efforts will cause a continued increase in this dependence on private-sector development. Part of the problem is the self-fulfilling prophecy of the environmentalist and no-growth critique of local government.[14] The critics' tendency to view local government as a servant of the developers undermines their ability to negotiate. Ironically, the ideology of the no-growth movement is feeding the growth machine.

Even if the grassroots movements were prepared to negotiate big-picture planning solutions, they would have to move beyond the economic and political constraints imposed by land-use policy and the market for land. Consider, for example, the prospects of an alternative vision based on two simple principles. First, the earth is not for sale at any price. Second, the physical bounds of life-and-work relations—rather than the superimposed authority of political or economic sovereignty—define the community, which is constituted by the relationships among humans and between humans and their nonhuman natural environment.[15]

Before we may be granted the luxury of imagining a better world, however, we should first come to terms with the world as it is, considering in some detail the promise of big-picture planning in the twentieth-century United States. I will simplify this ambitious task by focusing, in general, on the successes and failures of San Diego in progressing from the municipal plan of 1908 to smart growth in 1999 in general and, in particular, on San Diego County suburbs from 1970 to 1990. San Diego is a particularly appropriate case for analysis, partly because of its peculiarities as a poster child for progressive planning, especially during the Wilson years.[16]

In chapter 1, I focus first on the contradictory interests that plague contemporary U.S. communities, second on the irrationality of bureaucratic government, and third on the irony of popular participation. Chapter 2 provides the historical context of the speculative frenzy of 1970 to 1989, offering a brief history of San Diego and its suburbs. I then focus on Castleton, a particularly

interesting suburb, and Camelot, an upscale, one-thousand-acre planned residential community and resort-hotel project within Castleton. In chapter 3, I
consider the contradictory goals of affordable housing and growth control as
state, regional, and local actors attempted to impose, oppose, or accommodate
these demands between 1967 and 1992. Chapter 4 focuses on the conflict
between development and environmental interests, particularly as these were
contested and accommodated in Natural Community Conservation Planning of
the 1990s, and especially in the battles of the winter and spring of 1992.

In chapter 5, I discuss progress since 1992 and speculate about the uncertain
future, considering not just one, but various paths for planning. Specifically I
consider a retreat to a laissez-faire posture, with little more than local zoning
to interfere with the free market in land use; the possibility of sustaining a
cooperative public-private venture in which enlightened actors bargain for a
division of the earth into green (preserve) and white (development) segments;
and more aggressive state socialist or social democratic regulation closer to
what some scholars have proposed when comparing U.S. with British or other
Western European planning paradigms.[17]

Finally, I consider revolution, focusing on the limits and potential of urban
and suburban social movements for producing significant changes in the politics and economics of land use. Ultimately the challenge for these grassroots
movements is to reunite the alienated components of life and work in defining
our relationship to the earth. In that regard, we might consider the dream of
the Savoy Island Youth Hostel (or People's Pad) in Berkeley in the summer of
1969. Although defeated in city council by Model Cities, among others, and
decidedly lacking in theoretical and practical leadership, these hippies and
street people, perhaps instinctively, planted a garden. This, in the short run,
might be the most promising path toward reclaiming the earth. In any case, it
indicates one way in which life and work may be reunited. While some were
painting the cooperative housing units, others were planting socialism. If anyone had tended the garden, these efforts, if no others, might have borne fruit.[18]

Alternatively I consider the equally radical and decidedly feminist model offered
by Charlotte Perkins Gilman, who proposed a town planned by and for working-
class people as an alternative to the company town.[19] The problem in developing
a model is not technical or even economic. Ultimately, it is a matter of what local
residents are willing to fight for and how much they are willing to sacrifice their
private interests in the pursuit of public goods. Ultimately it is not a planning problem but a mobilization problem. How can we convince community residents to
reclaim and thus reconstruct their communities, investing their lives in working
together to place the public—parks, schools, utilities and services—at the center of
their communities, while constructing their private lives in the peripheral and
interstitial spaces of the community? We cannot plan the new community any
more than we can plan the communist, or workers', state. As we all should realize now that the dust of the Cold War battles has settled, intellectual and military
leaders must join and, ultimately, follow rather than lead. Thus the challenge is not
to articulate a plan but to listen to the voices of the grass roots.

Why San Diego Suburbs?

San Diego is the ideal location for an analysis of big-picture, comprehensive regional planning because it is an excellent example of a conservative yet progressive city with a long history of conflict between urban boosters and rural anti-industrialists. It is, perhaps, peculiar among postautomobile, postindustrial, postmodern cities because it still claims a large and largely undeveloped hinterland, the unincorporated area of San Diego County, as well as a sizable number of big suburbs. While it would qualify as a cutting-edge city on almost all of the typologies that sociologists and urban historians have offered, it is decidedly underanalyzed as a Sunbelt or informational city, perhaps because it lives in the shadow of its postmodern sister Los Angeles and its postsuburban neighbor Orange County.[1]

Historians and social scientists are still reconstructing the history of twentieth-century U.S. cities and suburbs. Thus far much of recent history has been defined in relation to the preceding epoch. We refer to the postindustrial economy, postmodern culture, and postsuburban society. In these terms San Diego has clearly moved from pre- to postindustrial between the development of its first municipal plan in 1908 and the development of its first Natural Community Conservation Plan (NCCP) in 1997. It has moved from "warfare to welfare" between mobilization for World Wars I and II and efforts to sustain Cold War defense spending. It has, perhaps, moved back from welfare to warfare, particularly during the years of the Reagan presidency. Clearly San Diego has changed from an industrial to an informational city. It has not, however, become postsuburban.[2]

San Diego, unlike its postsuburban neighbor Orange County, remains a metropolitan area in which finance and, to a lesser extent, commercial and industrial capital are centered in the urban core, the City of San Diego. Freeways and shopping centers have connected the central city with the northern, eastern, and southern suburbs, and black residents have been relegated to the interstitial spaces, particularly in the southeast San Diego community of Logan Heights and in Oceanside, the area adjacent to the Camp Pendleton Marine Base. Latinos are still concentrated in the southern border towns of Chula Vista, National City, and San Ysidro and in the eastern agricultural regions that became suburban boomtowns between 1970 and 1990.

Where Anglo and Latino suburbs meet is contested terrain, particularly on the southeastern edge of the suburban settlements. Mount Helix and San Miguel anchor the contested terrain between the eastern Anglo suburb of La Mesa and the southern Latino suburb of Chula Vista. Spring Valley, which separates La Mesa from Chula Vista, is divided into an Anglo northern segment (Casa de Oro) and a Latino southern segment (La Presa). The class and ethnic-racial divide adds hostility and the potential for violent clashes to the Spring Valley

Figure 1. San Diego County Cities, 2001
Base map provided by SANDAG

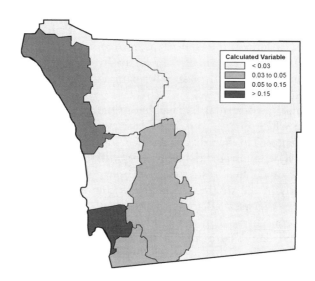

Figure 2. Percent Black Population in 1990
Major Statistical Areas in San Diego County
Base map provided by SANDAG

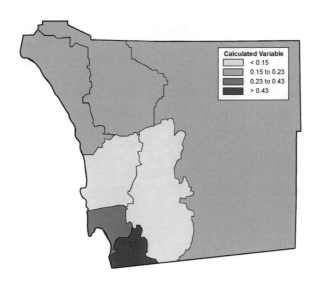

Figure 3. Percent Hispanic Population in 1990
Major Statistical Areas in San Diego County
Base map provided by SANDAG

high school football rivalry, which pits the Anglo Monte Vista Monarchs against the Latino Mount Miguel Matadors. Back in 1969 there were already violent confrontations, but they were limited to fisticuffs. Now that Monte Vista has become integrated (the first black family moved into the high school district in 1968), some of the racial tensions may have been alleviated. It was clear in 1992 that racial tensions were mounting in San Diego, but in contrast to Los Angeles in the wake of the Rodney King verdict, the violence was largely latent.

San Diego remains a segregated city, but in the western U.S. tradition. Blacks are concentrated in the urban core, and Latinos reside primarily on the rural periphery. So the two major minorities are more isolated from each other than they are from Anglo-Saxon whites. Latino segregation is less evident, however, since many middle-class Old Spanish families live in Anglo communities such as Mount Helix. Here it appears that class and race or ethnicity interact in the politics of suburban exclusion, a pattern quite unlike that found in black and white suburbs in the eastern states.[3]

In northern San Diego County the black population is concentrated in the northwest, near Camp Pendleton, and the Latino population is concentrated in the northeast, in Escondido. Once again Latinos appear to be less segregated than blacks. Wealthy Latinos can buy into Anglo neighborhoods. Thus, once again, class and ethnicity interact in the segregation of Latinos but not of blacks.

On balance San Diego suburbs are exclusionary in terms of class, race, and lifestyle. Aside from this exclusionary traditionalism, however, these suburbs are among the most progressive planning centers of the nation. Pete Wilson's election as mayor of San Diego in 1971 and as governor of California in 1990 placed San Diego in general and San Diego's suburbs in particular on the cutting edge of the quiet revolution in land use. Wilson exemplified the new perspective on land, which came to be viewed as both a commodity and a resource, as both a private and public good. In San Diego one can appreciate the contradictory nature of the seemingly arbitrary distinction between public and private, business and government. In the tradition of the navy town, the lines were always blurred. Consequently the San Diego County suburbs constitute ideal cases for analysis of big-picture plans for affordable housing, growth control, environmentalism, and natural and planned community development.[4]

Chapter One
The Prospects for Big-Picture Planning

> Things are changing. The real cost of disjointed, incremental building are [sic] coming home. People find they can no longer buy their way out of deteriorating conditions. Even the well-to-do cannot easily escape air pollution, traffic, and aircraft noise. The energy crisis, the threat of inundation by Los Angeles, have added to the sense of disquiet. . . . *Creative* action is required.
>
> Donald Appleyard and Kevin Lynch, 1974

In these words, spoken in September 1974, consultants hired by the San Diego city planning department challenged the city to begin an unprecedented regional planning effort to save San Diego County from the tragedy of uncontrolled growth.[1] Their nontechnical report, which was designed for widespread public dissemination, is entitled *Temporary Paradise?* This publication marked a sea change in city planning, which became evident in San Diego County planning departments beginning in the mid-1970s and spread rapidly so that by 1990 it had come to characterize progressive planning.[2]

What is Big-Picture Planning?

Temporary Paradise? was not simply a doomsday pronouncement. It was a model of big-picture planning that identified a series of values, or goals, and a detailed set of plans for realizing a clearly articulated vision of how the region should look not simply in the short run, but also in the indefinite future. In this regard the vision was comprehensive and regional, which is essentially the definition of big-picture planning.

The comprehensive nature of big-picture planning can be contrasted with the narrowly defined legal restrictions associated with zoning law, which merely imposes limits on the type of activity and the dimensions of the space within which physical structures might be constructed. Within the limits of approved use, setback, height, width, and bulk restrictions, traditional zoning allows a considerable degree of freedom for a variety of architectural and environmental plans. The city limits use and space under the legal right to maintain public safety and abate public nuisance, but any structure or use that is not explicitly illegal is permitted.[3]

Big-picture planning goes far beyond public safety and nuisance abatement in a proactive effort to develop space for the collective good.

The environmental plan will not simply be a plan for conserving nature, not
just for beautifying the city (although it will include those). It will deal with
six basic values, which might be thought of as the environmental rights of
any citizen: Livability . . . Access . . . Sense of place and time . . .
Responsiveness . . . Pleasure and Sensibility . . . Conservation.[4]

After professing these values as justification for comprehensive regional
planning, having already detailed the nature of good and bad development in a
series of discussions illustrated with photos and drawings, the authors close
with four questions and eight proposals:

1. Will San Diego and Tijuana continue as border towns. . . . Or can they
realize their role as a bicultural metropolis, the center of a great natural
region, safely sustained by the resources of that region?
2. Will San Diego grow as an extension of Los Angeles . . . or can it find a
new form [that] supports the well-being of its people?
3. Will the region make sure that its amenities are available to all its people, regardless of nationality or income?
4. How can this region organize itself to conserve and enhance the quality
of its environment, without losing touch with the local people in whose
name that quality is being conserved?[5]

Clearly the values and the questions suggest a planning vision that is comprehensive in scope and regional in scale. The planning vision transcends political boundaries in an effort to preserve natural communities.[6] Similarly, the
authors' eight proposals, all phrased in the imperative, transcend existing or
legally permitted limits in city planning.

1. Begin now to manage the . . . whole region in a coherent, effective way.
2. Save the shorelines, bays, valleys, and mountains, and restore them to
everyone.
3. Retard suburban development, and change its form.
4. Redirect growth. . . . Restore and enhance [urban neighborhoods]. . . .
Shift public investment to those existing localities and increase the measure
of local control.
5. Reduce dependence on the automobile.
6. Reach across the border. Treat San Diego/Tijuana as one unified metropolis.
7. Flatten the north-south social gradient [social and economic inequality
between the rich north and the poor south], and exploit the east-west
[inland-coastal] natural one.
8. Conserve water, conserve energy, conserve the land.[7]

The vision offered in *Temporary Paradise?* is enticing. Appleyard and Lynch
offer a picture of greenways, parks, and public transportation; the revitaliza-

tion of existing neighborhoods; and a truly diverse public transcending class and even national boundaries and sharing the bounty of this paradise by the sea. This is not a utopian dream, but a big-picture plan for a path toward comprehensive regional planning that might rescue San Diego from the imminent danger of uncontrolled growth. It is tempting to romanticize the vision and bemoan the fact that the city or county failed to pursue it with sufficient vigor. The problem, however, is not that city planners ignored the plan. Quite the contrary, San Diego followed the path of comprehensive regional planning much as it was outlined in *Appleyard and Lynch's report*. The San Diego Association of Governments (SANDAG) was established to facilitate regional planning. Citizen advisory committees were appointed and general-plan revisions undertaken. Metropolitan and even tricounty planning was instituted in an effort to develop more rational plans for habitat conservation. Public transportation projects were developed. When we look back with 20/20 hindsight, however, we discover that, in this case at least, big-picture planning failed to live up to its promises. Thus we might ask what went wrong. Why did the plan fail?

The Limits of Big-Picture Planning

One might argue that the big-picture planning vision offered by Appleyard and Lynch in 1974 was impractical—too radical to be implemented. For example, one section, entitled "The Public Sea," opens by proposing that "The entire sea front would be in public ownership . . . given to the people of the city, of all classes, to live near and to enjoy."[8] Such apparent radicalism notwithstanding, the authors were wedded to local control and democratic principles. Their recommendations followed, in general, the expressed interests of local residents, as best as they could be determined. Even the proposal for public ownership of the sea was not far removed from the spirit of the California Coastal Act, which voters had approved in 1972. If anything, the vision was not radical enough. The planners merely proposed a more progressive plan within the constraints imposed by the U.S. representative government and market economy systems.[9]

The major limitations of this vision are, first, the assumption that we share common values and, second, the assertion that given the value consensus the challenge is to find the most efficient means to achieve our goals. This quest for efficiency is the essence of progressive planning, but it tends to ignore the problem of interests. It ignores the conflicting interests of community residents and denies the interests of professionals. Thus professionals are viewed as objective or disinterested experts who are prepared to achieve our common goals, which are rooted in our shared beliefs and values and institutionalized in our laws. To appreciate this problem we need to move beyond a consideration of beliefs and values and on to a consideration of collective interests.

San Diego, like all U.S. metropolitan areas, is plagued by the contradictory interests of residents and investors. Even in the traditional bilateral negotiations between buyers and sellers of rural property, new uses proposed by the new property owner, the investor, routinely conflict with the interests of residents who defend the established use of land in their neighborhood. In fact, legalism, in the form of zoning law, developed to routinize and rationalize efforts to accommodate these contradictory interests.[10] This generated a second problem, however—the contradiction of legal rationality. The law, which is offered as a means to an end, inevitably becomes an end in itself. Mindless conformity to the letter of the law gets in the way of the ultimate goal—purportedly, to serve the public interest by maintaining safety and abating public nuisance. Instead, legalism serves the interests of lawyers and of those who can afford to hire the best legal services money can buy.[11]

In response to this bias in legal contests and to the more general problem of bureaucratic irrationality, a new form of land-use planning, characterized by trilateral negotiations among the developer, the citizens (residents), and the local government, has been established. Nevertheless, this new form of planning is merely another expression of the same general problem. The contradictory interests of investors and residents remain, along with the irrationality of legalism. This is, perhaps, most apparent in environmental regulations, particularly the National Environmental Policy Act (NEPA) of 1970, which establishes the Environmental Impact Report (EIR) as the legally mandated procedure for mobilizing local opposition to proposed land-use projects.[12]

Big-picture planning expands this new form of procedural justice through ad-hoc citizen advisory committees. First, it expands the scale of planning from municipal to regional. Second, it expands the scope from a narrow focus on project-by-project building permit approvals to the development and approval of comprehensive regional plans. This expansion of the scale and scope of the planning process increases the expense dramatically, virtually guaranteeing that only a Fortune 500 company can afford to invest in development projects. Thus, after one hundred years of planning we thus have professional bilateral negotiation. Instead of neighbors negotiating informal agreements, developers and municipal governments negotiate legally binding master plans. Particularly in the suburban cities that offer the most attractive investment opportunities, these master plans are critical components of the cities' general plans for future development.[13]

Thus planners have created a multimillion-dollar public spectacle: a media event with a cast of thousands, including various professional consultants, grassroots activists, and regional and national social-movement organizations, whose participation is subsidized by the cooperative efforts of big government and big capital. This increased scale of popular participation merely increases local government dependence on private-sector developers that have the interest and ability to pay the cost of big-picture planning.

Planning for Whom?

First and foremost, big-picture planning represents the professional interests of planners.[14] This is clearly articulated in *Temporary Paradise?* and is institutionalized in the San Diego Association of Governments (SANDAG) and in the development of regional affordable housing and habitat conservation plans. Although SANDAG is, at least nominally, a government organization—composed of municipal and county government officials—it is, for all intents and purposes, an organization proposed by planners, staffed by planners, and committed to professional planning.[15]

Similarly, affordable housing and habitat conservation programs were proposed by professional planners in order to promote professional planning.[16] To argue that planners are disinterested professionals is, in this regard, disingenuous. Planners are, in theory at least, motivated not by the selfish interests of residents or invesxtors but, instead, by their professional interests as planners. What this means is that big-picture planning represents two distinct and at times opposing interests: the professional interests of the planner and the class, status, or party interests of the planners' employers or clients.[17]

People who live and work in San Diego County, like their counterparts elsewhere in the United States, are in varying degrees organized in defense of their class and status interests. They support or oppose various components of big-picture plans to the extent that they perceive consequences for their particular interests. For example, developers, builders, and construction workers all expressed their class interests in the March 1993 federal decision to list the California gnatcatcher as a threatened species. Not surprisingly, labor and capital opposed this perceived threat to their class interests. They envisioned the loss in wages and profits that might result from federal protection of the bird, a loss that would prolong the depression in the building industry from which they had been suffering since the collapse of the savings and loan industry in 1989. Consequently, representatives from local unions appeared at the public hearings, held in San Diego in the winter of 1992, in some cases with picket signs proclaiming, "Carpenters Need Homes Too." Members of homeowners associations and environmental organizations also were present to defend their status, or lifestyle, interests.[18]

Three major class or status interests were organized and effectively represented in the struggle to control, or at least influence, land-use politics in San Diego in 1992. These interests clashed on the issues of what went wrong and what should be done to solve the problems caused by uncontrolled growth in San Diego from 1970 to 1990. The no-growth interest that proposed local ordinances in the 1980s and supported a no-growth mayoral candidate in 1992 was primarily an exclusionary suburban lifestyle, or status, interest. As such, the no-growth movement was able to accommodate conservatives and reactionaries who shared a rather pessimistic view of human nature and a decidedly simple explanation of the problem. The no-growth interest tended to argue that the major problem in San Diego is that there were simply too many people. Paradise had been lost to the horde of immigrants.

An opposing, yet decidedly conservative, class interest was that of the private-sector developers, who were generally represented by private-sector planners. From their perspective, uncontrolled growth was not a problem. Instead, it was the government that had ruined San Diego—and California—with rules and regulations. Dick, a private-sector planning consultant, explained, "Our government does one thing well—it fights wars." Another private-sector planner offered a similar critique. "Only government can take an idea whose time has come and wait until its time has passed." While some developers and private-sector planners were more enlightened than others and thus more likely to accept government regulation—or at least zoning—the developers generally opposed constraints on growth and on the free market in land and land use.

A third interest was the environmentalists, a status, or lifestyle, interest that included liberal and radical organizations, such as the Sierra Club and Earth First! respectively. What united the environmentalists was opposition to developer (or private-sector, free-market) control of the earth. The environmentalists, like the no-growth interest, tended to agree that the conspiracy of government and capital—particularly, developers—had ruined San Diego and were threatening the earth more generally. Development was the problem: even though we cannot turn back the clock, we can, at least, protect what remains of the natural habitat. Steve, the leader of Southern California Habitat Defenders, explained this perspective: "No growth would be nice, but it is not realistic. We need to concentrate on saving big pieces. Local government is controlled by special interests. CEQA [the California Environmental Quality Act] is not enough. They always wind up approving projects."

Liberal environmentalists, like Steve, attempt to save the earth within the limits of the existing representative government and market economy systems. Specifically, they attempt to buy land for public use and conservation or to use transfers of development rights, EIR mitigation, and other legal means to prevent development. Radicals advocate, in varying degrees, reclaiming the earth's resources for the people, repudiating private property rights, physically seizing or collectively occupying land, and sabotaging development or other enterprises (e.g., logging) that threaten the earth.

In 1992 the environmentalists (at least the liberal groups, such as the Nature Conservancy and the Sierra Club) attempted to cooperate either with the no-growth conservatives and reactionaries or with the enlightened conservative and liberal big-picture planning and development interests. Thus the more radical environmental interests were left out in the cold while the conservatives had been accommodated in the progressive planning solutions that the radicals and the reactionaries generally opposed. To the extent that the environmentalists made common cause with no-growth interests and opposed big-picture planning, they were flirting with exclusionary reactionary interests whose agenda seemed to contradict that of the inclusionary environmentalist interest, with its commitment to sharing the earth with all living creatures.

In any case, these conflicting interests and coalitions shaped the debate and the search for big-picture planning solutions that would reconcile affordable housing with growth control and habitat conservation with development. Choosing between these perspectives is not the goal in this analysis. It is more important to recognize the social, cultural, political, and economic bases of these interests, since any one of their perspectives is defensible. These partisan positions are rooted in distinctive class and community relations that typify the day-to-day lives of real people who are struggling to understand and to control—or at least to accommodate—the structural constraints that impose barriers to their quest for knowledge and power. These conflicting interests and unstable coalitions are critical in explaining the rise and fall of big-picture plans, including those for affordable housing and growth control and the Natural Community Conservation Plan (NCCP), the latest and most progressive big-picture plan for development and conservation.[19]

Aside from no-growth suburbanites, free-market developers, and environmentalists, there are other interested parties in land-use politics. Local government officials, lawyers, engineers, biologists, geographers, and, of course, city planners, are involved in varying degrees. They were conspicuous in San Diego County in 1992 in the struggle over the listing of the gnatcatcher. The professionals were major actors in the big-picture plan for habitat conservation that was being defended as an alternative or supplement to federal and state protection under the terms of the Endangered Species Act (ESA).

If we reject the assertion that these public-sector officials and private-sector professionals are disinterested, we need to explain the interests of these professionals. To some extent, as indicated in the case of the private-sector planners, these professionals represent the interests of their clients—either their employers or their constituencies. Beyond these often contradictory interests that public- and private-sector professionals represent, however, they also share a professional interest. Specifically with regard to land-use politics, the professionals share an interest in big-picture planning and, more generally, in progress as defined by professionalization. Each profession defends a narrowly defined interest in promoting its particular specialty, but collectively, all of these professions share an interest in professionalization that has been the bedrock of progressive reform since the opening years of the twentieth century.

Among those who promoted progressive reform in the early twentieth century were a variety of organized economic, political, and religious interests, including "a new class of specialists." This new class was, essentially, the professionals, who were particularly interested in progressive reform that promoted the goals of rational planning and professionalism.[20] Clearly city planners were part of that new class, which shared a professional interest in reform that was, and is, qualitatively different from the economic and political interests of capitalists and republicans.

Economic and political interests that supported reform supported it as a means to an end. To the extent that reform would facilitate capital accumulation and sustain republican control of the federal government it provided a means to achieve these goals and thereby served the interests of capitalists and republicans. Unlike capitalists and republicans, professional administrators—and professional planners in particular—supported reform as an end in itself. In a very real sense, city planning was developed and sustained by the Progressive movement. Thus planners have a professional interest in progressive reform, including big-picture planning, not as a means to an end but as an end in itself.

The interests of planners can be viewed as follows: First, planners have a professional interest in planning in general and in big-picture planning in particular, since this seems to be, or is becoming, the dominant planning paradigm. Second, as people who live or work in a particular locality, planners may have personal class, status, or party interests just like anyone else. Third, as consultants or employees for the public sector or private industry, planners represent and promote the class, status, and party interests of their clients or employers.

To the extent that planners are professionals and are committed to their professional approach, we should expect their personal or selfish interests to be secondary to their professional interest in planning and in serving the interests of their clients or employers. In fact, although we might think of the conflict between the personal and the professional as the quintessential moral dilemma, the conflict between the professional interest in big-picture planning and clients' or employers' interests is the major conflict facing the planning profession.

This does not imply, however, that big-picture planning is a radical endeavor foisted upon the public by professional planners in opposition to the mainstream economic and political interests of free-market conservatives and social-welfare liberals. Quite the contrary, big-picture planning is an attempt to accommodate all of the contradictory interests in the community. Specifically, the goal is to accommodate the inclusive interests of developers, who promote new land-use projects, and social welfare advocates, who demand affordable housing. At the same time, however, the plan must accommodate the exclusive interests of no-growth suburbanites, who want to protect their views, open space, and white, middle-class, suburban-family status from the encroachment of urban populations and land uses.[21]

Politically, big-picture planning is rooted in a progressive vision that recognizes the limits of a laissez-faire approach and attempts to balance the promise of technocracy with a commitment to democracy, or representative government. The conservative private-sector planner who defends the free-market interests of the private-sector developer shares with the more liberal public-sector planner and the enlightened developer an interest in big-picture planning. This is the progressive professional interest of all planners. Planning by professional planners is viewed from this perspective as far better than "ballot-box planning" through citizen initiative or piecemeal government regulation in the traditional legal bureaucratic mode. Liberals and conservatives differ primarily on how much public input and government planning versus private-sector input and planning is needed. In this regard, big-picture planning serves the interests of both liberals and conservatives who defend established institutions.[22]

Could Paradise Be Saved in 1974?

Appleyard and Lynch's 1974 report *Temporary Paradise?* challenged San Diego planners with the prospect of a paradise lost, but it also offered comprehensive regional, or big-picture, planning as the path toward salvation. Big-picture planning could accommodate the interests of conservative private-sector developers and liberal public-sector social welfare advocates. It could facilitate the inclusionary interests of big capital and big government, while at the same time accommodating the exclusionary interests of suburbanites. Thus big-picture planning marked the triumph of corporate liberalism and fiscal conservatism. Unfortunately, however, the paradise of 1960s San Diego was lost in the bargain.

Could paradise have been saved? In a word, no. Doing nothing would have resulted in a proliferation of bad development projects, such as early-1970s bedroom communities like Mira Mesa, which were ecologically and politically disastrous, concrete examples of the horrors of uncontrolled growth. Clearly, returning to a laissez-faire bilateralism or continuing with legal planning under zoning law was impossible. Public outrage and environmental awareness and increasing state and federal pressure for, among other things, affordable housing and environmental protection created a siege mentality in city planning departments. The sense of crisis would only increase as first the tax revolt and then the no-growth movement exacerbated the planning problem. A creative solution to an intractable planning problem—something like big-picture planning—was necessary. Within the limits imposed by the legal sanctity of private property and the free trade in land, labor, politicians, and policies, big-picture planning was perhaps the best technical solution possible. It was, however, a first-aid response to a systemic crisis. It stabilized the system by addressing the symptoms without treating the underlying systemic problems.

Big-picture planning as articulated in *Temporary Paradise?* offered an attractive alternative to the status quo. The authors proposed an ecologically viable natural community that was not divided by the artificial boundary of the international border and whose future development was geared toward sustaining and enhancing the quality of life for local inhabitants. As an alternative to the free-market approach of buying and selling the earth and its products in the interest of maximizing the size or stability of a marginal return on investment, big-picture planning is far superior as an ideal toward which we might strive. The problem is that the process of negotiating the big-picture plan merely exacerbates the systemic problems. The contradictory interests of life and work, the irrationality of legal rationality, and the problem of popular participation remain. They are, in fact, manifested on a larger scale as comprehensive regional planning replaces project-by-project zoning decisions.

The failure of planning is, simply stated, the inability to overcome the contradictory components of the free-market approach to political and economic control of the earth and its natural resources. Big-picture planning exacerbates the conflict between contradictory interests associated with public use versus private profit. When the scale and scope of planning is increased, the irrationality of legal rationality and the problem of popular participation are compounded. Accommodating contradictory interests within the confines of bureaucratic legal rationality became yet more difficult with the advent of the big-picture planning of the 1970s and 1980s.

The only way in which these systemic problems might be addressed is through a frontal assault on the system, specifically the free market in the earth and its products. With apologies to past and future dreamers and planners of utopias, there are no "quiet revolutions."[23] Unless we change the basis for land use from profit or investment to sustaining life, we will not overcome the systemic problems. To overcome systemic problems one must change the system.

How, in this new system, usage rights would be protected in the absence of private property and national authority is a premature concern. Given the collective capacity to seize control of the earth, one could imagine how that capacity could be sustained in abeyance to sanction usage rights. The problem of protecting the earth from its people is relatively trivial. The more serious problem is mobilizing people to battle national and international organizations, both monopoly capital and nation-states, that have been accumulating economic and political control of the earth in the self-destructive process of capital accumulation and state building, particularly in the last five centuries.[24] The problem, however, is not technical or even legal. It is essentially political. The only question is whether it is possible to mobilize sufficient popular support to reclaim the earth for the earthlings. In other words, are people ready to fight for a radical alternative to the status quo?

This truly radical vision is not, of course, the vision that was offered to the people of San Diego County in 1974. Instead, *Temporary Paradise?* offered a progressive big-picture planning solution to the problem of uncontrolled growth, or unregulated development, in San Diego County as of 1974. The content of some of the proposals may seem radical today, but the call for public ownership of the sea, for example, represented the interests of the people, or at least the voters, of California. It was the voters who, through the progressive tool of the citizen initiative, had proposed and ultimately adopted the California Coastal Act of 1972 to protect the coast from unregulated development.

In other areas the 1974 report anticipated—or, more accurately, promoted—the development of comprehensive regional planning. The report explicitly called for the organization of a regional planning authority, which is, essentially, what was organized as the San Diego Association of Governments (SANDAG). The report also presaged and promoted the development of comprehensive regional planning in the provision of affordable housing and in habitat conservation. Thus it offers an appropriate historical referent for evaluating the big-picture planning efforts of the 1990s.[25]

One might consider *Temporary Paradise?* as a product of the counter-cultural insanity of the 1970s or as a blueprint for big-picture planning in the twenty-first century. It depends on how much faith one maintains in the market economy, on the one hand, and representative government, on the other. For present purposes, we need only recognize that our attitudes are ideological blinders that will affect our evaluation of creative big-picture planning. The more critical point at this juncture is that such creative plans, including the more recent smart-growth plan, are not new. It is not for want of research and technical preparation that these big-picture planning solutions often fall upon deaf ears or fail to achieve their goals.

As Larry, head engineer for the Patterson Company, explained when I asked him about the difficulties of flood control in an environmentally sensitive local lagoon, "Sure we can do it. We can put a man on the moon. The only question is who is going to pay for it." Here, as in most cases, the planning problem was not primarily technical. As the consultants clearly recognized in 1974 and as public- and private-sector planners clearly recognize today, planning is political.

The barriers to big-picture planning in San Diego are not technical or even legal. California law actually promotes big-picture planning along the lines recommended by the authors of *Temporary Paradise?* State law mandates comprehensive regional planning in the provision of housing, including affordable housing. Growth-control and facilities management programs have thus far been local rather than state or regional initiatives, but the comprehensive regional planning authority that has been sustained in large part by state mandates for affordable housing has, at least in San Diego, begun to develop plans for regional growth control.[26]

In habitat preservation efforts, the State of California has been even more proactive, establishing the Natural Community Conservation Plan (NCCP) to facilitate the integration of local and regional preservation efforts in a statewide effort to conserve the wildlife communities of the state while still allowing for development. As regional planning authorities become more prominent and as the comprehensive plans for affordable housing, growth control, and habitat conservation become integrated into the regional planning process, California, and San Diego in particular, may provide the model for big-picture planning in the twenty-first century.[27] If big-picture planning is supposed to be an exercise in participatory democracy as opposed to technocracy, then San Diego might provide the best model. In any case, the competing authorities and the relatively large number of development companies make San Diego the ideal case for illustrating the political problems associated with big-picture planning, simply because the problems are so readily apparent.[28]

With this in mind we can consider in more detail the three major reasons that big-picture planning failed to protect the paradise of San Diego County in 1974. First, the planners had to accommodate the contradictory interests of those who live and work in the local community. Second, the irrationality of formal legal, or bureaucratic, authority continued to plague their efforts. Third, the problem of popular participation likewise confounded their best-laid plans. Although big-picture planning did not create these systemic problems, their scale increased dramatically as planning became increasingly comprehensive and regional.

Contradictory Interests in Community Politics

Communities as established in the U.S. federal system are plagued by contradictory interests that are inherent and irreconcilable. The boosters of the western frontier towns internalized these contradictions and reproduced them in the economic and political histories of their towns. The boosters platted a town, dividing it into lots that were then sold or donated to investors who promised to establish churches, hotels, restaurants, newspapers, and all of the amenities of a civilized metropolis. The booster press advertised the new town as the land of opportunity, in an effort to attract labor and capital to develop regional industry. The boosters also proclaimed their chosen community as a peaceable kingdom where persons and property were secure and public order reigned. Ultimately, however, to the extent that the boosters succeeded in attracting local industry, prosperity brought in its wake rancorous conflict within and between classes that undermined the boosters' claim of peace and public order. Thus the economic success of the boosters undermined their political control and inspired the organization of a variety of ad-hoc, class-based frontier governing authorities and indefatigable booster efforts to establish federally sanctioned territorial and state governments that might bolster and legitimate local efforts.

Quite apart from the class interests of frontier industrial classes, merchants and shopkeepers desired public order, which would facilitate predictability and thereby profitability in trade. Of course, like the industrial classes, they promoted local industry, since without industry trade could not be sustained. The townsfolk did not, however, defend the local industrial classes in their conflicts with national and international investors. Quite the contrary, local resistance to the intrusion of national capital investment and political incorporation engendered protracted political struggle that included both interclass and intraclass conflict and pitted local against national interests. In come cases the local struggle was between labor and capital, but in all cases, it was a struggle between local industrial and commercial interests.[29] This struggle between the inclusive interests of the town boosters and the exclusive interests of local industrial classes is institutionalized in U.S. municipal politics. It is, in some sense, the legacy of the western frontier experience.

The form of this conflict changed, however, as life and work became alienated in the course of capital accumulation and state building. We might distinguish, for example, the antebellum household economy from the early-twentieth-century industrial economy. In the latter, life and work were physically segregated. Men left home to go to work, women engaged in housework, and the separate spheres of men and women's lives became institutionalized. At this point class, or work, interests were distinct from and essentially in conflict with status, or home, interests. Increasingly, life became degraded as a subordinate if necessary enterprise that was valued only as a means to sustain work, which was valued only as a means to accumulate wealth or to earn a daily wage.

The fact that life and work were inseparable and that each served as a basis for sustaining the other underlines the contradictions and conflicts associated with the alienation of life and work in the modern, postbellum U.S. world. Life and work increasingly became opposite in form and content. Work was organized impersonally and rationally; it was based on principles of individual freedom that translated into equality of opportunity to buy or sell commodities, including labor power. This provided the basis for exploitation, through the purchase of others' labor power, and capital accumulation, which became an end in itself and engendered the inequality of condition that ultimately became a barrier to equal opportunity.

In contrast, middle-class home life was organized in a personal, child-centered, affective—emotional and thereby irrational—manner; it was based on principles of collective responsibility that translated into equity in the allocation of family tasks and in the development of individual potential. One might argue that the home was organized in the interest of developing and sustaining human potential, which was viewed as an end in itself. People were inherently important and were not inter-changeable or even comparable in either their needs or their capacities. Thus the family operated on the principle that each must receive according to need and contribute according to ability. The fact that needs and capacities varied across persons and across the life course was accepted. Since people were not viewed as means to an end, inequality in needs and capacities was not problematic.

Clearly there are class differences in the extent to which life and work conform to the characterization offered above. One might argue that home is becoming increasingly subject to the rational, objective organization of work, as the "rational" work world colonizes the "life" world. This does not alter the fact that life and work are alienated and that the experiences of life and work inspire contradictory interests that are manifested in class, race, and gender conflicts. Generally, the "life" interest is on the defensive, attempting to protect itself against the intrusion of work, which continues to dominate life, particularly in the United States. Thus, we might consider work to be the more inclusive (class) interest, which seeks to encourage the expansion of life-world efforts, particularly to encourage families as producers of labor and consumers of labor's products. The work world is also inclusive in the intrusive sense of imposing its demands on the family. In this regard, the family tends to promote exclusive (status) interests in sheltering family members from the demands of the world of work.[30]

Communities are plagued by the contradictory interests of life and work because they include all people who live and work in a geographically bounded region. As established by convention and sanctioned by law, U.S. communities are inherently both inclusive and exclusive. Cities and counties have geographic boundaries that define the limits of inclusion or exclusion, but these boundaries are not mutually exclusive, since cities are nested within counties. Furthermore, boundaries—both of counties and particularly of cities—are routinely contested. They change as the conflict between inclusionary and exclusionary interests waxes and wanes. The central city's right to annex unincorporated areas and suburban settlements' right to incorporate represent the contradictory interests of inclusion (annexation) and exclusion (incorporation). These contradictory interests are institutionalized in state law and thus shape the form and content of the politics of growth within metropolitan communities.[31]

Ultimately, however, cities and counties are subordinate to federal and state authority and are not legally allowed to exclude any U.S. citizens. Nor are they allowed to determine who is or is not a citizen. They can, however, define their boundaries and thereby include or exclude residents of certain areas. They can also impose zoning restrictions that exclude some types of land uses and thereby exclude some types of persons. Lot-size and density restrictions have traditionally been used to exclude low-status—particularly young, poor, unmarried, and nonwhite—residents. Homeownership is exclusionary by definition, and the suburban lifestyle represented by owner-occupied, detached single-family units with large yards has been institutionalized as the apex of the zoning pyramid. The single-family residence is the highest use, with commercial, industrial, and other uses constituting the base of the pyramid. Whether their inhabitants are owners or renters, rich or poor, black or white, single-family dwelling units are the most privileged land use, and zoning law is designed to protect them from the encroachment of less desirable uses. Single-family homes may be included in any zone (e.g., in multiple-family residential, commercial, or even industrial zones), but all other uses are excluded in single-family residential zones. There is, of course, discrimination in the way zoning law tends to defend the exclusionary interests of property owners, particularly in wealthy suburbs, and the inclusionary interests of the city, when ghetto property is condemned to make way for urban renewal projects. "The more land one owns, especially of the unused suburban variety, the greater the likelihood that exclusionary rights will prevail."[32] That is, however, an over-simplification of the dynamic process in which the irreconcilable inclusionary and exclusionary interests animate community politics.

There might be a tendency, at the neighborhood level, for exclusionary interests to increase as family wealth increases, but the major proponents of inclusionary interests are national if not international actors. Affordable housing is a case in point. Federal and state governments have imposed the burden of affordable housing on reluctant municipalities, particularly suburban communities. The exclusionary interests, on the other hand, are more frequently championed locally, in grassroots movements and citizen initiatives, including the California tax revolt of 1978 and, most recently, growth-control efforts.[33] Such interests have historically been rooted in racism, nativism, and suburbanism. This is apparent in a March 9, 1907, editorial in a suburban Chicago weekly, the Morgan Park *Post*, in which the editor urges the suburb's residents to incorporate as an independent municipality. "The real question is not taxes, nor water, nor streetcars—it is a much greater question. . . . It is the moral control of our village. Under local government we can absolutely control every objectionable thing that may try to enter our limits"[34]

The economic interests that underlie the conflict are fairly clear. Capital, or industry, is inherently inclusive and expansive, so defenders of the free market oppose any attempt to exclude profitable uses of land. On that point, even critics of capitalism recognize that the exclusionary interest of property owners is a barrier to productive enterprise. One might explain this conflict in terms of the suburban resident's interest in the use value of the family home, as opposed to the realtor's interest in its exchange value, or market value Clearly, however, the nature of the conflict is more complex. As indicated in analyses of nineteenth-century land-claim clubs, the distinction between the landowner, as sub-urb resident or family farmer, and the speculator is often difficult to maintain in practice.[35]

Most important for our purposes is the extent to which local government represents the exclusionary, or status, interests of the people, or of the family lifestyle, as opposed to the inclusionary, or class, interests of capital, or the workplace. Here I will argue that local government represents neither—or both. Most generally, the interest of local government officials is to secure their claim to office, whether they were elected or appointed. The extent to which they are dependent on the private sector, and especially on developers, in pursuing this interest varies considerably across time and place. In some times and places it appears that it is in the best interests of elected and appointed officials to serve the interests of the growth machine by facilitating development. In other times and places, officials' efforts to promote growth are a political liability.[36]

Consider, for example, the experience of the Castleton city planning director in the early 1980s, as described by Harry, a former city planning department employee. This case suggests support for the growth-machine perspective: the city planning director allegedly lost his job because he did not facilitate development. "'Facilitate quality development' was the motto of the city manager in the [early] 1980s. Shoot it [project proposals] down the [pipe]. A viable community is money in the bank. The planning director didn't survive because he couldn't do it fast enough. He was a regulator and didn't understand that he should facilitate."

On the other hand, consider the situation of the city council—and by extension the city planning department—in this same suburban city by 1986. Tommy, another former Castleton city planning employee, who is now the planning director in Farmington, explained that after 1986 Castleton citizens effectively opposed the growth machine. "In Castleton between 1981 and 1983 our motto was 'Our job is to facilitate quality development.' That changed amid citizen threats to throw out the council; growth control was adopted" in 1986.

The rise and fall of this suburban city's pro-growth governing coalition suggests two important conclusions. First, local government's interest in growth is variable and can change in response to the local economic and political climate. Second, local government officials are interested in controlling, or at least predicting, these changes. The economic and political turmoil associated with the building boom of the early 1980s did not serve the political interests of Castleton's elected and appointed officials, whose tenure was threatened or terminated as a result of the boom-and-bust cycles.

Local officials' purely political interest inspires them to attempt to accommodate the contradictory interests of federal, state, and local actors in order to maintain control and to keep their positions. Their professional interests, on the other hand, include a concern with how they might approach this task. For city planning officials, a professional interest in big-picture planning can facilitate efforts to accommodate other interests, but it can also create what appears to be the most common moral dilemma for professional planners—the conflict between professional interests and the interests of public- or private-sector employers. Doug, a program director in the Castleton city planning department, laments the fact that politics interferes with big-picture planning. "Any planner realizes the importance of big-picture vision," Doug explained. "The problem is that vision is constantly negotiated."

Beyond the professional interests of planners, the professional interest that predominates in U.S. government, particularly at the federal level, is law. Law provides procedural regularity and legitimacy, as well as an effective means for accommodating contradictory interests. Formal, legal, bureaucratic procedures can, however, create barriers to big-picture planning and exacerbate partisan political problems.[37]

The Irrationality of Formal Legal Authority

Particularly in the San Diego suburbs that we will be considering here, planning is a formal, legal, bureaucratic process. Planners at various levels of the bureaucratic structure evaluate formal proposals in the context of an existing set of laws and policies that are available for inspection in the files of the city planning department. Planning commissions and city councils are able to grant exemptions and, in fact, can change the rules, but even at these higher levels of the policymaking process, the decisions are essentially driven by the concerns of legal formalism. If a structure or development is in compliance with the law, then it can be built.

Doug explained that the city must obey the law even when the law is a barrier to big-picture planning or efforts to serve the public interest more generally. "Sometimes the rules get in the way," Doug said, "But staff can't violate the rules. The city must live within the limits of the law."

The city planning department has some room to maneuver, but it is clear that legal formalism is characteristic and that negotiation occurs within the confines of the written law. This creates frustration not only for angry neighbors, but also for developers and the private-sector planners who work for them. Bill, the vice president and local CEO for the Patterson Company, a major developer in Castleton, expressed this frustration as follows: "Public and private interests should cooperate. The problem is trust. We have constantly tried to promote creative solutions, but the city tends to walk with blinders on. They don't trust innovation."

Tom, Dick, and Harry, a group of planners who formerly worked for the Castleton city planning department but were in 1992 employed in the private sector, expressed similar frustration with the city and with public-sector planners in general.

> Harry: Regulation destroys creative efforts to attract people. Livability is a
> critical goal, [but] the city loses sight of this, focusing on setbacks, density.

Dick: The city is problem oriented, focusing on nitpicking.

Tom: When I was at the city, when a council member would call and complain about an approved project, [the planning director] would put together a new ordinance.

Dick: This sets up an endless chain of new regulations that makes for uncertainty and delay. [That is the] problem in knee-jerk, policy-by-policy regulation.

Legal formalism, or legal, rational administration by written law, is plagued by contradictory components of rationality. Law is established as means to an end, but in practice it is obeyed as an end itself. Bureaucracy engenders mindless conformity to the letter of the law. Consequently, the ultimate goal and its real-world implications are lost in the narrow-minded effort to apply the letter of the law.[38] Thus, as Doug suggested, "The law gets in the way."

The Benefits of Disinterest

Ironically, formal legal administration, or bureaucracy, creates delays and expenses that frustrate the interested parties who pursue legal remedies as a means to an end. Thus the parties to an employment or marriage dispute, for example, might find that the time and money required to obtain a legal settlement is prohibitive. Even county governments generally find due-process costs to be prohibitive, which is why county prosecutors plea bargain most of their criminal cases. It often seems that legal procedures merely postpone the inevitable and enrich private-sector lawyers in the process. However, it is not simply the lawyers but all "disinterested" parties who benefit from formal legal procedures.

For example, in 1992, the Sierra Club was suing Castleton and a host of others who had proposed a lagoon enhancement project, but the Sierra Club did not really care about the dredging of the lagoon. The lawsuit was an attempt to delay or, if possible, halt another project in another county. Dredging the lagoon was mitigation (compensation) for filling in wetlands in the other county, so the Sierra Club was opposing the lagoon project in order to prevent the wetlands project. City, state, and federal officials approved the project in 1987–1988, but the Army Corps of Engineers hesitated to approve it until the lawsuit was finally settled in 1994.

Between 1988 and 1994, the lawsuit was undermining the Patterson Company's plans to build a luxury hotel, which would be the centerpiece of Camelot, a one-thousand-acre master-plan community.[39] The Castleton City Council and the California Coastal Commission both supported the plans to dredge the lagoon in order to prevent the seasonal flooding of the coastal highway. Furthermore, California Fish and Game supported the lagoon enhancement project to protect the islands in the lagoon, on which the least tern, an endangered bird species, was nesting in the spring.[40] All of these parties were suffering as the legal battle continued. Meanwhile, the hollow shell of a luxury resort was over-looking a lagoon that continued to alternate between flood and swamp stages, threatening public transportation, endangered wildlife, property values, and the quality of life because it really stank during the dry season.[41]

The only parties who benefited from the protracted legal process of imple-menting the big-picture plan that was approved in 1988 were those who had no interest in the big picture. The Sierra Club was interested primarily in prevent-ing a project in another city and had no particular interest in the lagoon. Nevertheless, their lawsuit succeeded in delaying the lagoon project and in com-pounding the problems faced by all parties who were interested in the lagoon's future. But the Sierra Club's action only delayed the project. Like the no-growth interests who had opposed the Camelot project in the 1980s, the Sierra Club was not able—or not yet able—to fight its way into the decision-making process. Instead, its legal challenge might, at best, veto the proposed plan without offer-ing an alternative. In this case, even the veto power was merely a short-term gain. The Sierra Club could delay but could not stop the project. Ultimately, then, the only beneficiary in the protracted struggle to build the luxury hotel were actors who cared even less about the lagoon and the hotel, specifically, the Williams sisters, property owners who had secured the master-plan approval in 1988.

The Williams sisters didn't care if the hotel was built or the lagoon was dredged. As Bill, the local agent for the Patterson Company, explained, "They never intended to build." Their goal was to get the master plan approved so they could sell their property at an inflated price, which they did as soon as the plan was approved in 1988. Then the windfall profits were reinvested after the collapse of the building industry in 1989—it was a textbook example of buy-ing cheap and selling dear." The economic and legal crises of 1989–1994 expanded the opportunities for the Williams sisters to reinvest their profits from the 1988 sale, purchasing new land at bargain-basement prices. Thus while those interested in the future of the lagoon suffered, including Mr. Patterson, who had bought the property and hired Bill to oversee the project in 1988, those interested only in windfall profits, particularly the Williams sisters, benefited.[42]

The fact that the lengthy legal battle to gain master-plan approval served only the interests of the disinterested property owners who were pursuing windfall profits and had no particular interest in the lagoon or the hotel is char-acteristic of the problem of legal formalism, or bureaucracy. Legal formalism is antithetical to big-picture planning. Those who have an interest in the big pic-ture or in some tangible benefits that might result from the bureaucratic process will invariably lose to those who play the game as an end in itself. The specu-lators who fight for land-use rights as an end in itself and the professionals (developers, lawyers, and planning consultants) whom they hire will generally benefit in legal contests with actors who are interested in exercising land-use rights as a means to an end. Disinterest in the terms of the agreement or the substance of the land-use rights is an incredible advantage in the legal battle, since it allows the speculator to exploit or sacrifice advantages in a calculating manner that interested parties are generally unable to approach.

This inherent bias toward the disinterested party is the essence of the irrationality of formal rationality, as manifested in modern economic and political systems. In this regard, republicanism and capitalism are both irrational formal legal systems. They enable certain parties to exercise political domination, enforcing mindless obedience by bureaucrats, citizens, or workers to laws that do not serve their interests. Those who attempt to use the system as a means to an end (e.g., voters who seek particular policies or workers who work to earn money) invariably lose to those who play for the love of the game (e.g., planners, lawyers, and corporate capitalists). Ultimately even those who do not want to play the game as an end in itself are subject to the rules of the game and must play as if the game were an end in itself in order to compete with others. It is in this way that legal formalism becomes an iron cage.[43]

Focusing on the irrationality of legal formalism in land-use planning, we might conclude (as Tom, Dick, and Harry suggest) that as the planning process becomes increasingly bureaucratic, it also becomes increasingly conservative and regulatory. Rather than considering the big picture of what the community wants or needs, the routine process of permitting development is reduced to plan checking—verifying that the proposed development meets the letter of the law. This bureaucratic process tends to produce routine approvals of traditional projects and tends to discourage innovation. This is, however, an oversimplification, since the system does, in fact, reward creative efforts to manipulate the rules.

The Benefits of Overregulation

Ironically, legal formalism tends to reward those who are most committed to playing the game of circumventing the narrowly defined limits of the status quo. Tom, the head planner for Patterson and a former Castleton city planner, explained this irony: "The planning commission doesn't like to mess with our project because Bill comes, bitching and moaning, with lawyers. Bill will go directly to city council and bitch and moan if the planning commission doesn't . . . support him."

Bill frequently goes over the head of planning department or coastal commission staff and tries to win the battle with the council or the commission. He is particularly opportunistic in this regard. If he sees an opening, he'll complain about a condition in the hope of getting the council or commission to delete it, thus sending a message to the staff to back off. Tom, who works for Bill, also likes this sort of fight, but for him the strategy is not opportunistic but evasive. He's willing to pick a fight and lose in the interest of getting the permit. He will provoke a single-issue hearing, where the commissioners focus on a relatively unimportant issue, which they may or may not resolve. After discussing the issue, however, they always approve the permit.

This is a win-win situation for Tom, whose job is to secure approvals. Bill, who is in the business of maximizing potential profits and minimizing costs, prefers to pick fights that he can win. We might conclude then that Bill is more opportunistic and less manipulative than Tom. Nevertheless, they work well together, and most important for our purposes, the system tends to favor them because they are dedicated to playing the game. They play it either by seizing opportunities to gain new advantages or by conceding those advantages to gain approval for the larger enterprise.

Tom and Bill are willing to fight for or sacrifice specific advantages because they have no particular interest in the substance of the proposed development as a whole. Instead, they are professional negotiators, playing a game with their public-sector counterparts to determine who gets what they have requested from or recommended to the planning commission and the city council. Of course, ultimately what matters is not whether you win or lose but how you play the game. The players on both sides are skilled professionals who are dedicated to manipulating the formal legal procedures.

The irrationality of legal formalism provides professional developers and private-sector planners with two ways to manipulate the system. First, by appealing to the planning commission or the city council, the petitioner can challenge the injustice and irrationality of the public-sector planning staff's commitment to applying the letter of the law. Alternatively, the petitioner can negotiate with staff when the petition fails to conform to city policy but is not technically illegal. In such cases the developer's willingness to comply with the technical demands of staff provides a focus for commission and council hearings. This also tends to produce single-issue hearings, which tend to produce approvals.

From the city planning department's perspective, it is sometimes appropriate, or even necessary, for the developer to challenge the written rules, particularly when these seem to get in the way of big-picture planning solutions. Doug, a Castleton city planning department official, explained that if the developer's proposal is not in compliance with the letter of the zoning law, "we have to recommend denial. Sometimes staff will informally recommend for approval. They must let the petitioner make the case for discretion, but [they] can support [the petition] informally."

One such petition involved the Castleton city policy on gated communities, which was not being followed in a proposal the Patterson Company was preparing for the planning commission. At a private meeting held before the planning commission hearing, Larry, the engineer for Patterson, negotiated with Will, the city engineer, on how much space, or stacking distance, was required between the public street and the gated entrance to the proposed housing development.

In this case the developer did not have to appeal to the commissioners to overrule the city planning staff. Rather than demanding conformity to the letter of the law, the city engineering staff encouraged the project engineer to develop a better policy on gated communities.

Will: Policies are policies—not standards. We will ultimately have to revise the policy.

Larry: I want to work toward a solution that makes everybody happy rather than banging on the desk to get my way. Are you saying that we have to follow policy or can't have a [guard] booth?

Will: Guard-gated entries need a little work. We need to get a few on the ground and see how they are working. Or, if you could provide us with more information and specific problems and recommendations . . . I think eighty feet is arbitrary.

Because legal formalism is irrational, which all parties recognize to some degree, the professional developer or his planner can appeal to the planning commissioners by challenging or by complying with the unreasonable demands imposed by city planning staff. As the bureaucratic maze of regulation increases—with local planning commissions being supervised by city councils, and regional, state, and federal regulators adding additional steps to the approval process—this overregulation tends to facilitate the efforts of the professional developers and private-sector planners. Those who are willing to pit one regulator against another in an effort to gain new advantages or to fight pointless battles to prevent consideration of more serious issues can reap the benefits of overregulation. Bill, the Patterson Company's vice president, explained one of these benefits: Sometimes the "city allows us to do things [it might otherwise oppose] if the coastal commission approves. That works to our benefit. Like a kid whose mom says, 'if it's okay with Dad.'"

Like Bill, some city planning officials also recognize potential benefits in overregulation. Doug, the Castleton program director who supervised growth management and habitat preservation programs, explained that having the coastal commission review local projects was not necessarily a bad idea. Harry, a private-sector planning consultant explained rather cynically that Chuck, the Castleton city planning director, likes the diffusion of responsibility associated with overregulation. "The more fingerprints on the knife, the more difficult it is to prove guilt."

The diffusion of responsibility can also serve the interests of the private sector, especially large-scale corporate developers who are able to take advantage of opportunities, particularly those who retain professional lawyers and planners who are skilled in the game of negotiation. Specifically, Bill and Tom are able to reap the benefits of overregulation to the extent that they are prepared to be opportunistic or manipulative in challenging or accepting the unreasonable demands of regulatory staff.

The Irony of Popular Participation

Since big-picture planning is wedded to a commitment to representative government, incorporating popular participation into the planning process is a major concern. Accommodating the general public implies an effort to manage the conflict produced by the contradictory nature of community interests. Given residents' general disposition to oppose anything that might affect the neighborhood or property values, it seems reasonable to assert that neighborhood opposition to big-picture plans is inevitable. The critical factor is the extent to which the opposition is organized.[44]

There are regional and historical differences in the opportunities for grassroots opposition to land-use planning, but the environmental legislation of the 1970s was clearly instrumental in mobilizing potential opponents. The National Environmental Policy Act (NEPA) of 1970 and the California Environmental Quality Act (CEQA) of that same year require that the potentially interested public be contacted and informed of the potential environmental effects of any proposed project. If there are potentially significant effects, an Environmental Impact Report (EIR) must be prepared that details potential impacts of the project and considers possible alternatives, including the no-project option. This entails costly and time-consuming research.[45]

Most important for our purposes, the EIR provides a mechanism for potential opponents to identify each other and to share their concerns before meeting at a public hearing. If students of collective action were to design an experimental procedure to facilitate the organization of grassroots opposition, it seems unlikely that they would develop procedures more effective than those called for by CEQA and NEPA. Consequently, since 1970, particularly in California suburbs, organized opposition has been the rule rather than the exception.

In San Diego County suburbs, there are a variety of local organizations that are loosely affiliated with national or international social-movement organizations, most notably the Audubon Society, that can be mobilized in opposition. This mobilization is facilitated by the process of approving big-picture plans, which virtually guarantees that NEPA/CEQA procedures must be followed and that an EIR will be required. Thus, particularly in middle-class suburban settings with available resources, including time, money, and organizational and professional skills, organized interests can be mobilized and unorganized members of the community can become organized in the process of evaluating the project.[46] For public- or private-sector planners, the challenge of popular participation is to accommodate the contradictory interests of, first, established organized interests that are likely to conflict on the big-picture plan and, second, local residents who are likely to become organized in the course of the implementation of the EIR procedures.

Even in the public sector, popular participation tends to be viewed as something that needs to be managed and limited to the appropriate time and place. Doug, a Castleton city planning official, was clearly annoyed after attending an

NCCP meeting in Irvine (Orange County) that the environmentalists were badgering the state officials. As he explained, "It was not appropriate. It is appropriate at city council or planning commission meetings and at the Fish and Wildlife hearings, but not at [these meetings]. They are not dealing with project-by-project grading. We don't need to hear horror stories."

In big-picture planning, popular participation is managed in three distinct ways. First, concerned citizens representing organized or established interests are appointed to citizen advisory boards, where their public discussions, in tandem with private meetings of the experts, produce proposals that are then considered by the city council. Second, voters are sometimes asked to approve or reject proposed policies, either in the context of a partisan electoral campaign or a grassroots legislative initiative. Third, public opinion as expressed by potential or emergent interests in ad-hoc suggestions or complaints, public meetings, mass media reports, and private communications is ideally anticipated and preempted in big-picture plans. Generally, the aim of accommodating popular participation could be characterized as an effort to co-opt the organized and preempt the unorganized.[47]

Regarding the co-optation of organized interests, Tommy, the Farmington city planning director, explained the strategy as follows: "Vocal opponents often get co-opted: put on citizen advisory committees. [If] you are surrounded by people [throwing rocks] you need to bring them into the circle." Ideally the city hires a professional facilitator who is particularly talented in conflict management. One such facilitator, Lou, who ran the Habitat Protection Committee in Castleton, explained that his job is conflict management. "I was hired to play pivot in the process—[to be] demonstrably neutral. The city wanted to represent all the interests: Audubon Society, regulatory agencies, landowners. Other people came. All were treated the same. If the idea is to build consensus, even if there are bomb-throwers it is better to have them on the inside." A major part of the facilitator's job is "cooling out" organized interests that might otherwise sabotage the big-picture plan. The facilitator tries to gain their support for what the citizen advisory group ultimately proposes. In short, the goal is to co-opt the organized interests by incorporating them into the decision-making process.

Unlike organized interests, voters are more difficult to manage because their behavior is more difficult to predict. Nevertheless, one goal of big-picture planning is to anticipate the potential interests of voters before they become organized. This has been a major challenge because citizen initiatives have in some cases preceded city and county plans. Tom, the planner for Camelot, the Patterson project, explained the significance of voter interest as he realized it when he worked for the Castleton city planning department: "What amazed me was that the major goal was reelecting the city council. I thought the goal was good planning [but I] finally came to realize this." A less cynical perspective on the city's efforts to accommodate the interests of voters is offered by Lou, the citizen advisory group facilitator, who explained in 1992 how growth-control and environmental interests continued to challenge local government officials, who needed to anticipate what the voters would think of next. "Navarro," who was running for mayor of San Diego on an antigrowth platform in 1992, "shows that the growth management movement is not dead. Coastal sage scrub in now the concern. [Before it] was wetlands. What next? [We] need to anticipate and prepare."

In attempting to anticipate and prepare, this suburban city initiated a major revision of its general plan for future development. Chuck, the Castleton city planning director, at a breakfast meeting for developers and other interested parties held at a country club in a neighboring city in the spring of 1992, explained the strategy: "We need to take the whole package to the [city residents] to make sure of approval for the direction we plan to take in the future. We felt the general plan was legally adequate but needed improvement so that we can preempt challenges once development commences."

As difficult as it is to anticipate the interests of voters, public opinion is even more slippery, yet equally important as a potential problem that must be anticipated. As Tommy, the Farmington planning director, explained during a 1992 interview in his office, "For the past four years we've had a slow-growth council. Now they are concerned with economic development [and] have established an incentive program for attracting investment. Public opinion and the press are major factors in shaping council, thus city policy." Private-sector planners generally agree that public opinion is critical in influencing city planning decisions.

> Dick: The fear of having the wool pulled over their eyes and unleashing public outcry [prevents] government from working with developers.

> Tom: Phone calls about approved projects scare the planning department.

> Harry: The telephone is critical. If people are calling city hall there is a problem. Otherwise, everything is fine.

Local governments attempt to shape as well as preempt popular opinion, particularly by engaging in the public relations efforts that surround general plan revisions and, of course, elections. In the most progressive California cities, like Castleton, city council meetings are televised and thus become a critical component of government efforts to serve, to shape, and to anticipate public opinion.[48]

The major challenger that San Diego suburban governments were facing in their efforts to manage public opinion and accommodate popular participation in 1992 was the coalition of no-growth and environmental interests. These interests seemed to be coalescing in an unstable coalition that accommodated contradictory (exclusive and inclusive) interests, generated considerable support among voters, and to a large extent shaped public opinion by appealing to the general suspicion of government and big business. Lou, the citizen advisory group facilitator, described the coalition: "Local environmentalists are noisy constituents who get placed on committees. There are two distinct points of view that are overlapping in this city: one, environmental issues are important, and two, growth is bad."

These converging or overlapping interests are fundamentally contradictory with regard to local land-use planning. Most generally, environmentalism is an inclusive interest that defends the idea that the earth should be preserved for everyone, including plants and animals. As a practical matter, environmentalists favor high-density, small-footprint development within already settled areas and preservation of the still unsettled, natural areas. Dan, a state NCCP official and an environmental biologist, explained:

> Good development means small footprint—build up, not out; build inside (don't expand) the urban area.
>
> [Higher density is better?] Yes.

The no-growth movement, on the other hand, is generally an exclusive interest dedicated to maintaining existing low-density suburban communities and keeping everyone else (including the developers) out. The common interests uniting environmentalists and no-growth advocates are limited to exercising veto power: stopping unwanted development. Thus they can only create planning problems by opposing development. They are unable to negotiate solutions because their ultimate goals are contradictory.[49]

Some environmentalists realize this problem but assume that it will go away. Steve, the leader of Southern California Habitat Defenders, described the problems of and possibilities for this coalition: "No-growth people are potential allies. They will eventually see the trade-off and will recognize what is the lesser evil: open space and the village concept [of development]. No-growth people are reacting to a real problem, but they are people that you can talk to." It is not clear, however, that environmentalists will be able to convert their no-growth allies to environmentalism, given their contradictory interests. Thus it seems that this coalition will continue to be limited by its conflicting interests. The only collective interest is opposition to local government and developers, whom coalition members tend to view as co-conspirators or powerful elites who effectively control land-use planning.

Their commitment to this conspiracy theory of land-use politics severely limits the influence of both environmental and no-growth interests, quite apart from their difficulty in cooperating with each other. Their crude version of the growth-machine or power-elite theory not only limits their ability to negotiate with local government, but also becomes something of a self-fulfilling prophecy. To the extent that they mistrust local government and treat public and private planners and even environmental consultants as the enemy, they foster cooperation among enlightened developers and public and private planners and consultants, who support big-picture planning as an alternative to ballot-box planning by citizen initiative.[50]

No-growth and environmental interests might appear to be a potent weapon in local land-use politics, but members of this coalition believe that they have no influence. When I was in the field in 1992, I was amazed at how widespread this attitude was. At a Castleton city council meeting that approved an EIR that would allow the city to move forward on a long-awaited plan for widening a major thoroughfare, the local no-growth and environmental interests seemed remarkably resigned to what they considered inevitable. Emma, a middle-aged woman who lives outside of the town but frequently attends city council meetings in Castleton, offered what seemed like token opposition, suggesting that she felt obliged to say something. Yet more perplexing was the mere token support offered by Ruby, who spoke on behalf of the local Audubon Society representative.

Ruby is an elderly woman with long, straight white hair, a Latina who carries herself with the aura of a Native American chief. Sometimes I felt that she was mentally and spiritually far removed from the mundane activities that we were observing. Because she was one of the concerned citizens who attended the Castleton Habitat Protection Committee meetings, we saw each other frequently. When I saw her outside chambers, just before that 1992 city council meeting, I chatted with her briefly and asked her what she thought of the final agreement. She seemed resigned and said, "they [presumably the government and the developers] had it all figured out from the beginning."

That surprised me, because Ruby is an activist. Didn't she think that her opposition mattered? In retrospect, I am also surprised because she later spoke in support of the EIR. Ruby and her colleagues, like the environmentalists at the NCCP meeting in Irvine, seem to think that local government and developers are engaged in a conspiracy. Regardless of how the concerned citizens try, they can never do more than delay the proceedings, which is generally what they succeed in doing.

Even when locals participate in the citizen advisory groups and are thereby able to influence the negotiation process, they tend to use disruption as a primary tactic, relying, as one city official suggested, on the recitation of horror stories and demands for some type of action. Consequently, they tend to get preempted, even when they have already been co-opted. At the Castleton habitat-conservation citizen advisory group meetings, for example, local environmentalists, including Carl, the local representative of the Audubon Society, frequently raised tangentially relevant issues regarding illegal grading or other questionable practices they had observed, in some cases in other cities. These concerns were taken seriously, however, as indicated in the following discussions at citizen advisory committee meetings:

> Carl: There was a story on the lagoon [in the local paper]. A tenant farmer has filled the creek with sediment. Farmers should be required to do erosion control.

> Doug (Castleton city planning program director): We need to study the possibility of controlling farming [and its effects]: erosion and encroachment on habitat.

> [at the next meeting]

Doug: We have a draft of revisions to the municipal code on the grading ordinance.

Carl: We need to incorporate erosion control—the California Coastal Commission recommended an amended erosion plan.

[Doug assures Carl that the city will work on it]

One might argue that raising the concern with grading ordinances was inappropriate in a committee designed to develop a big-picture plan for habitat conservation, but part of the business of these committees is cooling out opposition to city plans. Thus Doug, the same city planning official who complained about environmentalist horror stories at the state-level NCCP meetings in Irvine, welcomed the opportunity to preempt local concerns by presenting an ordinance that was apparently already under consideration. In this case, it seems that Carl was satisfied by the preemptive revision of the grading ordinance, the details of which would be negotiated between public- and private-sector planners and eventually presented to the planning commission, then to the city council.

Like city officials, developers and their private-sector planners routinely attempt to preempt community opposition to their plans. Tom explained that he routinely used plateau bargaining: asking for more than he really wants so he can make concessions or allow the planning department to "hold the developer's feet to the fire." Like single-issue hearings, plateau bargaining creates a win-win situation. The neighbors are appeased, the city gets to regulate, and the project gets approved. Particularly when seeking approval for big projects, like a master-plan, or planned community, proposal, the developer plays politics in much the same way as elected officials. Bill, Tom's boss, explained his strategy: "You need to win community support. We set up community meetings: forums of 200 people and coffee klatches with just a few people. We got ideas, incorporated them, and met again with new plans. We had met [so many times] with so many [people] that there were over 100 people in support at the city council meeting. You have to be like a politician running for office: walk the streets, shake hands, and kiss babies."

It is clear that grassroots movements and social-movement organizations could affect land-use policy and land-use decision making, but it seems that the professionals, public- and private-sector planners in particular, manage the opposition better than the opposition manages itself. Even when the opponents are included in the negotiation process, they tend to be exercising veto power at best. Most often they seem to be diverting attention from big-picture planning efforts or delaying the process through disruption. The irony of popular participation is that it increases the cost and complexity of the planning process and thereby increases public-sector dependence on developers—the only parties who are willing and able to pay the cost of pursuing big-picture solutions.

The inability to coordinate the diverse factions of antideveloper interests, the

unwillingness to trust local government and to pay the cost of providing public goods, and the lack of professional experience and orientation in the game
of legal formalism reduce citizen influence dramatically. If the citizens were as
manipulative and opportunistic as the professionals, they might fare better in
the negotiations. Even then, unless the citizens were willing, first, to confront
the contradictory interests of liberal environmentalists and reactionary no-
growth advocates and, second, to pay taxes or otherwise contribute to the cost
of producing big-picture planning solutions, they wouldn't be able to expect to
control land-use planning.[51]

Liberal environmentalists are becoming vested interests who are satisfied to
delay development though lawsuits or to be co-opted or preempted in big-picture
plans. Ultimately the environmentalist organizations, and particularly the major
actors such as the Sierra Club and World Wildlife, compete with local government for support from the grassroots. To the extent that the environmentalists
ally with no-growth interests in opposition to developers and city government
officials, as they did in 1992, they are driving local government into the arms of
private-sector developers. Unless they change this strategy, the problem of popular participation will become yet more serious, and the irony of popular participation will likewise increase.

Chapter Two
Locating the Development Site:
Sociohistorical Context

> If we judge by Mira Mesa [in the inland corridor along Highway 15
> between Escondido and downtown San Diego], it seems that present sub-
> urban growth is too rapid, too poorly coordinated with public services, too
> expensive and homogeneous, too destructive of the land, inappropriate in
> form, and in the wrong place.
>
> Donald Appleyard and Kevin Lynch, 1974

Despite partisan bickering and disagreements about who is to blame, it is clear
that uncontrolled growth in southern California suburbs in the 1970s and
1980s inspired the development of comprehensive regional, big-picture, planning. The urban planning professionals who were hired by the City of San
Diego to evaluate local planning problems and possibilities recognized in 1974
what now seems obvious.[1] The growth of San Diego suburbs, particularly in the
inland valley connecting San Diego to Riverside, was, simply stated, out of control. San Diego residents who were less sophisticated described the inland
empire as a cancer. It was Los Angeles making an end run around Camp
Pendleton (the U.S. Marine Corps base on the coast north of Oceanside) and
invading San Diego via Escondido along what had been Highway 395 and soon
became Interstate 15.

With 20/20 hindsight even nonresidents now recognize the seriousness of the
problem of uncontrolled growth in San Diego's suburbs circa 1970. For example, when asked in 1992 to characterize bad development, Dan, a state-level
Natural Communities Conservation Planning (NCCP) official and environmental biologist, replied, "The Inland Empire along Highway 15 from
Riverside south to Escondido [and especially from] Temecula north to
Riverside. People are commuting two hours plus. Twenty thousand single-
family dwelling units were completed but never occupied."

Bad development and uncontrolled growth do not in and of themselves
explain the nature and scope of change in land-use planning since 1970,
however—neither in the United States in general nor in southern California in
particular. Public policy changes must be analyzed in the context of ongoing economic and political struggles that both inspire and confound policy-making
efforts. In this case, a series of economic and political crises between 1970 and
1990 created incredible opportunities for a variety of interests to mobilize in
opposition to extant land-use policy and to shape the direction that land-use pol-

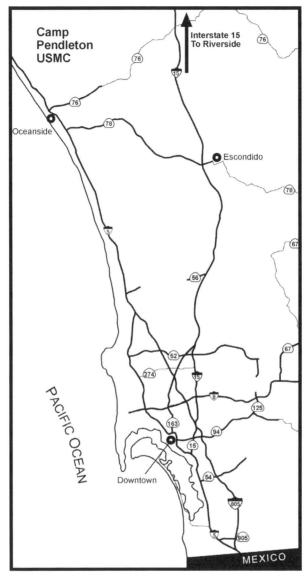

Figure 4. San Diego County Major Highways, 2001
Base map provided by SANDAG

icy would take in the 1990s. This was particularly true in southern California, especially in the fastest-growing suburban region of San Diego County.[2]

Old, Great Society, liberals interested in affordable housing clashed with new, environmental, liberals interested in protecting wildlife and natural resources. Both clashed with traditional free-market conservatives, who were interested in protecting private property from government regulation. New Federalist conservatives challenged the old and new liberals by offering a new form of cooperation between government and the private sector. In the old New Deal corporate liberalism, public money provided infrastructure for private enterprise. In the New Federalism, the private sector provides public services. The New Deal governing coalition made private enterprise and private space increasingly subject to public scrutiny. Under the New Federalist regime, however, public works and public space became increasingly privatized.

In some sense this New Federalist vision triumphed, at least in San Diego County, but it was not unopposed and it did not survive unscathed. Clearly there were contradictory interests, both locally and nationally. There were legal challenges on the "taking" issue and on the duties associated with meeting regional housing needs in compliance with general-plan guidelines. Furthermore, there were fiscal challenges associated with the tax revolt in California and with Reaganomics more generally. Finally, managing opposition to development, particularly opposition from the liberal environmental and reactionary no-growth interests, was a major problem that shaped the nature and scope of big-picture planning solutions in unanticipated ways.[3]

Thus, what the progressive coalition of big-picture planning advocates ultimately succeeded in creating was not the environmental-populist picture offered by the authors of the 1974 report to the City of San Diego, *Temporary Paradise?* Neither was it exactly what the New Federalist conservatives envisioned. Instead, it was something of a progressive compromise between new liberals and conservatives. It was, ultimately, the package that its promoters were able to sell.

The good news for progressive planners and for liberals in general is that growth would no longer be uncontrolled, subject only to the whims of investors or to their perception of consumer preferences. There would be no more Mira Mesas. Instead, there would be schools and fire stations, more open space, more parks, and more serious efforts to conserve natural resources. In this regard, the old, free-market, conservatives lost, although private-property rights were not abandoned. The bad news for liberals, and particularly for old liberals, was that development would be geared toward commercialism and the privatization of public space. In this regard, the new conservatives won.

The prize, of course, was the regional development plan, through which, between 1970 and 1989, San Diego was transformed from the "unconventional city" into "Yuppie Heaven."[4] The transformation did not happen overnight; it occurred in fits and starts over the course of two decades. The first push was political protest, particularly by environmentalists, as marked by the first Earth Day celebration in 1970. There were tremendous political and economic opportunities in 1970 in the wake of the political challenges and economic prosperity of the 1960s. These opportunities declined markedly by 1980, in response to the combined effects of economic depression and conservative reaction. Then in the Reagan years (1981–1988) speculative frenzy reached its peak, fueled by the triumph of social conservatism and fiscal irresponsibility. This brought a second wave of political protest, notably the no-growth movement of the late 1980s. The savings-and-loan crash of 1989 and the ensuing protracted economic depression marked the end of this short cycle of economic and political crisis. In San Diego County—and particularly in the building industry, the leading edge of 1972–1989 boom—the depression lingered until 1996. Since then, as we entered the twenty-first century, smart growth has become the watchword, and it has looked like déjà vu all over again.

Now that the dust is clearing, we can ask, first, how the socially constructed city and county of San Diego changed between 1970 and 1990. Then we can consider the extent to which either the product or the production process constitutes a revolutionary change in land-use politics.

From Unconventional City to Yuppie Heaven

As a project, Yuppie Heaven does represent something new. The reconstruction of downtown San Diego and the extension of regional development along the lines now promoted as smart growth are producing a leisure world for the physically active and financially secure. It resembles Disneyland in some ways, but it clearly is not just for kids. The Wild Animal Park near Escondido is Adventure Land. Julian, in the eastern mountains near Cuyamaca Rancho State Park, is Frontier Land. Horton Plaza and the Gaslight District, downtown, is Main Street. Seaport Village, the new convention center, the ferry connection, and the parallel universe on Coronado Island resemble the Pirates of the Caribbean (both the Navy and the Yacht club are central to this reconstructed harbor land). The problem, however, is that even with the inclusion of the Tijuana Trolley, San Diego still falls short of the Disneyland adventure via monorail. Here in Yuppie Heaven the visitor rents a BMW and travels from attraction to attraction on freeways. The well-prepared visitor is careful to orient travel away from the stream of commuters, who clog the freeways with automobiles, thereby contributing to pollution, road rage, and the generally unpleasant long-term effects of life in the fast lane.[5]

Yuppie Heaven is a wonderful place to visit, but I wouldn't want to try to make a living there. Many, if not most, local residents, however, consider it to be a major improvement over what preceded it.

In the 1960s there were local bars and restaurants in the satellite communities, but no nightlife downtown, except for the sailors, strippers, and prostitutes. The El Cortez hotel, with its glass elevator and big-band orchestra, was the only respectable club downtown. Of course, there were Anthony's Fish Grotto on the harbor and the boat that offered dinner and dancing on Harbor Island cruises. There were, as well, the Hotel Del Coronado, where *Some Like It Hot* was filmed on location; the Marine Room and La Jolla Beach and Tennis Club in La Jolla; and the Del Mar Hotel and Racetrack, along with the Carlsbad Raceway, in North County. And there was, of course, Tijuana. But there was nothing going on in San Diego County after dark that would inter-

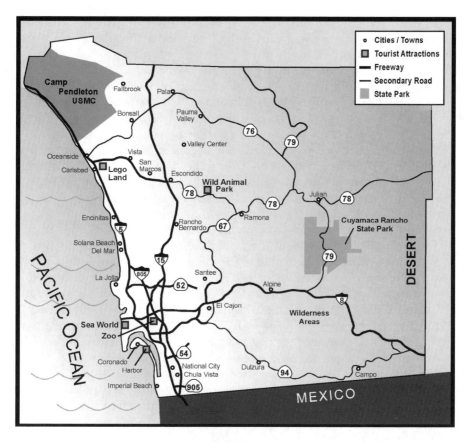

Figure 5. Yuppie Heaven
Base map provided by SANDAG

est a wealthy, cosmopolitan business executive. In fact, most of the hotels and restaurants that accommodated business travelers were located in Mission Valley—actually, in adjacent Hotel Circle—in the middle of nowhere.[6]

San Diego had considerable natural attractions in addition to its golf courses. Balboa Park, located uptown, had been reconstructed as the fairgrounds for the Panama and California Expositions of 1915 and 1916 to celebrate the opening of the Panama Canal. Today Balboa Park is home to multiple museums and the world-famous San Diego Zoo. There was also Sea World, which opened in 1964 in Mission Bay, where hotels were springing up in the late 1960s in the space between Old Town, which had yet to be reconstructed as Margaritaville, and the Mission Beach Boardwalk, with its prereconstruction deteriorating amusement park and shabby beach cottages. There were mountain and desert parks (Cuyamaca and Anza-Borrego), miles of public beaches, and hundreds of thousands of vacant acres, particularly in the North County inland hills and valleys and the East County sagebrush and tumbleweed plains.[7] Before the elaborate freeway system was built in the 1960s and 1970s, there were lots of wide-open spaces and relatively little development. San Diego was, in short, a developer's dream: a virgin land ready for the taking.

Between 1970 and the savings-and-loan crash of 1989, despite opposition from the political extremists on the right and the left, the paradise of San Diego in the 1960s was lost. San Diego County was reconstructed as a Yuppie Heaven, with natural resources like the harbor developed for commercial use as tourist attractions or yuppie playgrounds, where the wealthy can stroll at their leisure. These attractions were built to accommodate automobile rather than pedestrian traffic. They are surrounded by secured parking that creates a guarded perimeter for the walled city of conspicuous consumption on the inside while effectively keeping the street people on the outside.

Seaport Village, for example, is conveniently located near the convention center and theoretically within walking distance of the Gaslight District, but it is difficult to make that trip on foot. As in most of San Diego, there are no pedestrian routes. The path on foot follows cars right into the parking lot, conveniently located in front of the village entrance. Even Horton Plaza, an old square with a war memorial where sailors and prostitutes held midnight services, was reconstructed in 1985 as a suburban-type shopping mall. The plaza is an enclosed, private commercial district, with secured parking and guarded entrances that all but prohibit pedestrian access despite the plaza's location right in the center of town.

The Wild Animal Park, an enclosed space for jungle creatures, was constructed from 1969 to 1972 in the north-central region. This park has a fenced perimeter within which wild animals run free while the humans are caged or otherwise confined at a safe distance from the wildlife. Located on the eastern edge of the Inland Empire between Escondido and Ramona, the Wild Animal Park is on the periphery of the North County suburban freeway, Highway 78, which ends abruptly in Escondido then meanders through the surface streets of the city and eventually becomes a rural highway that leads to the park. Past the park Highway 78 meanders again, this time through northeast San Diego County, intersecting Highway 67 in Ramona and leading eventually to the growing tourist town of Julian, which still lacks freeway access to the Disneyland-like attractions of the west.[8]

In fact, Yuppie Heaven has serious access problems that confound efforts to include yuppies while excluding the poor and the wretched. The problem is twofold. First, the coalition of no-growth and environmental interests effectively opposed freeway expansion in the 1970s and 1980s. Some of the freeway links that were already on the drawing board when *Temporary Paradise?* was published in 1974 were effectively delayed by popular and planner opposition and were still not completed twenty years later. Certain booming suburban and exurban locations, such as Poway, continue to suffer for lack of easy freeway access, and it is unlikely that an eight-lane freeway will ever link Adventure Land and Frontier Land. Perhaps those problems will be solved if the smart-growth coalition can sustain itself and the economy does not collapse

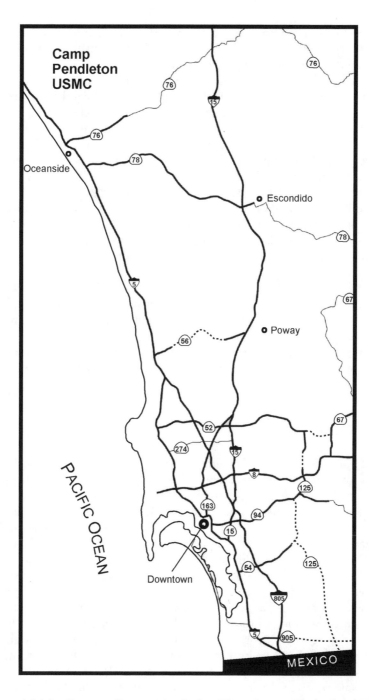

Figure 6. Major Freeway Construction in San Diego County, Planned and Under
Construction in 2001 (Indicated with Broken Lines)
Base map provided by SANDAG

before these revitalized projects are completed. As I finish writing these words in December of 2001, the jury is still out on the prospects for economic recovery, despite the patriotic feelings and the drums of war.

The other problem is at the opposite extreme of the class and status continuum. The Gaslight District is designed to create yuppie nightlife on the streets of the inner city. This creates a serious problem for selective policing that represses the indigenous lower-class street life to facilitate the expansion of suburban middle-class street life. This requires more discrimination than policing the trolley, where security officers just try to keep "ghetto youth" from taking free rides downtown. In the Gaslight District, the problem is distinguishing drunk and rowdy but otherwise respectable yuppies from vagrants. This is the same problem that authorities face in policing Rush Street in Chicago, or Bourbon Street in New Orleans, or Times Square in New York. Ultimately it is much easier to distinguish people by race and gender than according to class and status. Even sociologists are still struggling with that problem.

Whether Yuppie Heaven is an improvement over the unconventional city is a matter of opinion. Yuppies and environmentalists, including downtown office workers, tend to like it. Downtown small business owners and shopkeepers complain loudly that revitalization is not bringing any street traffic into their businesses. Nobody seems to be listening to the grumblers, however, or to people of color, poor people, and labor, all of whom seem to have been excluded from the progressive alliance promoting big-picture planning and, more recently, smart growth.

A Quiet Revolution?

Yuppie Heaven is not what the authors of *Temporary Paradise?* envisioned. In fact, in some ways neither the content of development projects nor the general mode of producing new projects has changed very much from the form and content of development in the previous decades. There were two major changes: first, the suburban freeway and shopping mall was introduced to the inner city in the revitalization of downtown commerce, second, and most important, the scale and scope of planning increased dramatically. This is the story of "big picture" planning. It is comprehensive (increased scope) and regional (increased scale). Nevertheless, it is still free enterprise planning for profit and planners for hire. In that sense, there has been no radical change. The bankers and business who built the suburbs came home to roost in the 1980s (the Reagan years, 1981–1988). Following the lead of Mayor Pete Wilson (1972–1982), the bankers and businessmen who had promoted suburbanization after World War II became environmentalists and growth control advocates in the 1970s. In the process, they gradually moved from the freeway and shopping center development model to the big-picture planning model that inspired the construction of Yuppie Heaven.

Generally San Diego grew out in the 1960s and 1970s and then grew up in the 1980s. The general pattern for growing out was firmly established by 1960.

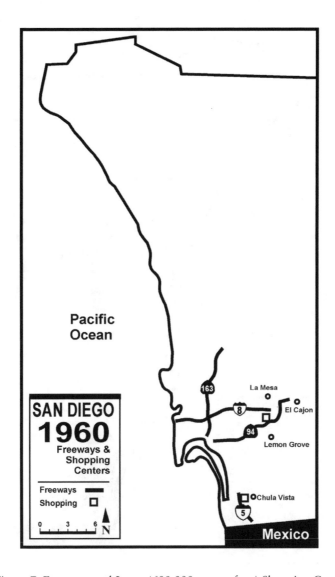

Figure 7. Freeways and Large (600,000 square foot) Shopping Centers
in San Diego County, 1960
Base map provided by SANDAG

Suburban expansion followed freeway construction and was, in turn, followed
by regional commercial development (suburban shopping malls). In 1948 the
first freeway was built. The Cabrillo Freeway (which became Highway 163)
linked downtown San Diego to what would become Mission Valley. The following year the streetcar system closed, marking the triumph of freeway-and-
shopping-center development at the expense of the walking city.[9]

In 1960 two large suburban shopping centers opened. College Grove, since

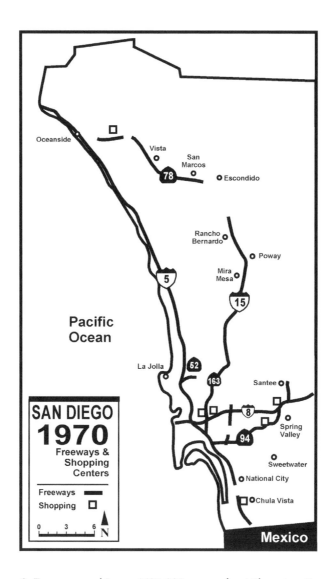

Figure 8. Freeways and Large (600,000 square foot) Shopping Centers,
San Diego 1970
Base map provided by SANDAG

renamed Market Place on the Grove, was located on Highway 94, a freeway
that commenced downtown and extended in 1960 past Lemon Grove to the
entrance of La Mesa and Spring Valley at Spring Street and Campo Road.
Although Highway 80 (which would become Interstate 8) was not yet completed through La Mesa, there was a temporary freeway connection from Highway
94 to Highway 80, which continued into El Cajon. The two major east-west

freeways (Highway 80 and Highway 94) were not yet linked, but freeway service to the eastern suburbs was far better than to the south. The Chula Vista
Shopping Center also opened in 1960 in the southern suburb of Chula Vista on
the most extensive segment of Interstate 5 that had been completed at that time.
This freeway segment, however, was connected to nothing. It brought the southern suburbs closer to Tijuana, Mexico, than to downtown San Diego or the rest
of San Diego County. More progress had been made on the northern freeway,
Highway 163, which commenced uptown and extended to what was then
Highway 395, the road to Escondido that later became Interstate 15.[10]

In the 1960s four new suburban shopping centers were opened. Mission
Valley, opened in 1960, was located north of downtown where Highway 163
(the Cabrillo Freeway) met what became Interstate 8. This regional shopping
center was built in the flood basin of the San Diego River despite the objections
of the city planning staff. Grossmont Center was built in La Mesa near what
later became the connecting link (Highway 125) between the major east-west
freeways (Interstate 8 and Highway 94).[11] In 1969 Fashion Valley was added
adjacent to Mission Valley on Interstate 8, on the opposite side of Highway
163, establishing this area as the commercial center for the north city and for
the county as a whole. At the same time Plaza Camino Real opened in North
County between Oceanside and Vista, off Interstate 5 on a segment of Highway
78 that was not yet connected to anything else.

The San Diego County freeway system continued to develop, particularly to
the north and the east. By 1970 freeway service to the eastern suburbs extended beyond La Mesa, where Highway 94 and Interstate 8 were linked via
Highway 125. Interstate 8 was freeway well beyond the eastern border of El
Cajon, and Highway 67 provided freeway access to Santee, which was the
fastest-growing city in the eastern suburbs. Progress on the southern freeways
extended Interstate 5 all the way to National City, but the gap between Chula
Vista and National City remained. Sweetwater, just east of Chula Vista, was the
fastest-growing southern suburb, but the region still lacked freeway access. The
most extensive freeway construction was north of downtown, particularly
along the coast. Interstate 5 was extended past Oceanside as part of the
statewide project and provided freeway access to Orange County and Los
Angeles. The inland route extended Highway 163 along what had been
Highway 395 but had since become Interstate 15, thus providing freeway
access from downtown to Rancho Bernardo, just south of Escondido.

The east-west links between the coastal (Interstate 5) and inland (Interstate
15) freeways were not yet established in 1970, however. In North County, San
Marcos, the fastest-growing suburb in the region, had freeway access to
Escondido and Vista, but Highway 78 did not yet provide freeway access to
Interstate 5 on the coast or Interstate 15, which was still not freeway between
Rancho Bernardo and Escondido. Similarly, further south, by May 1970
Highway 52 had been extended from Interstate 5 to what would eventually
become Interstate 805, but it did not yet connect the coastal and inland free-
ways. The gaps in freeways and commercial services in the North City region

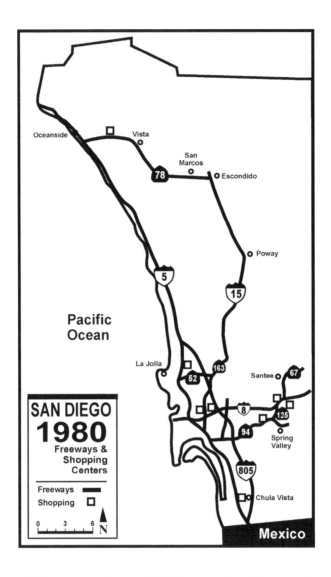

Figure 9. Freeways and Large (600,000 square foot) Shopping Centers,
San Diego 1980
Base map provided by SANDAG

created acute strain on existing services, because this was the fastest-growing region in the county during the 1960s. North and east of the first completed stretch of Highway 52, between the coastal freeway (Interstate 5) and the inland freeway (Interstate 15) were a series of instant cities. In University City, just north of the first completed section of 52 in what became the Golden Triangle formed by Interstate 5, Highway 52, and Interstate 805, population increased from just over 150 persons to well over 14,000.

North and east of University City, the instant cities of Mira Mesa, Rancho Penasquitos, and Rancho Bernardo extended along the western side of Interstate 15 to its end. On the eastern side of Interstate 15 the small town of Poway, which had a population of just over 5,000 in 1960, had added over 9,000 additional residents by 1970. Virtually all of the new construction was of single-family dwelling units, although there were condominiums and apartments built in the coastal North City region, south and west of the suburban explosion. These units accommodated the overflow of the University of California at San Diego (UCSD), just west of Interstate 5 on the cliffs above the ocean on the northern edge of the wealthy coastal community of La Jolla.

The completion of Interstate 805, which by 1972 ran south from Interstate 5 to Interstate 8, then by 1975 extended farther south to rejoin Interstate 5 just north of the Mexican border, relieved some of the pressure, particularly for the coastal communities. Highway 52 did not reach Interstate 15 until 1988, however, and it did not reached Highway 125 until 1998. The South Bay Freeway (Highway 54) stopped at the edge of Spring Valley. One proposal called for extending 54 into East County, across 94, and on to Interstate 8 east of El Cajon. At the same time Highway 125 was to go north to Poway. Perhaps if the freeway extensions had continued Highways 67 and 78 would have provided freeway access to Julian, but public outrage and big-picture planning alternatives suggested a different path. In a nutshell, environmentalists in the 1970s and no-growth advocates in the 1980s combined to severely limit the planned expansion of the San Diego freeway system.

In the midst of the controversy surrounding the uncontrolled growth of San Diego County suburbs, two distinct paths were leading toward a new big-picture plan that has ultimately become smart growth. The San Diego city planning department commissioned the analysis of development problems and possibilities that ultimately produced the 1974 report, *Temporary Paradise?* Meanwhile, the Comprehensive Planning Organization of the San Diego Region (CPO) published a different report in 1972 calling for regional planning to provide affordable housing. Then when *Temporary Paradise?* was published, the consultants who had produced the report recommended cooperation with the CPO and the establishment of a regional environmental planning and design authority. Thus these two independent analyses of environmental and affordable housing problems and possibilities led potentially conflicting interests down a converging path. The result was the creation of the San Diego Association of Governments (SANDAG), the regional planning authority that projects needs and recommends plans for regional housing and transportation and, most recently, environmental planning, habitat conservation, and all that is now subsumed under the big-picture plan called smart growth.[12]

This is not to suggest, however, that the growth of suburban San Diego County in the 1960s and 1970s was not planned or patterned. It was, in fact, planned to follow a general pattern of freeway expansion that facilitated commercial and residential development. This is just a modern variant of the nineteenth-century booster plan, where a hotel, a newspaper, and a real estate office were established in an effort to attract the transcontinental railroad. The

problem was that railroad builders and town builders were not always cooperating. Sometimes railroad builders built competing towns. At other times
town builders built competing railroads. In both cases the development of
transportation, commercial, and residential services were not synchronized.
And in addition to the challenge of attracting industry, there was the problem
of the uncertain development of boomtowns that might become ghost towns
almost overnight.[13]

The boomtowns of San Diego County in the 1960s and 1970s all fit the
pattern of expanded freeway access and commercial enterprise in the form of
shopping centers. The problem in 1970 was that neither freeway access nor
commercial services were keeping up with the building boom. University City
boomed in the 1960s, but the North City freeway triangle was not completed
until 1972. Until then University City residents were limited to Interstate 5—it
was the only way in and out via freeway. In a similar vein, University City is
bounded by regional shopping centers, all of which opened after the building
boom and after the freeway triangle was completed. University Towne Centre,
just north of University City, opened in 1977, and La Jolla Village Square, just
west of Interstate 5, opened in 1979. Claremont Square, just south of Highway
52, did not open until 1997.

The eastern and southern suburban boomtowns of the 1960s faced similar
problems with lagging freeway and commercial services. Santee boomed in the
1960s, but the extension of Interstate 8 and Highway 67 did not reach the suburb until 1968. The Parkway Plaza Shopping Center at the intersection of
Interstate 8 and Highway 67 did not open until 1972. Sweetwater was the
booming southern suburb in the 1960s, located at what became the intersection
of Interstate 805 and the South Bay Freeway (Highway 54). That segment of
Interstate 805 was not completed until 1975, however. The South Bay Freeway
opened in 1985 and didn't connect to Interstate 5 until 1990. Even then it did
not offer freeway access to the eastern suburbs or anywhere else. In fact, the
extension of Highway 125 to Highway 94 is still being constructed as I write
these words (in February 2001). Although Sweetwater and surrounding communities still lacked adequate freeway access until 1990—they were tied to
Interstate 805 as the only way in and out—they were at least served by the
Sweetwater Road Town and Country Shopping Center, which opened in 1975,
and the Plaza Bonita Shopping Center, which opened in 1981. These malls
occupy the northwest and southeast quadrants of the intersection of Interstate
805 and the South Bay Freeway (Highway 54).

In this regard, one might argue that Mira Mesa, and Interstate 15 development between San Diego and Riverside, was exceptionally poorly planned.
Mira Mesa is located on Highway 163 just above what would become
Highway 52, but that freeway connection was not completed until 1988. Even
then, as the flurry of growth-control measures subsided and the savings-and-
loan crash of 1989 approached, Mira Mesa and the Inland Empire remained
relatively isolated and lacked adequate commercial services. North County

Fair, fifteen miles south of Escondido, opened in 1986, but that was the only freeway-accessible major shopping center north of Mission Valley. Until Highway 52 was completed in 1988, offering freeway access to the University City Golden Triangle, it was easier for Mira Mesa residents to go to Mission Valley.

Just south of Escondido a small commercial center with freeway access opened in 1983, but it was in Rancho Bernardo, a more or less self-contained retirement community. The young families that moved into Mira Mesa and Poway in the 1960s and 1970s, like most middle-class San Diego suburban families, found that Mission Valley and Fashion Valley provided better commercial services. The problem with Mira Mesa, however, was that there were no local shopping centers—or even schools and fire departments. Thus the tragedy of Mira Mesa, which everyone seems to recognize as an example of bad development, might be considered the exception to what generally has been planned development and controlled growth, both before and after the San Diego city planning department commissioned the analysis that produced *Temporary Paradise?*

The Poway problem was similar but not quite as bad. The plan for the North City freeway system had included Highway 56, which was supposed to connect to Interstate 5 just below Del Mar then run through Mira Mesa, across Interstate 15, and into Poway. At the same time, Highway 125 was supposed to connect Poway with Santee to the south. Thus, even if the Highway 67 freeway were never extended to Highway 78, Poway still would have direct freeway access to the coast and to the eastern suburbs. Fortunately—or unfortunately, depending on how one views freeway expansion—one of the legacies of the big-picture plan offered in *Temporary Paradise?* was the decision not to build Highway 56 and not to extend Highway 125.[14] Thus Poway continues to suffer not so much from bad planning as from a change of plans that occurred in the middle of a building frenzy. It is only since prosperity has returned and smart growth has become the watchword that construction on Highways 56 and 125 is advancing. Perhaps this time the connections will be established before popular protest or economic depression undermines efforts to complete the big-picture plans for the region.

Although the best-laid plans were not always realized, it is clear that even prior to big-picture planning, suburban development in San Diego County was planned. The planning was less comprehensive and less regional in scale and scope, and some of the most ambitious efforts, such as Mission Valley, were implemented over the protests of the city planners, but the freeway-and-shopping-center pattern of suburbanization was planned. The obsolescence of the streetcar system was, as in Los Angeles, planned. The choice is not between planned and unplanned growth. The critical questions are: Planned how? Planned by whom? Planned toward what end?

Prior to the big-picture, comprehensive regional planning that was implemented in the 1970s, private-sector developers and state highway, state and federal housing, and local planning departments each pursued their respective plans, often without very effective coordination. Then, in response to the recommendations of various planners working on different pieces of the puzzle, and equally important, in response to increasing demands by environmentalists, proposals for big-picture plans emerged and ultimately converged as the cutting edge of progressive planning efforts. Big business and big government paved the way for what ultimately developed as a coalition that also included major environmentalist organizations.

In San Diego, as in the United States in general, the Rockefeller Brothers Fund sponsored big-picture planning. Its task force introduced itself in 1973 as follows: "The Task Force on Land Use and Urban Growth was created in the summer of 1972 by the Citizen' Advisory Committee on Environmental Quality (a body established by presidential executive order in May 1969)." Its members included Lawrence Rockefeller; Henry L. Diamond, commissioner of the New York State Department of Environmental Conservation; Pete Wilson, mayor of San Diego; Vernon E. Jordan Jr., executive director of the National Urban League; Harvard and M.I.T. academics; and vice presidents from Bank of America in California and Manufacturers Hanover Trust in New York.[15]

One might characterize the general perspective of the task force by the land-use authorities cited in the preface of its report. The first named are Fred Bosselman and David Callies, the authors of *The Quiet Revolution in Land Use Control*.[16] In a nutshell, the task force, following Bosselman and Callies, argues that the public attitude toward growth, and toward land-use in general, has changed. Consequently, land-use policies have also changed, on a "revolutionary" scale and scope without adequate central corporate and federal government administration.

Thus this first citizen task force was assembled to promote local, state, and federal policies that might establish a balance between environmental and development interests. It concluded that it was necessary and desirable to incorporate the concerns of environmentalists. Consequently, the Rockefeller Brothers Fund convened the Environmental Agenda Task Force, which included a veritable who's who of mainstream organized environmental interests. The New Federalist coalition included big government, big capital, and big environmentalists. Conspicuous in their absence were representatives of the labor, women's, and Civil Rights (or Black Power) movements. The New Federalists were in some ways like the progressive Republicans of the early twentieth century, except that women were conspicuously absent from the late-twentieth-century progressive coalition.[17]

Bosselman, Callies, Pete Wilson, and the Rockefeller brothers all viewed big-picture planning as a revolutionary change in land-use planning. For them, however, change that is effected without bloodshed—or in some cases the lack of change despite bloodshed—is revolutionary. Rebellion and revolutionary struggle, from their perspective, is chaos or crime. A revolutionary situation in which multiple authorities claim to control the state is, from their perspective, anarchy.

Here I offer a distinctively different perspective on social change. I assert that out of crisis comes progress but not revolution. San Diego County suburbs responded, and are continuing to respond, to the contradictory demands for affordable housing and growth control and to the conflicting if not contradictory demands of federal, state, and local conservation programs. In many cases the suburban cities have developed or are in the process of developing new general plans for development. In other words, there have been or will be substantial changes in the rules governing who gets to build what, and where.

The product—Yuppie Heaven—is new and improved. The production process (big-picture planning or smart growth) is bigger and better. The bottom line, however, is still the predominant concern for the bottom line. In other words, this is planning for profit and planners for hire. It is merely the latest version of cooperation between local government and national or international corporations, in this case with the whole world watching.

San Diego and the Speculative Frenzy, 1972–1989

Only by viewing the growth of San Diego County in historical perspective can we appreciate the nature and significance of the speculative frenzy of 1972–1989.[18] Contrary to popular mythology San Diego was not a sleepy Mexican farming village prior to the arrival of U.S. military forces during World War II. In fact, the U.S. military invasion came almost a century earlier, in 1846, when U.S. sailors arrived to enforce their nation's claim to San Diego. In 1867 Alonzo E. Horton arrived in San Diego and initiated the first major development project, purchasing at bargain basement prices what would become the territorial base of the City of San Diego. He then proceeded to construct his city on the harbor, displacing the old town, which has since been reconstructed as a tourist attraction.[19]

By 1900 San Diego was a thriving metropolitan community with a population growing at a rate of 76 to 87 percent per decade, far above the rates for California (44–65%) and the nation as a whole (15–16%). Although the population boom slowed during the Great Depression, population still increased by 38 percent between 1930 and 1940. The rate of population increase peaked at 92.4 percent between 1940 and 1950 and remained high (85.5%) until 1960, then declined precipitously (to 31.4%) thereafter.[20] Thus the boom of the World War II era was a return to the exceptionally high rates of growth that San Diego had been experiencing before the Great Depression.

Viewed in this historical context the population and building boom of San Diego County in the 1970s was relatively trivial. Population increased 37 percent in the 1970s and less than 35 percent in the 1980s.[21] This is comparable to the rate of growth experienced during the Depression years. Whatever happened in the 1970s and 1980s that inspired the tax revolt of 1978 and the no-growth movement of 1986–1988, it was not exceptional population growth. That had occurred much earlier.

What changed most dramatically was the industrial base that supported the increase in population. The late-nineteenth-century settlement had established trade and manufacturing, but the growth of these industrial sectors was most impressive after the establishment of military bases and military contracting companies during World War II and in the subsequent Cold War years. By 1956 manufacturing exceeded trade as the major county employer. Between 1947 and 1956 manufacturing jobs more than doubled, increasing from 20,783 to 47,731. Between 1949 and 1956, employment in retail and wholesale trade increased more modestly, from 29,866 to 39,154.[22]

The relative abundance of manufacturing jobs was particularly important in sustaining a growing population of consumers, because manufacturing jobs generally pay better than sales jobs. In 1967 the combined payroll for sales (retail and wholesale) and services was $451,629,000 in San Diego County. The comparable manufacturing payroll was $521,100,000. This disparity in payroll was sustained despite the growth of sales and service positions between 1956 and 1967 (in wholesale trade, for example, the number of employees increased from 7,076 to 11,805, an increase of 67%, while manufacturing jobs increased at a rate of 33%).

By 1972 sales and services had surpassed manufacturing as the employment base for the civilian labor force. Not only were there more jobs in retail sales (77,605) than in manufacturing (64,900), but the total payroll for manufacturing ($658,000,000) was exceeded by the combined payrolls of retail ($416,492,000), wholesale ($139,386,000), and service ($285,817,000). Still, while manufacturing offered just over 32 percent of the jobs in these four industrial sectors, it accounted for nearly 44 percent of the total payroll. Thus manufacturing continued to offer better-paying jobs, but there were relatively fewer jobs in that sector compared to the expanding opportunities for low-paid employment in sales and services.

Well-paid jobs that engage labor in productive enterprise were not declining in San Diego County between 1969 and 1988, but the rate of increase in manufacturing wages (5.95) was dwarfed by the rapid increase in service (11.7), finance, insurance, and real estate (11.2), and wholesale trade (10.2) earnings. The growth sectors of the economy were speculation and trade. This fueled the construction boom and the rapidly increasing cost of living in an economy that produced more money than products.[23]

Between the world wars, during World War II, and to a lesser extent in the Cold War era, the San Diego service economy was subsidized by federal government employment, particularly military employment. Earnings from government employment increased only fourfold (4.2) between 1969 and 1988, however, making government one of the slowest growth sectors. Furthermore, the federal share of wages paid to government employees has been declining relative to the share paid by local and state governments. Between 1983 and 1988, earnings from military employment increased only 25 percent and federal civilian earnings increased only 29 percent while earnings from local and state government employment increased 65 percent.[24]

State and local government employment is approaching the level of federal military employment in number of jobs and has already exceeded military employment in total earnings. In 1990, there were 138,672 military jobs and 132,697 jobs in local and state government. As early as 1988, however, earnings for local and state government employment ($2,985,817,000) had surpassed military earnings ($2,832,132,000). Thus military earnings are not even sufficient to pay the salaries of local government workers, and certainly not the salaries of the service and retail trade workers ($10,649,231,000), who are far more numerous.[25]

In sum, the postmodern, or postindustrial, economy of San Diego from 1972 to 1989 produced paper profits through speculation but produced an insufficient quantity of material objects that might maintain their value when the speculative bubble burst. At the same time, the base of consumer spending was eroded by the expansion of low-paid retail and service jobs. Not only do these jobs offer lower salaries, but they also tend to offer limited, if any, job security and benefits, thus contributing to the vulnerability of the postmodern economy when depression follows inflationary speculation.[26]

Not only was wealth redistributed in favor of the wealthy, particularly the financiers, during this period, but risk was also redistributed, as financiers enjoyed federal insurance and workers lost unemployment and health insurance. Thus in 1989, when the savings-and-loan industry collapsed, taxpayers provided welfare for the wealthy but offered no relief for the poor. The profits generated from "paper entrepreneurialism" had produced no tangible products that the public might claim in compensation for bailing out the financiers. "Unlike the production of goods and services, 'fiddling with' money produces few new jobs and no consumer goods. Policies based on outdated assumptions about the intrinsically beneficial nature of entrepreneurial activity tend to exacerbate the situation. . . . In the case of savings and loans, the abstract theory of 'trickle down' yielded the harsh reality of 'trickle up,' as taxpayers foot the bill for the casino extravaganza."[27]

In San Diego in particular, the basis for speculation and "fiddling with" money was land, and the speculative frenzy involved the futures market in land use. Developers attempted to gain new usage rights to land that was held by speculators, who then might sell as the market value of the land increased with the newly acquired usage rights. Since usage rights are granted by city or county government, local government was a critical actor in the speculative frenzy, performing as regulator and booster for investment companies seeking to profit from rapidly appreciating land values and thus expanding employment opportunities in state and local government.

The essential economic process is clear. Between 1970 and 1990, the United States experienced a short cycle of boom and bust. Within this twenty-year cycle, there were shorter phases of boom and bust. After the depression of 1970 to 1971, for example, there were boom phases in 1972–1973 and again in 1976–1978 preceding the bust phase of 1980–1982. Then between 1983 and 1989—roughly during the Reagan presidency—came the most protracted boom of the cycle. This was followed by the depression of 1990–1991, which still lingered from 1992 to 1996, particularly in southern California.

The boom-and-bust cycle of 1972–1989 was most dramatic in California, where Gross Domestic Product (GDP) increased annually by as much as 8.3 percent (in 1972) and averaged 3.9 percent for the twenty-year period. Although the boom was most spectacular in the 1972 recovery from the depression of 1970 the most sustained growth occurred between 1983 and 1989, when GDP annual growth in the state ranged from 3.8 percent in 1989 to 7.7 percent in 1984. Then the economy collapsed. In 1991 California posted its first decline in GDP for this period, surpassing, if only modestly, the national rate of decline (2.0% versus 1.8%).[28]

The boom was particularly spectacular in San Diego, where Mayor Pete Wilson (1972–1982) and Governor Ronald Reagan (1967–1975) facilitated efforts to develop and redevelop the city and county. Reagan, among other actions, reduced California's state taxes by $4 million between 1971 and 1975, thereby facilitating trickle-down economic prosperity.[29] Windfall profits were encouraged by local and state efforts to facilitate private-sector initiatives and cooperative development efforts. These efforts, the experimental case for what Reagan would later offer as federal policy, defied the logic of corporate liberalism (big government, capital, and labor). Indeed, the boom in San Diego, which represented the epitome of the Wilson-Reagan economic growth policy, defied the logic of New Deal economic policy. How could the San Diego economy boom if the government was shrinking?

The economic growth of San Diego between 1972 and 1989 was based on a giant pyramid scheme in which surplus capital was invested in speculation on land-use futures. Development, particularly in the early years, followed the rapidly proliferating maze of freeways, expanding in all directions to create suburbs—or boomtowns in the case of Poway and San Marcos—in the outlying rural areas. Some of the booming regions of early years, Sweetwater and University City, for example, which flourished between 1960 and 1970, were not cities at all but unincorporated regions of San Diego County or part of the City of San Diego. Mira Mesa was another such booming nonentity. The boom of the 1970s, in contrast, was particularly focused on vacant land in what had been outlying areas but soon, with the completion of the freeway system, came to be expanding suburban cities.[30] In the 1980s the City of San Diego was redeveloped. Thus, San Diego grew out in the 1960s and 1970s and then grew up in the 1980s.

What distinguishes the period of 1972–1989, then, is not growth, but the nature of growth within a county that had been growing steadily since 1900 and was booming in the postwar years. After World War II the marriage of big government, capital, and labor gave birth to the military-industrial complex, which sustained the early boom in Sunbelt cities like San Diego.[31] What distinguishes the Wilson-Reagan economic development policy of the 1970s from the boomtown growth of the 1950s and 1960s is that by 1972 well-paying manufacturing jobs—with health and retirement benefits—were no longer driving the booming economy as they had in the earlier decades, when industrial workers could afford to buy the houses that were being built. In fact, the base of the 1970s San Diego economy was, essentially, speculation and trade. Consequently, without the moderating effects of industrial unionism and federal employment contracts, the cycles of boom and bust were more dramatic, less predictable, and more dangerous, particularly for workers and their families.

Political Challengers and Contradictory Demands, 1970–1990

Needless to say, the boom-and-bust cycles of speculative frenzy between 1972 and 1989 generated political crises nationally as well as locally, beginning with the beleaguered Nixon administration of 1968–1974. The Nixon administration was vulnerable to political challenge in the early 1970s. The growing strength of the environmental movement was evidenced on Earth Day in 1970. The continued vitality of the antiwar movement was confirmed by the march on Washington in April 1971. The federal elections of 1970 indicated that both parties were vulnerable to new challenges, and a variety of laws were passed in an attempt to preempt the challengers. In 1970, for example, eighteen-year-olds were granted the vote and the Equal Rights Amendment passed Congress and moved into the state legislatures for ratification. In response to environmentalist concerns, the National Environmental Policy Act (NEPA) and a more stringent version of the Clean Water Act were passed. Also, the Environmental Protection Agency was established.[32]

On the basis of these accomplishments, his promise to end the war in Vietnam, and some signs of economic growth in 1972, Nixon survived the challenge. He continued to offer concessions to environmental and antiwar interests, signing the Clean Water Act and the Coastal Zone Management Act in the election year of 1972, and the Endangered Species Act (ESA) in 1973. In 1973 Nixon also successfully negotiated the end of the Vietnam War and the end of the draft. Nevertheless, 1973 also brought new opportunities to challenge the government, as the Supreme Court granted abortion rights in *Roe v. Wade* and the energy crisis threatened an untimely end to the economic boom of 1972 and 1973. Finally, the Watergate scandal threatened the president with impeachment in 1973 and 1974. Nixon resigned in August of 1974.[33]

Meanwhile, in California, Wilson and Reagan, in their plan for redeveloping San Diego and reinventing government, were attempting to preempt federal authority and local grassroots pressure for environmental regulation. Voters, however, impatient with the state legislature, mobilized a successful citizen initiative that imposed the California Coastal Act on local zoning authorities in 1972. Especially in the southern part of the state the California Coastal Commission tended "to 'correct' the decisions of more lenient" zoning authorities. Thus the San Diego County building boom was challenged particularly effectively along the coast, which explains, in part, why overbuilding, or bad development, was particularly evident in the inland corridor between 1973 and 1975. Then as the California economy was beginning to boom once again in 1978, voters who were dissatisfied despite the Reagan tax cuts and anxious about inflated real estate prices successfully mounted another citizen initiative to roll back local property taxes.[34]

The Coastal Act of 1972 and especially the tax revolt of 1978, which produced Proposition 13 had major effects on land-use planning in San Diego

County. Nevertheless, with Reagan in the White House a new wave of prosperity—or at least of construction—developed in the boom years of the mid-1980s. At that point, in the rapidly growing suburbs of San Diego County the citizen initiative was used again, this time in local elections, in an effort to reduce growth.[35]

Thus in each of the boom phases of the boom-and-bust cycle of 1972–1989, the citizen initiative imposed new demands that were added to the already growing set of conflicting state and federal requirements. The Coastal Act initiative was passed, in 1972, just as the California economy started to boom. The tax revolt of 1978 came near the end of the next boom, which had begun in 1976. Then, just as San Diego County was booming again, 1986–1988, local and regional growth control was imposed by citizen initiative (or in efforts to preempt such initiatives).

Clearly grassroots opposition to the Wilson-Reagan development policy was, in part, what inspired San Diego County suburbs to search for big-picture planning solutions. Aside from the exclusionary interests of grassroots community-based movements, suburban planners were also challenged by the often contradictory demands of state and federal authorities. California had developed its own environmental regulations in an effort to preempt federal challenges. The California Environmental Quality Act (CEQA) of 1970, for example, preempted federal NEPA standards. The federal Endangered Species Act (ESA) of 1973 also became a major stumbling block for efforts to encourage development in San Diego. CEQA regulations are procedural. They are designed to ensure that the environmental impact of approved projects is assessed and that the interested public is made aware of the options, including the no-project alternative. ESA, however, was a "wild card."[36]

It appears that the ESA was aimed originally at preventing federal development projects from interfering with federal preservation efforts. In 1978, however, the Supreme Court ruled that the law also applied to private development projects. That marked the beginning of growing uncertainty and increasing legislative efforts to balance the goals of conservation with the perceived need for economic growth. Congress amended the ESA in 1978 to allow for exemptions in cases where the benefits of development might outweigh the cost of species extinction, and it created a committee, which became known as the God Squad, to decide whether certain species would be exempt from protection. In 1978 the God Squad ruled against the Tennessee Valley Authority and in favor of the snail darter, an endangered fish species. Between 1978 and 1982 whenever a new species was listed for protection, only an act of the God Squad could allow development to continue.[37]

Not surprisingly, the most significant legislation for enabling development despite the incidental destruction ("taking") of endangered species came during the Reagan years. The ESA was amended in 1982 to establish the basis for the Habitat Conservation Plan (HCP), under which the taking of endangered species could be "mitigated" by preservation efforts. This legislation paved the way for big-picture plans, such as Natural Community Conservation Planning

(NCCP), that would allow for development in the southern California counties of San Diego, Orange, and Riverside. These counties were the target for this experiment in big-picture planning because they contained the bulk of extant coastal sage scrub, the habitat for the California gnatcatcher, a bird species listed by U.S. Fish and Wildlife Service as threatened in 1993. The precipitating event for the NCCP, however, was the protracted struggle between timber and preservation interests over the spotted owl in the Pacific Northwest. The spotted owl controversy became a campaign issue in 1992 as Clinton and Gore attempted to court environmentalists while remaining responsive to the need for economic development.[38]

Thus, the Wilson-Reagan development policies and the accompanying speculative frenzy inspired grassroots opposition to uncontrolled growth, to property tax increases based on inflated housing prices, and to bad development, particularly along the coast. The exclusionary demand for growth control and the often conflicting demands of state and federal programs—affordable housing versus preservation, for example—created serious planning problems in suburban cities that were seriously strapped for cash in the aftermath of the tax revolt,. Ultimately the search for creative solutions led local officials to the developers—the only parties willing and able to pay the cost of finding a big-picture solution. As Dan, a state NCCP official and an environmental biologist, explained in 1992: "Developers are by and large more enlightened than government officials. Most [government officials] have their jobs because they were concreting the city and county (e.g., Pete Wilson in San Diego). They are slow to realize that the rules of the game have changed." With that in mind, we can consider how suburban San Diego County governments accommodated these contradictory local, state, and federal demands between 1972 and 1989.

Accommodating Contradictory Demands

The environmental movement and environmental legislation created major problems for local planners in their negotiations with developers. New construction along the coast required conformity with requirements of the federal and state authorities that were protecting the coastline, the wetlands, and the endangered species that inhabited the coastal region. Environmental legislation created a complex and expensive bureaucratic maze, complete with Environmental Impact Reports (EIRs) and high-paid consultants. This increased the cost and complexity of obtaining building permits and produced a short-term decline in project approvals and a long-term trend toward big government, big capital, and large development projects.

Tommy, the Farmington city planning director, explained in 1992, "There were in the 1980s small guys, but most [developers] now are large firms with three-piece suits and UCLA degrees. After Proposition 13 the small guys disappeared as the cost went up." As the bureaucratic regulatory maze became more complex, the benefits of overregulation accrued to the developers and private-sector planners who were prepared to be opportunistic and manipulative. In the short-run, however, regulation tended to interfere with development.

In 1974, in the wake of the Endangered Species Act (1973), the California Coastal Act (1972), and the California Environmental Quality Act (1970), only 14,900 new dwelling units were approved in San Diego County. The lull was only temporary, however. In 1976, 29,100 new units were approved. In 1977 the number reached 36,400. Clearly the developers and the city planners had accommodated the environmental regulations by 1977, at which point they faced a new crisis—the property tax revolt of 1978.

The tax revolt proved to be a protracted problem especially for planners and developers of residential units, because the prospect of revenue in the form of property taxes was a major incentive for the city to promote residential development. Without the promise of these tax revenues, cities were hard pressed to approve new units, which would require public expense for utilities, roads, schools, and so on. To make matters worse, the tax revolt problems were compounded by the Supreme Court decision, also in 1978, that subjected private development projects to the regulatory power of the ESA. Between 1979 and 1982 the number of units approved per year dropped below 20,000—falling to 7,500 in 1982.

Nevertheless, even the tax revolt was eventually accommodated. In the wake of still further amendments to the ESA, this time under the auspices of the Reagan administration, approvals climbed from over 20,000 in 1983 to a peak of 44,100 in 1986. This exceeded the previous peak of 36,400 in 1977, achieved just prior to the tax revolt and the Supreme Court decision. Developers could envision the economic and political crises that unbridled speculation and uncontrolled building were likely to engender, so they were rushing master-planned community projects through the bureaucratic maze, hoping to gain approval before the bottom fell out of the market or the citizens rebelled. This boom suffered somewhat during the flurry of growth-control measures adopted between 1986 and 1988: annual approvals fell to 30,600 in 1987 and to 28,600 in 1988. Then when the savings-and-loan crisis hit the newspaper headlines in 1989, the speculative frenzy was over. Between 1989 and 1993, annual approvals fell from 18,700 to 5,800.[39]

The causes and consequences of the speculative frenzy of 1972–1989 can be debated. Most important for present purposes, however, is the fact that the rules of the planning game have changed dramatically since the boom cycle opened in 1972. Since 1970 land-use planning has involved more laws and less tax revenue (particularly since 1978), more citizen participation, and greater reliance on the creative solutions provided by developers. Planning has become big business, combining big government and big capital in a dialectical relationship of conflict and cooperation.

In 1992, Tommy, the Farmington city planning director, summarized these changes as follows: There are more constraints on cities, imposed both by the state and by citizens. "The general plan is now taken more seriously. There is more ballot-box planning and more citizen involvement." Furthermore, the tax revolt of 1978 increased local government's dependence on developers. "Proposition 13 had major effects, particularly in bedroom communities. . . . For the next four to five years, cities looked for creative solutions. Developers were required to pay more fees. . . . Farmington and Castleton have the highest fees in the county."

Public- and private-sector interests agree on the basic chronology. The short-term effect of the tax revolt and the extended regulatory authority of the ESA was a sharp decline in housing unit approvals. Within the next five years, however, suburban cities were able to entice developers into providing infrastructure and public services as mitigation for environmental impact. In fact, the CEQA procedures adopted in Castleton resulted in EIRs that included "Public Facilities Fees to cover the need for any additional facilities" as mitigation for the fact that the "proposed development would significantly impact police services within the City."[40] Thus environmental regulation provided a means of extracting public services and special fees that might sustain suburban cities in the aftermath of the tax revolt. Particularly in the case of CEQA regulations, which are procedural in nature, the elaborate planning process increased both the bureaucratic legal formalism of applying the letter of the law and the trilateral citizen-developer-government negotiation that was increasingly coming to characterize the politics of city planning.

Growth control was a major challenge in the rapidly growing suburban cities. In varying degrees, however, these suburban cities were able to entice developers to cooperate in preempting local growth-control initiatives with facility management plans. In two San Diego suburbs that were particularly challenged by the contradictory demands of growth control and affordable housing, developers were enticed into big-picture planning efforts, in one suburb for a medical-industrial complex, and in the other for upscale housing developments that would provide open space and trails, habitat conservation, and even affordable housing. Some of these developers were willing to pay any price for project approvals that might bring windfall profits before the bubble burst, which it did in 1989.

Developers who cooperated with local government in preempting citizen-initiated growth control during the boom years and who continued to support local government in the development of affordable housing plans became increasingly important in efforts to co-opt grassroots opposition groups during the bust phase, when cities revisited their general plans. The enlightened, cooperative developer is a critical actor in trilateral negotiations, particularly during a bust phase, when no one is building but everyone is talking and planning for the future. Tommy, the Farmington city planning director, described this aspect of the new world of urban planning: "We get developers to communicate with neighbors and bring them into the planning effort. . . . A few developers know how to do this. . . . Some developers get involved in the community and do things [make charitable contributions, and so on]. That eases approval." Tommy went on to explain how developers are learning to play politics: "Hiring local agents helps. The Williams sisters tried to railroad the

Castleton planning department. Then they hired Bill, who would schmooze with neighbors and lobby Congress."

Schmoozing with neighbors and cooperating with local government was increasingly important in the slow-growth period after 1989. During this bust phase quite a few suburban cities made major revisions to their general plans. Of five contiguous cities in what had been the fastest-growing region of the county in the 1970s. Farmington thoroughly revised its general plan in 1990, and all of the others were engaged in major revisions between 1989 and 1997. Clearly these revisions were intended to accommodate grassroots concerns as well as the concerns of the developers. In 1992 Castleton officials prepared pamphlets encouraging citizens to participate in the general-plan revisions: "Through a series of Town Hall Meetings, Community Workshops, and a Children and Youth Outreach Program, the Public Review Program will ensure that the General Plan addresses the needs of all Castleton citizens and reflects the community vision of what Castleton should be."

At a meeting for developers and other interested parties held at a regional country club in spring of 1992, planning directors from these five suburban cities offered an olive branch to the building interests. They hosted a lovely buffet breakfast and tried to gain support for their ongoing public relations efforts, projected changes in planning policies, and general hesitance to approve new projects in the interim. Chuck, the planning director from Castleton, began his speech with a bad joke, "I'm glad I was not asked to talk about current development." Only one building permit had been approved in the first quarter of 1992, so the audience wasn't laughing. Chuck continued to be upbeat, however, like a stand-up comic who was dying up there but wouldn't give up on his monologue. He briefly described "long-range plans [for] getting our general plan in shape and getting ready for economic recovery."

The update process in Castleton combined private meetings with developers and consultants, which produce technical reports and feasibility studies, with various types of public meetings in which interested parties added their comments and expressed their concerns regarding the plans developed by the experts. There were three different types of public meetings: citizen advisory committee (CAC) meetings, workshops, and hearings. CACs were appointed to discuss the most controversial issues, particularly open space and habitat conservation. These committees included the noisy neighbors, the large landowners, the developers, and representatives of organizations such as Save Our Open Space, Friends of Castleton Lagoon, the local Audubon Society, and so on. They were led by a facilitator and operated in tandem with executive committees composed of experts. In the course of lengthy discussion, the opposition was worn down or won over. Then there were public review meetings, or workshops, for the general public to discuss the CAC plan. Finally, public hearings, as required under NEPA and CEQA, were held. The opposition had usually been worn down or won over before the public hearings began, so final approval was anticlimactic—a celebration of the popular will and a parody of the democratic process.[41]

The process of co-opting and preempting potential opposition during the general-plan update is in many ways similar to what the enlightened developer does in gaining community support for a project. Of particular interest in the context of accommodating contradictory demands is the fact that city governments cooperated with developers in preempting citizen growth-control initiatives at the height of the building boom. Since then, during the bust of 1990–1992, the cities were actively courting citizen involvement in general-plan revisions. In efforts to accommodate contradictory demands, these city governments attempted to preempt challengers during the boom phase and then co-opt them during the bust phase.

Five San Diego Suburbs

The suburban boomtowns of the 1970s faced their most serious challenge from the contradictory interests promoting affordable housing, growth control and habitat conservation.[42] Earlier, in the 1960s, development at the northern edge of the City of San Diego, just inland from the quaint coastal residential and commercial settlement of La Jolla, was fostered by the cooperative efforts of public and private interests. Since the development was not part of La Jolla but was located on vacant land that lay within the legal bounds of the San Diego, this expansion was legally negotiated without much apparent controversy.[43]

After a major highway system (Highway 52 and Interstates 5 and 805, which form the Golden Triangle) was built through this section of the county, the legal development in the area continued.[44] The rate of growth was declining, however, as areas on the edge of the city offered fewer possibilities for windfall profits and as legal constraints on coastal and wetlands development increased. After 1970, with new residential development and increased environmental regulation, this sort of development and the expansion of the highway system was much more problematic. Federal, state, county, and city authorities were more involved, and public notification procedures tended to generate grassroots opposition to widening the highway or adding housing units to an increasingly populated area.

Once the regions on the edge of the city were developed and the highway system was expanded to provide rapid transit throughout the county, that which had been considered rural was within the reach of suburban development. Consequently, between 1970 and 1980, the pull of undeveloped land and the push of declining opportunities on the edge of the city inspired speculation in the future development of rural areas that might become suburban. The suburban cities selected for analysis here became middle-class suburbs between 1970 and 1980. They are located in the part of the county that experienced the most dramatic rate of growth at the height of the speculative growth boom and the grassroots political movements.[45]

San Diego County was not experiencing unusually high rates of population and housing growth in the 1960s. County population increased by 31 percent (compared to 27% in the state), housing increased by 34 percent (30% in the state). In the 1970s, however, two things changed. First, San Diego's population growth far exceeded statewide growth. Second, housing-unit growth far exceeded population growth. This general pattern of overbuilding was characteristic of the period. Statewide population growth was only 19 percent, but the number of housing units increased by 33 percent statewide. San Diego County population increased by 37 percent (nearly twice the state rate), with the number of housing units increasing by 60 percent.

Our five suburban boomtowns display an exaggerated version of this general trend, although each experienced its own distinctive pattern of growth. Only Waterton and Farmington were really cities in 1970, with populations over 25,000, and both had already been growing rapidly in the 1960s. Waterton's population increased by 62 percent, and Farmington's increased by 125 percent between 1960 and 1970. Waterton continued to boom in the 1970s, with population increasing by 89 percent and the number of housing units expanding by 124 percent. Farmington also continued to grow, but the rates of population (75%) and housing (100%) growth actually declined from that of the 1960s. Belleville, a small but fairly well established working-class suburb, sustained its population growth rate of 45 percent and increased its rate of housing growth only modestly (from 64% in the 1960s to 73% in the 1970s).

The boomtowns of the 1970s were Paradise and Castleton. Paradise, a virtual nonentity in the 1960s, experienced population growth of 349 percent between 1970 and 1980, with the number of housing units increasing by 346 percent. Here there was no overbuilding. In Paradise new residents were arriving as fast as relatively inexpensive new suburban homes could be built. In Castleton as well the rate of population and housing growth increased dramatically in the 1970s, but here there was considerable overbuilding. Castleton witnessed a 138 percent population increase and a 198 percent increase in the number of housing units between 1970 and 1980. Despite this overbuilding, Castleton, unlike its neighbors, was becoming an increasingly wealthy suburb.

Except for Castleton these were not particularly wealthy communities compared to San Diego County as a whole. The four cities other than Castleton reported lower median family income and lower median value of owner-occupied housing not only in 1970, but in 1980 and 1990 as well. They were decidedly suburban, however, reporting average or slightly higher than average rates of owner-occupied dwellings. Even Castleton, the wealthiest community in this section of the county, reported household income ($10,000) and housing values ($25,000) that were only moderately above the county figures ($10,000 and $22,000 for housing values) in 1970. Between 1970 and 1980, however, Castleton became a wealthy suburb, with median income ($26,000) and housing values ($123,000) far exceeding the county average (median income: $20,000; housing: $91,000) for 1980. Meanwhile, Paradise, although not particularly wealthy, was the fastest-growing bedroom community in the county. Population more than tripled in the 1970s, and owner-occupied homes constituted 76 percent of all occupied units in 1980.

In varying degrees, then, these five contiguous suburban cities experienced the most dramatic effects of the building boom between 1970 and 1980, and they faced the challenge of accommodating the contradictory demands of state and regional authorities, who demanded affordable housing, and local residents, who demanded growth control. Of the five communities Castleton faced what might be considered the most serious challenge. It managed, however, to preempt the challengers by enticing developers to cooperate during the boom, in 1986, and then to co-opt local opposition leaders in producing the general-plan update after the bust, in 1991. This modern-day success story warrants scrutiny.

The Kingdom of Castleton

Castleton is one of the many suburban San Diego County municipalities that boomed during the speculative frenzy of 1972–1989. This particular suburban city developed in fits and starts as stagecoach, railroad, and finally highway access provided a basis for speculation and development of the inland agricultural lands and the coastal resort locations. From the beginning there was a tension between the coastal zone, with its potential for tourism, and the inland area, with its potential for agriculture. Nevertheless, for more than a century, local boosters have promoted the development of seaside resorts and agricultural production, attempting to entice investment and creating transportation and irrigation systems. Prior to World War II, however, such efforts were only marginally successful. Fancy hotels were built, farms were irrigated, and lands were subdivided for development, but the boomtown never boomed. Agriculture was sustained, however, and coastal resorts succeeded, in varying degrees, in enticing tourists throughout the boom-and-bust cycles of the developing economy prior to 1945.

After the war the boosters struggled to convince the coastal and inland residents to incorporate and thus reap the benefits of the postwar boom, developing local facilities, particularly water and sewer systems, under local authority. They faced an uphill battle, however, as many of the coastal development interests were opposed to incorporation, preferring the more certain path of annexation by Waterton, while many rural residents were opposed to change in any form. The conflicts among the inland agricultural and residential interests, the coastal development interests, and the Castleton boosters characterize the development of this community and that of other San Diego County coastal cities and towns. Although the boosters won the battle for incorporation, it is not clear that they have won the war; they have certainly not resolved the conflicting interests of local residents.

The coastal interests, for example, have been exceptionally ill-served by the boosters. What was the main drag of the old beach town has deteriorated. There is one old hotel and one pre–Coastal Act restaurant on the only Castleton beach that is readily accessible to bathers. On the other hand, there is only a single ugly cliffside condominium development, on the ocean side of Highway 5, and there are no shabby beach cottages, biker bars, boardwalks, or amusement parks. The window of opportunity for oceanfront development between the freeway construction of 1970 and the Coastal Act of 1972 was too small to allow the production of anything like Venice Beach or Santa Monica Beach and Pier in Los Angeles, or even Mission Beach and Pacific Beach in San Diego.

Castleton does have a huge lagoon, which erosion, neglect, and abuse from too many years of quasi-industrial agriculture had turned into an ecological disaster by 1992. The lagoon alternated between summer swamp and winter flood phases, effectively destroying the market and use value of the entire region, from the eastern edge of the stinking swamp to the western edge of the frequently flooded coastal highway. Fixing the lagoon was part of the big-picture plan of the 1980s. Meanwhile, Castleton expanded to the east of Highway 5, creating a modern downtown and civic center as far away from the lagoon as possible while maintaining easy freeway access. The upscale residential areas of the 1970s were also far from the lagoon, in the hills east of the new downtown, but new developments, particularly large-scale planned communities, shopping centers, and industrial parks, came to be spread throughout the expanding municipal region.

In the 1960s and particularly in the 1970s, Castleton annexed adjacent land to facilitate the building boom in residential and commercial units. Thus the population of Castleton increased 111 percent, from just over 4,000 in 1950 to more than 9,000 in 1960. Over the next decade it jumped another 62 percent, to almost 15,000 in 1970; the increase included nearly 800 residents in areas annexed since 1960. The biggest boom was in the 1970s, when population grew 138 percent, to over 35,000, by 1980.[46] This boom in the 1970s was both cause and consequence of the cooperation between big government and big capital in the political economy of land speculation, preservation, and development. In Castleton, as in other suburban San Diego cities, "free-market populism" (or petit bourgeois revolt) emerged in the form of environmentalism in the late 1960s and early 1970s, tax revolt in the late 1970s, and growth control in the 1980s.[47]

One observer, writing in 1976, offered insights into the popular unrest and anticipated at least the nature of the grievances if not the specific forms of local rebellion. "These cities have permitted developers to increase the number of multifamily apartments along the bluffs. . . . Many people are concerned about the possibility of overload on community facilities . . . and [about] tax increases. . . . Finally, all found their local autonomy somewhat reduced by the creation of the Regional Coastal Commission in 1972."[48] All of these concerns were expressed in Castleton, inspiring the city council, in 1988, to order an update of the city's general plan for future development. This update was accompanied by a massive public relations effort in 1991 to 1992.

On balance, this suburban city provides a particularly instructive case for analysis—not because it is typical of the San Diego County or the United States, but because it illustrates the speculative frenzy and the economic and political crises, including the environmental, open-space, and growth-control movements.[49]

Castleton has a long history of boosterism and promotion of economic development, although the boosters have struggled against opposition from the outset. Nevertheless, even in the wake of the local growth-control movement, the city continues to present itself as progressive. "Castleton's progressive city government legislates a unique balance of public services and planning strategies to meet the current and future needs of the citizenry. Though committed to economic growth, the city is critically sensitive to [its] unique ecological position."[50] On this note, we might consider the progressive vision of Castleton as viewed from the developer's perspective in the context of a master-plan, or planned community, project proposed in 1983.

The Project

The Patterson Company describes the history of the Camelot project in its promotional literature as follows: "Camelot is located . . . on 1,000 acres adjacent to the Castleton lagoon. The beginnings of the master-planned resort and residential community date back to 1979, when the Williams sisters purchased the property."

By reading between the lines of the promotional documents and supplementing this account with five months of observation and intensive interviews with the major players, it is easy to reconstruct the process of planning this project in the context of what we already know about the city and the speculative frenzy of 1972–1989. First, in 1979 the Williams sisters attempted to "railroad" the city, as Tommy, the lead planner for Castleton on the project in the 1980s, put it as he described the initial attempt to gain master-plan approval. Bill, the local CEO for the Camelot project, described that experience as follows: "The Williams sisters were running this project out of [their national office] and hired an L.A. group [to get master-plan approval] between 1980 and 1983. Then they hired me to mend fences." Bill identified himself as "a third-generation San Diegan"—obviously an insider. Plus, he was the president of a national developers association—clearly a pro. "But the plan was high density. They didn't take into account the land, etc. We had to figure out what the coastal commission would accept. I talked to Dick [a consultant and former city employee] about that. It was hard to convince the Williams sisters to start over, but they were getting nowhere."

Here we see the benefits of using local agents. Bill is a San Diegan, and he used former city planning department staff, Dick and Harry, as consultants. He even hired a full-time planner for the project—Tom, a former city employee who had gotten fed up and was prepared to work for the other side in the interest of pursuing creative planning solutions. Also on staff were Larry, an engineer, who worked with city engineers on creative solutions to technical problems, and John, a construction manager, who made sure the bulldozers were ready to roll on cue and generally managed the construction of roads, sewers, and so on. (The developer does not build houses, just infrastructure). There were also Millie, the marketing director; Pat, an assistant planner; and a host of administrative and clerical workers.

These folks worked well together. They were highly educated and highly motivated, bright and ambitious, and thoroughly versed in the formal and informal ways of planning development in Castleton. They complemented each other nicely. Bill was something of a cowboy politician—very California, very smooth, but sometimes a little reckless and impetuous. Larry, the engineer, was more conservative, but he modeled his behavior, even his dress and professional associations, on those of his boss. Although he told me that he would like to get out of this rat race and go to graduate school, Larry seemed like future developer material. Tom, the head planner, was the real insider—a professional planner who had been hired in the city planning department by Tommy, a childhood friend who later became the city's lead planner for the Camelot project and then became director of planning in Farmington. Tom had also worked with the consultants, most of whom were former city employees. As a law school dropout, he even had a legal background, and he seemed comfortable talking to the project attorney, who was kept on retainer and charged the developer by the minute for telephone consultations.

Schmoozing with neighbors and informally negotiating with city planning officials were Bill's forte, and he was also a force to be reckoned with when lobbying state and federal officials and pleading his case at public hearings. Bill was involved in the most important negotiations and attended the most important public hearings. The day-to-day bureaucratic process was the domain of Tom and Larry. Bill was more concerned with the big picture.

Bill explained his strategy for gaining master-plan approval: "By 1985 we had a new plan and the city was more receptive. I was unable to spread out a thousand-acre map. It was too intimidating—too vast. So we divided it into a checkerboard of planning areas and did one per week—visited the site and looked at the plans." Bill explained that he and the city planners had pretty much solved the problems before putting together the formal proposal. "By the end we had worked through all the major problems. I met with Tommy, planners, and engineers and negotiated area by area. We had already agreed on the basics before putting together the master plan." Nevertheless, the CEQA procedures virtually guaranteed that organized opposition would emerge, particularly in a wealthy suburb like Castleton. "CEQA created lots of controversy. We got lots of comments and tried to incorporate them into the plan. Thus the revised plan had solved most of the problems." When I asked specifically about plateau bargaining, Bill denied that he used that ploy. "We were not asking for more than we wanted [but] the owners never intended to build [so] they didn't care about dropping the number of units."

The master of schmoozing, Bill was able to get the best deal possible from the city by using his political skills to gain support from the community. "We developed a community outreach program [because] we wanted to challenge the conventional wisdom that the developer comes in with a plan and crams it down throats. We wanted to convince citizens [because] staff work in fear of council and council works in fear of constituents." Despite overwhelming local support, however, Bill faced strong opposition from the California Coastal Commission. Castleton had not established a local plan, so Camelot had to go before the state commission, whose members were not particularly concerned with the interests of local government or even local residents. "The coastal commission staff conditioned 'No hotel.' We had a fall-back position—deed restrictions, etc., giving more than the staff asked. Plus we had 150 people in support. If you follow the Coastal Act you can work with them." Bill explained that Patterson had not had a problem with the coastal commission and that in some ways it had benefited from the extra layer of regulation. By 1992, however, he wanted the city to organize its own local coastal plan to eliminate the additional delays and expense.

Once the master plan for Camelot was finally approved, in 1988, the Williams sisters sold the project to Mr. Patterson. He retained Bill and his staff to carry out the relatively routine formal legal process of preparing each segment, or planning area, of the project for final approval so lots could be sold to builders with some confidence that Castleton would issue building permits. Tom was in charge of obtaining the necessary approvals and permits, beginning with section one of the master plan, which required tentative maps for each of the six neighborhoods surrounding the golf course. Once the city and the coastal commission staff approved the final maps, these planning areas were sold to builders. Then similar plans, with tentative maps, were submitted for two additional residential sections and for each of the twenty-five to thirty neighborhoods that would eventually be built in those two sections of the project. When I arrived in the field in January 1992, section one had been built except for the resort hotel, and eight of the planning areas in section two were in various stages of approval. I had the opportunity to follow seven planning areas through the various stages of the approval process in the winter and spring of 1992.

The major problem in 1992 from the developer's perspective was that the rules were changing. Castleton was trying to negotiate an affordable housing agreement whereby 15 percent of all new housing would be affordable for low-income families. This was a major problem for an upscale development project, but all tentative maps were encumbered with the condition that the developer must reach an agreement with the city on the provision of affordable housing. Castleton was also working on a habitat preservation program that would accommodate the anticipated listing of a bird species, the California gnatcatcher. Since the bird nests in the rolling hills on prime development sites, this was a problem as well.

A third problem was a plan to dredge the lagoon as mitigation for a project in another county. The Sierra Club was suing the city and delaying the dredging project. Meanwhile, the cycles of flooding and the stagnant water contributed to the nervousness of resort hotel investors. It seemed unlikely that the hotel would attract new investors, or convince old investors to come back on board, before the lagoon preservation project commenced. Meanwhile, Bill,

Tom, and Larry were struggling with temporary measures that might provide creative solutions to the short-term problems of flooding, which was a problem for the city, and stagnant water, which was a problem for the developer.

As if this were not enough, the economic depression and the failure of the savings-and-loan industry created serious problems for planners. Tom wanted to obtain approval for the planning areas in section two that might contain sensitive habitat or gnatcatchers. He also wanted to get approval of the tentative map for section three, which contained both sensitive habitat and gnatcatchers, before the bird was listed or before the rules changed again and he was required to preserve more or pay more in order to secure development rights.

Since the master plan did not vest development rights in Castleton—in fact, developers do not have vested rights until the foundations are in—there were incentives for moving quickly. Tom wanted to get instant approval so that he could sell to a builder, who could put in the foundations before the rules changed. It was, however, difficult to move quickly because the depressed housing industry offered few incentives to build. It would be difficult to sell these lots to a builder, and the tentative map would expire if grading did not commence in a timely fashion. Thus Tom was between a rock and a hard place. Castleton planners were regulating his project to death, in his opinion, and were stalling because they were apprehensive about what the general-plan update might produce. The future looked bleak, so he wanted to expedite the approval process, but he was concerned that he might lose development rights if he engaged in premature grading that was not followed in short order by the construction of houses. These were hard times in the industry, and desperate times produced, on occasion, equally desperate measures.

The greatest source of anxiety was the prospect that the California gnatcatcher would be listed as a state or federal endangered or threatened species. The master plan and the tentative maps for sections one and two had already been approved. What remained was primarily a routine bureaucratic process of negotiating the conditions that would be imposed on the tentative maps for section three and for each of the eight remaining planning areas in section two. The Castleton city planning department had routinely encumbered each approval with conditions regarding local facilities, special tax districts, erosion control, winter grading (which required a special permit), open space, building heights, and so on—the planning department routinely imposed between fifty and one hundred conditions. There were, however, three new conditions that the developer was attempting to negotiate.

First, the city conditioned its agreement on the provision of affordable housing. Second, the coastal commission staff had imposed a new condition requiring a survey of gnatcatchers if grading was proposed during nesting season. Third, the city stipulated that the property owner must agree to participate in a yet-to-be-established drainage assessment district to provide revenues for a city drainage plan that was still on the drawing board. This was the most odious of the new conditions and the one that the developer fought all the way to the Castleton City Council.[51]

Fighting City Hall

The first public confrontation with the city council on the drainage assessment district condition came during a fairly routine request for tentative map approval, required so the developer could begin rough grading to prepare the site for roads, sewers, and so on. Bill had chosen to use the planning commission hearing on this map as part of his continuing assault on the drainage issue. The developer had already protested the assessment in writing and before the planning commission. In the prehearing meeting where they discussed the conditions and tried to anticipate problems, Tom had informed the city planning department that he would object to the condition. The planning commission had already refused to strike it, and the developer had appealed to city council. Thus the expression of opposition to the drainage assessment district during the planning commission meeting might be considered strategic: the developer went on the record as opposed to the condition while it was preparing for the council meeting.

Bill attended the planning commission meeting, along with Tom and Larry. Before the meeting the project staff talked about their prospects for defeating the drainage assessment condition, joking about taxation without representation and the idea of wearing feathers—an allusion to the Boston Tea Party. At the planning commission hearing, however, there was no public spectacle. Compared to city council meetings, planning commission meetings are usually downright dull. There are virtually no impassioned speeches, and the only drama is in waiting for the results of the vote. Even after many meetings I found it very difficult to follow the concerns of the planning commissioners. In Castleton, for example, one commissioner was always concerned about the material used to construct fences, although it was never clear why that was relevant and how it influenced his vote on a permit.

This particular meeting, despite its obvious importance for the Camelot project staff, was characteristically boring. The city planning department recommended approval of the tentative map with the specified conditions, and the commission asked the petitioner if he had any comments.

> Bill: This meeting can be short. We've raised this before. The property is already taxed [and] I don't know where this will end. The city is supposed to provide services. We object to [the drainage assessment] condition.

> [after some unrelated discussions that led nowhere]

> Commissioner: We will not vote on [this] condition. We had two votes last time.

The planning commission then unanimously approved the tentative map, and Bill immediately filed an appeal to the city council.

When the city council heard the appeal from the planning commission hearing, the discussion was much more animated. The city planning department staff made a fairly routine report but noted that there was some controversy at the planning commission hearing regarding the drainage assessment condition.

Council: Why is this condition not more specific?

Staff: We didn't know when we wrote it what would be involved. We are in the process of preparing a program for drainage control. It got more specific when the question was raised.

Council: If we didn't have this financial crunch this condition wouldn't be here.

Staff: Maybe. We have been advised to cut corners. We now require developers to maintain a desilting basin. We will have to spend some money on maintenance.

This public display of conflict between the planning staff and the council was quite amusing and was obviously staged for the benefit of the television audience. Part of what makes Castleton City Council meetings a true carnival of public government is the fact that the proceedings are televised.

Council: We will have to do this citywide in order to qualify. These projects would not have to provide for the rest of the city?

Staff: No. Just for their drainage.

Mayor: Are there other developments that will be in the district that do not have this condition?

Staff: No.

City Manager: There is no district yet.

Clearly, the elected officials were making quite an effort to appear to be fair in this matter.

Mayor: There is a problem with some residents being required to pay without voting while others get to vote.

Council: Does this mean that the developer will not have the right to object if the district is formed?

City Attorney: Yes.

Staff: We would prefer to have a citywide district, but we would need to have a hearing in which people are allowed to protest. Ten percent opposed would require an election.

In ongoing discussion it became clear that one council member and the mayor were concerned about the fairness if some could protest but others could not. Bill was then recognized and he gave a rousing speech.

> Bill: Like the mayor said, [this is like the] Boston Tea Party. We have already paid. We can't pay more. Most important, we want the right to speak. We will not "escape." We have paid our fair share and will pay our fair share. We would like to remove the condition from the other two tentative maps also.

> City Attorney: We can't remove the condition from the previous planning areas, because the period for appeal is over.

One member of council asked for scenarios with and without the condition. Another member declared opposition to the condition. The first agreed and moved to delete the condition. A third seconded the motion. The motion passed; the condition was removed. The motion to approve the negative declaration and the tentative map passed unanimously.

This is a good example of a single-issue hearing. There was no discussion of any other condition or finding, and the council and the mayor were very much involved in determining what was fair, in this case in response to the letter of protest they had received from the developer. Ultimately, as Tom predicted, after the debate the council voted unanimously to approve the project. This is also a good example of an opportunistic challenge to the unreasonable demands of the city planning staff. Bill was always ready to take advantage of any opportunity in the ongoing negotiations with the city. He seemed to enjoy winning the battles, while Tom was more focused on the war. This was not due primarily to a personality difference but was their division of labor in negotiating for land-use permits.

In this case, the developer won. The drainage assessment district condition was stricken from the grading permit. In other cases the developer negotiated for creative solutions that no other actor had the interest or ability to provide. These creative solutions were expensive. Tom estimated that the affordable housing agreement alone would cost Camelot at least $250,000 (not counting the staff time consumed in the negotiations). Preserving gnatcatcher habitat was also an expensive proposition. Tom, in a presentation to the coastal commission, claimed that the gnatcatcher occupied the most valuable property in the project. He estimated that Mr. Patterson, who had bought the project in 1988, would lose $20 million when Camelot was finally completed, due to the expense of developing creative solutions each time the city or the state changed the rules of the game.

Those of us who have difficulty imagining how we could gain or lose $20 million might find it difficult to sympathize, but Mr. Patterson had bought late, in 1988, just before the bubble burst. Also, although he was not involved in the construction of housing, he was much closer to construction (he sold to builders) than the previous owners had been. Thus the story of Camelot is not the story of the wicked Mr. Patterson or those naughty Williams sisters conspiring with government to rape the land for fun and profit. The speculative frenzy was not about building houses. It was about buying and selling land and speculating in usage rights. By the time Mr. Patterson purchased the property, the boom days were drawing to a close, and the prospects of windfall profits were bleak.

Whether building luxury housing is a good or bad thing is a matter of personal opinion, which need not concern us here. The insanity of land-use planning and development is the primary concern, including the benefits of overregulation and the irony of popular participation. One could easily blame the speculators or the regulators or the exclusionary grassroots movements.[52] But after spending some time with the interested parties, I am convinced that these are not bad or malevolent people. Particularly if we focus on the big players—the Nature Conservancy, the state-level Natural Community Conservation Planning (NCCP) staff, the executive and middle-management city planning staff, and the directors and middle-management staff of the largest development firms—we find highly educated professionals in search of big-picture planning solutions. The problem is not the actors—these are the best and the brightest. The problem is the system—the free market in land and development for profit, with plans and planners for sale. This should become increasingly clear as we look at the creative solutions developed to solve the problems of affordable housing and habitat conservation. Then we can return to these big-picture, systemic concerns in considering the prospects for planning the postmodern community.

Chapter Three
Affordable Housing and Growth Control:
Contradictory Interests in Permitting Development

> Cities are caught between city council [support for] growth control and [state] requirements for affordable housing.
> Ken, San Diego Association of Governments (SANDAG) official, 1992

Perhaps the greatest problem and the most promising possibility for developing big-picture, comprehensive regional planning lies in efforts to accommodate the contradictory interests of state and federal actors who are promoting the inclusionary interest of affordable housing and local actors who are defending the exclusionary interest of growth control. This is the greatest problem because it reaches to the heart of the inherently contradictory interests that characterize community politics in the United States. At the same time, however, this problem offers the most promising path toward big-picture planning.

Like most social problems and progressive solutions of the late-twentieth-century United States, the affordable housing–growth-control conundrum appeared early on the east and west coasts and has since invaded middle America. Ramapo, in Rockland County, New York, a pioneer in growth control, in 1969 offered an early version of a facilities-management program in which the developers would provide public services. The neighboring state of New Jersey pioneered court-ordered affordable housing quotas in 1983. The New Jersey Supreme Court fired the opening volley in 1975, when the first Mount Laurel decision overturned the restrictive zoning that was a barrier to affordable housing.[1]

California state and local governments were, if not the first, at least among the leaders in big-picture planning to accommodate demands for affordable housing and growth control. The growth-control movement in San Diego was locally based, in the suburbs, during the 1980s, but in the 1990s, SANDAG developed plans for regional growth control. Since 1988, when voters approved the idea of developing a regional growth plan, SANDAG has been actively involved in big-picture plans that encompass not only affordable housing and growth control but also habitat conservation. Thus San Diego provides a model for comprehensive regional planning efforts to accommodate the contradictory interests of state and local actors.[2]

Affordable housing and growth control are already institutionalized in local general plans for development, in the housing element and in the projected housing and population limits for the city when it is "built out," or fully developed. The problem is in the way state law mandates affordable housing, as opposed to the way citizen initiatives mandate growth control. The state law allocates regional shares of new housing, including affordable housing, on the basis of the city's ability to provide it, and it allocates "fair shares" of subsidized housing on the basis of local population needs. This not only is big-picture, comprehensive regional planning, but also is fairly radical politically. Essentially, the State of California is applying the principle of "From each according to his ability, to each according to his need."[3] On the basis of this formula, rapidly growing suburban cities with vast tracts of vacant land and increasing employment opportunities must shoulder an inordinate regional share of new housing, including a larger number of affordable homes. Cities with a larger population of relatively poor persons have larger fair-share obligations for providing housing subsidies for poor households, but not necessarily larger regional-share responsibilities for providing new, including affordable, housing.

Unlike California state affordable housing law, citizen growth-control initiatives are based on the reactionary, exclusionary principles of restrictive zoning—specifically, the idea that those already living in the city have the right to keep others out. These citizen initiatives attempt to limit annual growth by imposing caps, or annual limits, on new housing units permitted within the city. It is in this way that the interests and programs are contradictory. The rapidly growing suburbs that are most capable of accommodating new affordable housing are least willing to do so.[4]

Suburban cities were challenged by the contradictory demands for affordable housing and growth control to the extent that they suffered the combined effects of speculative growth, grassroots resistance, and a substantial state-mandated affordable housing burden. Thus the most challenged San Diego County suburbs can be distinguished as follows:

1) they experienced speculative growth (overbuilding) between 1970 and 1980,
2) their citizens were organized and capable of demanding growth control by citizen initiative, and
3) SANDAG imposed on them substantial regional-share responsibilitiesfor new, including affordable, housing units.

All suburban cities were facing a serious challenge, but on the basis of these criteria, Castleton faced the most serious. However, Castleton managed to preempt citizen demands for growth control and to co-opt developers by adopting an elaborate alternative to growth limits. Castleton was successful in preempting grassroots-imposed growth control and still accommodating state-mandated affordable housing because with large tracts of vacant land that were becoming increasingly valuable, it was the most attractive candidate for massive infusions of capital. Thus the city was able to entice large landowners into paying the cost of developing a big-picture planning solution.

As both the most challenged and the most successful in preempting citizens and co-opting developers to accommodate the demands of the State of

California as represented by SANDAG, Castleton captures the essential contradictions of Sunbelt growth, particularly during the speculative frenzy of 1972–1989. The problem is speculative growth. The symptoms are the contradictory demands made by citizens and regional authorities in response to uncontrolled growth. The solution is increased cooperation between local government and private-sector development companies.

In this case, the citizen growth-control initiative merely increased the city's dependence on the developer. The developer was the critical actor at every step. First, it provided expertise and support in preparing and implementing an elaborate growth management plan to preempt the citizen initiative. Then it was instrumental in preparing the plan to achieve affordable housing goals without violating the terms of growth management. Finally, the developer paid the cost of actually building affordable housing units, that is, the developer's staff negotiated with the city, prepared plans, and designated lots, which were sold to the builders who eventually built the affordable housing.

Contradictory Interests in Development

Environmentalists often resent the implication that growth control and affordable housing are contradictory demands. From their perspective the solution is simple: the state should impose high-density housing on the reluctant suburbs. This would minimize ecological damage and also reduce housing costs. The problem, according to the environmentalists, is that the developers oppose this solution. Steve, the leader of the Southern California Habitat Defenders, explained his position as follows: "Developers will not build affordable housing because estate homes sell for more money. Local government needs to impose minimum density. Portland [Oregon] did, and they have lots of affordable housing. Low density is a problem." Steve suggests that there is room for compromise. "We need to find a win-win solution—transfer development rights and offer a fair market price for the land." Even Steve recognizes that citizens, including growth-control advocates, would not support his creative solution of high-density private-sector development and government purchase of habitat. He explained: "Development should be within the urban area, and it should be infill, transit oriented, and greater density. Local government is pro-growth, pro-sprawl, [and the] general public sees higher density as evil. They don't understand the bigger picture." Steve ultimately concludes that the conspiracy of local government and private-sector developers is the root of the problem. If only we could forego the problem of local government and local citizens, we could accommodate Steve's version of growth control and affordable housing. "EIRs, consultants, and city councils controlled by developers are the problem. I like central administration, but that's not the American way—in England it works [but I'm] not sure for the U.S."

Public-sector planners are understandably much less contemptuous of local governments and the concerns of their constituents, and they are much more likely to recognize that growth control and other political concerns are at least constraints on a city's ability to provide its regional share of new, and particularly affordable, housing. The Regional Housing Needs Statement (RHNS) for the San Diego region recognizes these political problems, but concludes that local governments will have to find a way to solve them. In the discussion of governmental constraints, the RHNS offers the following observation: "Governmental constraints include: land-use controls/growth management, building codes, processing fees, and site improvement costs. [The housing element] must identify the steps that they will take to remove such constraints."[5]

The city is not required to meet its regional or fair-share goals as allocated by SANDAG or as adopted in its housing element. A legally defensible housing element must, however, indicate what the courts might judge to be good-faith efforts and reasonable progress. As SANDAG explains, "The law recognizes that the needs will likely exceed the resources." The city must, however, "establish the maximum number of housing units that can constructed . . . [and] a program which sets forth a five year schedule of actions . . . to achieve the goals and objectives of the housing element" (Sec. 65883[b])."[6]

Thus SANDAG does not really impose quotas on local governments. It simply estimates San Diego County needs for additional housing units, including affordable units, and for housing subsidies to accommodate low-income households.[7] SANDAG predicts the fit between population and housing growth and recommends how many new units, including affordable units, will be needed and how many households will need rent or mortgage subsidies.

In 1990 the projection was for 162,229 new units to be added between 1989 and 1996. Since cities would not be able to revise their general plans until after the RHNS was published in July of 1990, however, SANDAG provided a five-year (1991–1996) goal of 108,801 new units. In order to accommodate the need for affordable housing, 23 percent (25,024) should be affordable for very low-income (less than 50 percent of county median income) households, 17 percent (18,497) affordable for low-income (51–80 percent of median) households, and 21 percent (22,846) affordable for moderate-income (81–120 percent of median) households. Finally, 39 percent (42,434) should be provided for all other households, including those that make more than 120 percent of the county median income and those who choose to spend more than 25 percent of their income on housing.[8]

It was hard to imagine during the building depression of 1990–1996 that the county might add over 100,000 new units during those years, since only 225,894 new units were added during the boom years of 1980–1990.[9] Nevertheless, in 1990 it was not yet clear that the boom was over. In any case, these were targets, not requirements. SANDAG officials realized by 1992 that the prospects for achieving these goals were less certain than had been the case in 1984 when the economy was still booming, or especially in 1981, the year of the first RHNS, when the biggest boom was yet to come.

The housing needs projection for 1991–1996 was only part, and quite probably the least controversial part, of the report. SANDAG also estimated that

173,787 households would require housing subsidies and recommended that 21,728 subsidies be acquired countywide as a five-year goal.[10] Perhaps the most controversial part of the plan was the way in which the burden was to be distributed across cities and unincorporated areas. This allocation—or re-allocation—plan was the most radical part of the report.

SANDAG, in compliance with state law, allocates regional shares of new housing needs on the basis of each city's or unincorporated area's ability to provide housing. Generally locations, such as outlying suburban areas, that have been experiencing rapid growth in new housing units and employment opportunities and still have vacant land for new development are expected to shoulder an inordinate regional share of new housing units, including, of course, affordable housing. As SANDAG explains, "regional housing needs are defined and distributed [according to]: market demand for housing, employment opportunities, availability of sites, the availability of public facilities, commuting pattern, type and tenure of housing need, and the needs of several disadvantaged segments of the housing market (including farm workers). Thus, the RHNS addresses the factors identified in the State requirements."[11]

On the basis of this formula, in 1990 the largest regional shares were allocated to the largest and most populous areas: the City of San Diego was assigned 40.5 percent, and the unincorporated region of the county was assigned 19.1 percent. These two areas contained just over 66 percent of the 1980 population, but they were not growing nearly as rapidly as the outlying suburban areas. The suburban boomtowns of the 1970s and early 1980s were allocated larger shares than their population and territorial size would suggest because growth was a factor in the calculation of regional shares. After the City of San Diego and the large unincorporated area of the county, the largest regional shares were allocated to five contiguous suburban cities that had boomed in the 1970s and continued to boom in varying degrees in the 1980s.[12]

Unlike regional shares of new housing units, fair shares of households requiring housing subsidies were based, in part, on the concentration of poor people in the community. Consequently cities like San Diego and Chula Vista (south of San Diego) with large black or Latino populations and large areas of substandard housing and poverty had fair shares that were larger than their regional shares (43 versus 40.5 and 4.9 versus 3.3, respectively). The need for housing subsidies in these cities was greater than the need for new housing, including affordable housing. Since growth was also incorporated into the calculation, however, rapidly growing suburban cities still had substantial fair-share responsibilities for housing subsidies. The five suburban cities with the largest regional shares after San Diego and the unincorporated area all had fair shares that were smaller than their regional shares. Nevertheless, one of these suburban cities, Castleton, was allocated a larger fair share than any other city except for San Diego, despite the fact that Chula Vista, for example, had more than twice the population and substantially more low-income households.[13]

All five suburban cities, Castleton in particular, had inordinately large regional-share responsibilities, which would require continued growth. They also had substantial fair-share responsibilities, which would require that each city obtain housing subsidies. The goal was to redistribute the burden of affordable housing and subsidized housing from the central cities to the rapidly growing suburbs. Part of the problem with this plan, however, aside from the fact that the developers and private-sector planners were opposed to it, was that suburban residents did not generally want the building boom to continue. In fact, three of the five suburban cities discussed above (Waterton, Belleville, and Castleton) faced citizen-initiated growth-control measures in the late 1980s.

Particularly in these suburban boomtowns, contradictory state demands for affordable housing and citizen demands for growth control challenged city planning departments. Each of the citizen initiatives would have imposed annual limits, or caps, on new housing unit approvals that would have made it impossible for the city to provide its regional share of new housing units. To make matters even worse, 40 percent of these new units were expected to be affordable, which means essentially that the suburbs were expected to build cheap apartments despite the exclusionary interests of local residents, most of whom were homeowners. As Tom, the Camelot project planner, explained, this was not the people's choice. "The affordable housing program is asking cities to facilitate a building boom in multiple-family dwelling units. That clearly is not what the people in Castleton want."

Confounding Economic and Political Problems

The contradictory demands for affordable housing and growth control created major planning problems, particularly in the suburban boomtowns and particularly in the early 1990s. The challenge for local planning authorities was compounded by a series of economic and political crises associated with the speculative frenzy of 1972–1989. It is difficult to separate cause and effect in this case, because the economic and political crises were intimately linked in the cycles of boom and bust and the cycles of political challenge that characterized the two decades of speculative frenzy.

The economic and political crises associated with the Wilson-Reagan economic development policy and the speculative frenzy of 1972–1989 did not create the contradictory interests of citizens and state. State demands for and citizen opposition to affordable housing predate 1972. The State of California has required that municipal general plans include a housing element that "identifies the housing needs of the city and recommends ways to meet these needs" since 1967. Citizen opposition to affordable housing dates back to 1950, when voters amended the California constitution to require voter approval in a referendum for "any state public body . . . [to] develop, construct, or acquire . . . low rent housing project[s] for persons of low income."[14]

Clearly, then, the contradictory interests of state and citizen predated the economic and political crises of 1972–1989, but the speculative growth and the boom-and-bust cycles of that period exacerbated the planning problem. First of all, the boom-and-bust economy drove housing costs through the ceiling, creating increased demand for affordable housing, particularly at the height of the boom phase. Then the bust phase of 1989–1996 all but foreclosed the prospects of enticing developers to provide affordable housing.

At the same time, local government was increasingly challenged by contradictory and escalating demands from state legislatures, citizens, and the California courts. By 1989 the demands for affordable housing and growth control had reached a fevered pitch. But with the savings-and-loan collapse and the economic depression, the possibility of accommodating these demands in yet another big-picture planning solution appeared bleak.

The initial demand for comprehensive regional planning in the provision of affordable housing began, in San Diego, in 1972. The Comprehensive Planning Organization (CPO) of the San Diego region recommended that the county establish a regional planning organization—what would become SANDAG—and create comprehensive, regional affordable housing policies, which would be adopted by the state in the 1980s. The CPO's report emphasized that these steps were desperately needed. The San Diego Housing Authority was clearly unable to meet the needs of the local population. "After a FHA market analysis indicated a need for over 2,000 public housing units in the Region, San Diego Housing Authority, with a waiting list of 6,900 households, applied for 2,000 units, and was awarded 150." Similarly, the report continued, the private sector would not respond adequately to the need for affordable housing. "Although over 20,000 housing units have been built in the Region in the past year, to the point of excess in higher price ranges, most of the housing needs and deficiencies identified in this report have remained unaffected."[15]

The Areawide Housing Opportunity Plan of 1981 and the Regional Housing Needs Statements of 1985 and 1990 were essentially specifications of the general policy proposed in 1972. What changed was not the interest in redistributing the burden of affordable housing but the intensity of the political pressure applied in demanding that each city provide its regional share of new housing units and its fair share of housing subsidies for low-income households. In 1972, as the speculation on land-use futures and the building boom in suburban housing commenced, neither state nor local governments had been particularly concerned with the problem of providing affordable housing.

It was not until the bust phase of 1980–1982, in fact, that the state mandated regional allocation of fair-share responsibilities and made suggestions for regional-share responsibilities. In the first round of housing element revisions at the peak of the 1985–1986 building boom, it was not clear that either city or state governments were taking the affordable housing mandates very seriously. Cities were not required to meet regional-share goals or even to explain in their housing element revisions why they were unable to provide the suggested number of affordable housing units. The only requirement was for fair shares of housing subsidies, and even here it is not clear that there were any carrots or sticks other than lawsuits.[16]

The 1981 RHNS had estimated that 132,838 households in the San Diego region would require housing subsidies in 1985. The three-year goal (October

1981–October 1984) for the county as a whole was 10,002 households, but only 9,096 were accommodated during the six years from 1980 to 1985, when the first revision to the RHNS was required. Four years after the 1981 RHNS was published, fully 47 percent of the jurisdictions had not met their three-year goals. The City of San Diego, for example, had achieved only 66 percent of its three-year goal.[17]

Those jurisdictions in the more rapidly developing outlying areas were generally more successful, however. Only one of the suburban boomtown cities failed to achieve its three-year goal by 1985, and that city achieved 80 percent. Similarly, the unincorporated area of the county achieved 89 percent of its goal. On balance, because some jurisdictions far exceeded their goals, San Diego County achieved 91 percent of its three-year goal in the six years between 1980 and 1985 despite the performance of the underachievers, notably the City of San Diego.[18]

At that point, in 1985, when regional housing needs were assessed for the first round of housing element revisions, the five-year goal for the county was 16,613 households, of which San Diego City was to accommodate 7,601 (46 percent). When each jurisdiction's progress was evaluated in 1986–1987, fully 84 percent of the jurisdictions had failed to meet their two-year goals, many of them falling far short; only three had exceeded their goals, by 127 to 234 percent. This time the City of San Diego achieved 95 percent of its goal by offering subsidized or guaranteed affordable housing for 2,887 additional households in 1986 and 1987. With the remarkable progress of the city and the efforts of a few overachievers, 84 percent of the county's two-year goal was achieved.[19]

A regional share of new housing units based on projected population growth had been included in the 1985 RHNS, but this was not translated into specific recommendations for each jurisdiction. Between 1985 and 1990, however, the legislature specified the requirements for determining each jurisdiction's portion.[20] Thus local efforts to include affordable housing in all new development projects were inspired in part by changes in state and regional policy for determining housing need. Consequently, many inclusionary municipal housing ordinances appeared for the first time after the second round of housing element revisions in 1991.

In fact, it was not until this second round of revisions, which occurred during the depth of the post-boom depression, that San Diego County cities began to develop strategies for meeting both their fair-share responsibilities for housing subsidies and their regional-share responsibilities for affordable housing units. By that time, however, SANDAG and city officials realized that the 1991–1996 goals were, at best, impractical. The skyrocketing cost of housing in California, and particularly in San Diego suburban boomtowns, between 1972 and 1989 had exacerbated the problem of housing affordability and had inspired increasing demands from state authorities and growing opposition from local residents. Each city revised its housing element in 1991 and established goals based on the projection of regional needs and its assessment of what was reasonable, given the nature of economic and political constraints.

Quite apart from the interests of land developers, the exclusionary interests of California voters are a major constraint on government efforts to provide affordable housing. This is fairly clear in the legislative history of California. In 1950 voters amended the state constitution to require voter approval for the construction of low-income public housing projects. In 1978 six San Diego County cities had public housing referenda on the ballot, and voters defeated half of these.[21]

Environmental restrictions imposed by federal and state authorities have also confounded efforts to provide affordable housing. Although the California Environmental Quality Act of 1970 (CEQA) procedures did not substantially reduce new housing construction, they clearly increased the complexity and the price of gaining permission to build. Additional complexities and expenses were added when the California Coastal Act was imposed on local governments by citizen initiative in 1972. Then in 1978, when the U.S. Supreme Court determined that the Endangered Species Act of 1973 (ESA) regulations applied to private developments, the costs and complexities increased once again.[22]

A less direct but still important constraint on the provision of affordable housing is Proposition 13, a 1978 voter initiative that substantially reduced property taxes and imposed the requirement of a two-thirds popular-vote approval for future tax increases. This state law has dramatically reduced local government resources and contributed to a variety of problems associated with "the fiscalization of planning." Local governments are encouraged to seek out sales-tax-yielding commercial development projects at the expense of residential development, and they have become increasingly dependent on the fees they charge developers and on the conditions they impose for project approval. The idea that the developer can pay for public services and even build the infrastructure, including streets, sewers, and schools, appeals to local voters but leads to even greater dependence on the willingness to build.[23] So far the developers have not revolted, but it is clear that local governments are becoming increasingly dependent on developers, rather than homeowners, as the source of funds for public projects.

The local government's fiscal dependence on development fees tends to inspire government support for increased development, but the voters have placed yet another obstacle before their elected officials. In the 1980s San Diego County voters initiated a flurry of growth-control measures. At the same time they replaced prodevelopment politicians with local leaders who would support growth management; environmental, or neighborhood, protection; and related measures that would put the elected officials on a collision course with local developers, whose fees were needed to provide public services.[24]

Thus there were a variety of constraints on local government efforts to provide affordable housing, including the fact that neither voters nor developers wanted low-income projects in their neighborhoods. Why did local governments provide affordable housing in response to state and regional affordable housing demands when there was virtually no voter support for them and considerable opposition? Simply stated, they feared lawsuits.[25]

The City of San Diego nearly reached its two-year fair-share goal for 1986–87 after falling far short in 1985, in large part because of prodding from the courts. In 1985 the state appellate court decided that San Diego could not approve a permit for a planned residential community until the city could indicate substantial progress in its efforts to "conserve and improve the condition of existing housing stock." After that decision all San Diego County cities began to consider the adequacy of their plans and the evidence of their progress. Although it is difficult to determine cause and effect here, it is clear that the City of San Diego, and particularly the central city, experienced a population boom in the 1980s. In fact, roughly 45 percent of all housing units added in the City of San Diego in the 1980s were built between 1985 and 1987 in the wake of the court decision.[26]

Clearly a major inducement to provide affordable housing is the desire to avoid lawsuits. Not only might poor or homeless residents (or their designated representatives, such as Legal Aid) sue the city, but anyone opposing any development project might sue on the grounds that the city cannot approve the project until it makes substantial progress toward providing its regional share of affordable housing. That is the legacy of the San Diego lawsuit. Even if no one in the city wants affordable housing, a program must be in place to protect the city from a lawsuit that challenges the housing element of its general plan.[27]

Of course, even developers might rattle legal sabers or even sue the city in opposition to affordable housing or growth control or both. Thus free-market conservatives are exaggerating the extent to which the courts are consistently ruling against the developers.[28] Nevertheless, the California courts have inspired city governments, particularly in San Diego County, to develop inclusionary housing ordinances to meet their regional-share obligations for affordable housing.

San Diego County suburban cities were developing their housing elements as the speculation in land-use futures was taking off. The contradictory demands of state and citizens, for and against affordable housing, were exacerbated by the economic and political crises of 1972–1989. Environmental challenges were initially accommodated, but the cost of Environmental Impact Reports (EIRs) and coastal zone approvals increased the difficulty of providing affordable housing and made local governments more dependent on private-sector developers.

The boom and bust cycles of 1972–1989 facilitated grassroots challenges to already beleaguered local governments. The boom of 1972 brought the opening round of regional planning demands to accommodate affordable housing, but also facilitated grassroots opposition, which led to the Coastal Act of 1972. The second boom phase of 1976–1978 brought increasing demands for affordable housing, the regulatory encumbrance of the ESA, and ultimately the tax revolt. The biggest boom of the cycle came in 1983–1986. Reagan's New Federalism, including new amendments to the ESA, facilitated the building boom, which inspired increasing state demands for affordable housing, this time bolstered by the California courts and confounded by a flurry of local growth-control movements. This was the frenzy of contradictory demands that preceded the general-plan housing element revisions in 1991. At that point the task of accommodating the contradictory interests appeared insurmountable.

Accommodating Contradictory Interests

Even before the California Appellate Court ruled against the City of San Diego in 1985, plans were underway to revitalize the central city. In fact, the redevelopment of downtown San Diego was part of Mayor Wilson's plan, and it was during his tenure, 1972–1982, that most of the projects were initiated. Equally important in this process were private developers, particularly Ernest W. Hahn, who was instrumental in the exurban developments of the 1960s and 1970s, including Fashion Valley in 1969.[29]

Hahn turned to the revitalization of the central city beginning in 1974, when he was chosen by the Centre City Development Corporation to guide the redevelopment efforts. The problem with earlier efforts to redevelop downtown was that they had failed to bridge the gulf between the downtown day and night life. Appleyard and Lynch described this problem as follows: "The new office area downtown has elegant buildings, well-designed landscaping, and elaborate street furniture. Most of the time, it seems empty of people, while Horton Plaza, brash and tawdry, is packed with action. It will be unfortunate if the renewal program banishes this liveliness and substitutes for it an empty space ringed by bank fronts."[30]

The Horton Plaza downtown redevelopment project did not simply banish the liveliness of sailors, prostitutes, single-room-occupancy (SRO) hotels, and small businesses, including restaurants that delivered food to the SRO residents. Instead, it imported suburbia, providing parking, shopping, dining, and entertainment in what became the "enclosed and protected space" of the new Horton Plaza.[31] As the owner of one local restaurant explained, however, the new plaza doesn't bring any business downtown. People drive in and drive out without setting foot on the downtown streets or sidewalks. The fact that the plaza offers the enclosed security of a suburban mall is probably one reason why it has been so successful.

What makes Horton Plaza the ultimate postmodern[32] experience is that it has essentially reconstructed the modern suburban shopping center in the center of the downtown area. Like suburban developments, it is designed for automobile access. In fact, it is not at all clear how a pedestrian can access the shopping center from the street. It took me half an hour to find a street exit from the mall, and I still got lost when I returned on foot, even though I used to deliver Italian food from a restaurant across the street. Once outside, I could find the Italian restaurant and the other downtown businesses, but the single-room-occupancy hotels were gone and business outside the plaza bubble was definitely not booming.

The new Horton Plaza is a commercial fantasyland for suburban residents and, perhaps, tourists, but it that offers little to the traditional lively denizens of the old Horton Plaza. For the downtown residents, there is, however, an upside to this story of central-city redevelopment. In response to increasing pressure that culminated in the 1985 lawsuit, affordable housing was incorporated into the development package.

The Horton Plaza service entrance, from which workers exit and refuse is expelled, opens onto high-rise subsidized housing units built in the style that the French have labeled "rabbit cages." While it is not clear that these high-density structures are better than the SROs and low-rise apartments buildings they replaced, it might be the case that the location of this affordable housing at the service entrance to the suburban fantasyland is functional. This is probably as close as the resident downtown population will get to the suburbs, and the plaza's service entrance might be convenient for local residents who work there. It will not, however, replace the benches and the war memorial in the old Horton Plaza as a place for poor people to hang out.[33]

In any case, the fact that Hahn and Wilson were already in negotiation for this massive redevelopment project facilitated efforts to integrate affordable housing into the big picture. By 1992 Wilson was governor and growth control was the battle cry in the San Diego mayoral contest. The redevelopment of San Diego was at that point essentially completed, so the city was not particularly challenged by the contradictory demands of growth control and affordable housing, having accommodated the latter in Horton Plaza prior to the clamor for growth control. In 1992 Ken, a SANDAG official, explained City of San Diego redevelopment efforts. "Redevelopment after Horton Plaza has been vacant-land infill. Classic [tear-down-and-rebuild] development was done in Horton Plaza—commercial and cheap apartments, HUD units, other subsidized and market rate [units]. That was completed in the early 1980s."

At the county level, however, in 1992 SANDAG was still attempting to accommodate the contradictory demands of affordable housing and growth control after gaining approval from voters in the 1988 election.[34] Much of the regional planning in 1992 involved efforts to help suburban cities to develop inclusionary ordinances that required developers to provide affordable housing as part of a master plan for large-scale development. Generally these suburban cities, which had experienced the most dramatic growth in the early 1980s, were the most challenged in 1992.[35] Ken explained, "Between 1980 and 1985 we sat down with each jurisdiction and looked at their general plan. All but a couple had adequate plans through 1990. We have since concluded, however, that between 1996 and 2001 there would be four to seven jurisdictions with greater population and housing growth than their general plan allowed."

SANDAG is somewhat sympathetic to the challenge faced by suburban cities but also sees the big-picture solution as a move away from traditional patterns of suburban development and toward high-density, transit-oriented development, as promoted by environmentalists. Ken explained, "Cities are not happy, but cities are not responding to reality. The reality is that you can't build affordable housing on estate lots. You've got to have densities of twenty-five to thirty-five dwelling units per acre. Suburban cities have eighteen to twenty maximum."

SANDAG tries to work with these cities, helping them to respond to the challenge. SANDAG helped Paradise, the fastest-growing bedroom community in the county, to negotiate for a medical-industrial complex that would include affordable housing. As Ken explained, "Paradise developed inclusionary policy and ordinance requirements—15 percent affordable, density bonuses, SROs. To avoid ghettoization they built in design criteria and standards." Ken went on to explain that developers in Paradise were willing to cooperate in order to get vested development rights. "We told the city that they need to develop a policy. They could declare a moratorium and put all on hold or could work with one developer and see if we could work out a policy. Now we are working with three developers. Developers are getting development agreements [vested rights] and are conditioned to build affordable housing."

This is essentially how rapidly growing suburban cities managed to accommodate the demand that they provide their regional share of affordable housing. To the extent that they were able to co-opt developers and preempt citizen demands for growth control, they imposed affordable housing conditions on new developments, requiring that the developers meet a quota of affordable housing units or pay fees in lieu of providing the housing. However, some cities were more willing and able that others to accommodate the contradictory demands for growth control and affordable housing in this big-picture plan for future development.

Suburban cities that were experiencing speculative growth, or overbuilding, between 1972 and 1986 found it difficult to accommodate the contradictory demands. The challenge was especially great in suburban cities that faced citizen-initiated growth-control measures and substantial demands for regional shares of new housing units. Facing the most serious challenge were the five contiguous suburban cities that in 1990 had the largest regional-share responsibilities after the City of San Diego and the unincorporated area.

Three of these five cities—Waterton, Belleville, and Castleton—faced citizen initiatives demanding caps, or annual limits, on new housing approvals in 1986 and 1987. All three of these cities had experienced speculative growth, particularly in the 1970s. In Waterton, population increased 89 percent in the 1980s, while the number of housing units increased 124 percent. The city was relatively built out: only 36 percent of its land was vacant and unencumbered by development rights or some sort of constraints on use. Because Waterton did not have particularly expensive homes or wealthy residents in 1980 or even in 1990, its regional share of new housing from 1991 to 1996 constituted only a 15 percent increase over 1990 housing units, and just 13 percent of the new units were to be affordable.

Nevertheless, the results of Waterton's 1987 citizen initiative threatened to limited annual approvals to 800 per year, thus foreclosing the possibility of meeting regional-share goals and threatening development projects that had already received preliminary approval. Waterton had attempted to preempt the citizen initiative with a growth-control plan that would have allowed for development, but the city ordinance failed to defeat the citizen initiative, and annual caps were imposed. Then the developers sued Waterton for refusing to permit its tentatively approved projects. This complicated the planning problem, but the city was able to finesse the building caps. It continued to issue building permits for previously approved projects and thus exceeded the limit of 800 new units every year until 1992. By that time, the continuing depression had substantially reduced new approvals even in cities without growth-control ordinances.

Although it had failed to preempt the citizen initiative and to co-opt developers—at least, the lawsuit suggests that the city did not get all the developers on board—Waterton did manage to develop an inclusionary ordinance to provide its share of affordable housing. As the Waterton planning director explained at a breakfast meeting at a local country club, "We adopted a housing element last October [1991] with an inclusionary ordinance for every unit approved since May 1991. We had originally planned to include all units, but we negotiated for 'since May 1991.'" There was a lawsuit involved, but the planning director did not mention it. "Ten percent of housing must be affordable or developers must pay in-lieu fees of $5,800 per unit, which has since been lowered to $3,900." More negotiation is implied here but the planning director did not offer any more details about it. "We're working through a tight budget. [The major zoning change] in 1986 was a revised land-use map. In 1988, [it was the revision of] a zoning ordinance/map that had not been thoroughly revised since 1958." Obviously the beleaguered Waterton city planning director was struggling to accommodate the demands of developers, some of whom were willing to take their case to court along with citizen demands for limited growth and state and SANDAG demands for affordable housing.

The neighboring suburb of Belleville, which also faced a citizen initiative, seemed to be more successful, at least in preempting the citizens. Belleville adopted a council-initiated growth-control plan that imposed annual limits of only 500 units, effective in 1987. As in Waterton, this goal was not immediately achieved. Building permits were issued for tentatively approved projects so new approvals did not fall to 500 until 1990. Although Belleville was more effective than Waterton in preempting citizens, it was not much more effective in co-opting developers, partly because it was nearly (77 percent) built out in 1990. The city was attempting to develop an inclusionary ordinance and an elaborate facilities-management program that would require that new developments provide facilities including schools, parks, drainage systems, and other public goods, but that was still on the drawing board in 1990.

Castleton, the third suburban city that faced a citizen initiative was arguably the most challenged. Population had increased 138 percent and housing units nearly 200 percent in this suburban city in the 1970s. In 1990 Castleton had the largest regional and fair-share obligations, but in 1986 it had faced an initiative that would have foreclosed the possibility of meeting those goals. It also was in negotiation with a number of developers with partially or tentatively approved projects, including Camelot, a thousand-acre project that was approved in 1987 to be developed as a master-plan upscale residential community with a resort hotel and country club. Castleton's regional share of new housing units was over 11,000 for 1985–1990. If the 1986 growth-control initiative had passed, Castleton would have been legally unable to meet its regional-share goals. More important, the city would not have been able to permit already approved master plan units, and it might, like its neighbor Waterton, have faced developers prepared to sue for their rights. Instead, Castleton managed to preempt citizens and co-opt developers during the building boom in 1986. Still, the city still fell far short of its 1990 goals.

Paradise and Farmington, the two suburban cities that did not face a citizen initiative on growth control, were less challenged because their citizens were not mobilized in opposition to uncontrolled growth. Farmington boomed in the 1960s, when population and housing units increased by roughly 125 percent. Farmington was still growing in the 1970s, but the rate of growth declined to a 75 percent increase in population and a 100 percent increase in housing units. The city was nearly built out, and its land was not as valuable as in some neighboring suburbs, so Farmington was less challenged by demands for affordable housing. This city did thoroughly revise its general plan in 1990, but in 1992 it was still struggling to develop inclusionary ordinances and facilities-management plans. The problem, as Tommy, the city planning director, explained, was that they couldn't get the big developers to cooperate. "We're trying to entice them . . . [but] it is difficult because the city is almost (about two-thirds) built out. We can't get the big developers to put in the infrastructure."

Paradise, the other suburban city that did not face a citizen initiative, was the fastest-growing bedroom community in the county. It faced a different sort of challenge because it was less than 50 percent built out, but lacked an employment base. Thus, ever since the property tax revolt of 1978, Paradise had lacked a tax base to sustain future development. This city was able to entice developers, however, and with the assistance of SANDAG it negotiated for inclusionary ordinances as part of the big-picture plan for the medical-industrial complex. Thus here, as in Castleton, the developers were enticed to pay the price for a creative big-picture planning solution to the contradictory and increasingly serious demands for growth control and affordable housing.[36]

Affordable Housing in Castleton

Castleton was arguably the most challenged by the contradictory demands for affordable housing and growth control. This city had experienced speculative growth in new housing units in the 1970s, faced a citizen initiative to impose building caps in 1986, and was allocated the largest regional and fair shares of any of the suburban cities. Nevertheless, Castleton was able to preempt citizen demands, and because it had considerable vacant land that was becoming increasingly valuable, the city was able to co-opt big developers, including Patterson and Peterson. Thus Castleton adopted an elaborate alternative to annual growth limits and an inclusionary ordinance that required developers to provide affordable housing.

Castleton had boomed during the 1970s, when population increased 138 percent and the number of housing units increased 198 percent, increasing the vacancy rate from 6 percent in 1970 to 11.2 percent in 1980. This building boom in expensive homes created a wealthy suburb in what had not been a particularly wealthy regional city. In 1969, median family income in Castleton was only 3 percent higher than the county median ($10,129), and Castleton's median value for owner-occupied housing was only 14 percent higher than the county median ($22,349). By 1979, however, median family income was 28 percent higher than the county median, and in 1980 the median value of owner-occupied housing was 37 percent higher than in the county as a whole ($91,000).[37]

When Castleton prepared its housing element in 1981 to accommodate the suggested goals of the RHNS, the expectation was that the city would add over 7,000 new housing units between 1980 and 1985 and would provide housing subsidies for over 300 households. With the extended economic depression of 1980–1982, however, Castleton added only slightly more than 5,000 new units. The city was able to provide subsidies for over 300 households, however, and seemed confident as the building boom had recommenced in 1985 that it could provide subsidies for nearly 700 additional households, thereby approximating its projected fair share for 1981–1991.[38] In 1985, as it completed its first required revision of the housing element after the regional fair shares were allocated, the city expressed its confidence: "Castleton's population has exhibited a rapid rate of growth, more than doubling from 1970 to 1980. The rate of growth is expected to continue."[39]

This optimism was short lived. In 1985 the city was committed to "facilitating quality development" and did not have much concern about the recommendations and mandates related to affordable and subsidized housing, but that changed dramatically in 1986. After the California appellate court found against the City of San Diego in 1985, and the citizen initiative for imposing building caps qualified for the ballot in 1986, Castleton faced what was arguably the greatest challenge in efforts to accommodate the contradictory interests of local citizens and the state.

Facing these contradictory demands, Castleton turned to developers. The developers were prepared to pay any price to maintain the building boom, so they were ready to help. The fact that there were a couple of large development companies (Patterson and Peterson) that together held over 4,000 acres of Castleton land greatly facilitated the cooperative effort. A group of private-sector planners who were formerly employed by the city explained the situation: The Castleton voters put a measure on the ballot in 1986 to impose caps on new development. Large developers worked with the city to create a facilities-management program as an elaborate alternative to building caps. Under the terms of this program, the developers would build the infrastructure and public services, including schools, as part of their master-plan communities.

Tom: In 1986, all development stopped. The city turned to developers, finally. . . . Growth management was essentially a developer project.

Dick: The assumption by developers was here is a plan we can live with.

The facilities-management program established sectors within the city and planning areas within each sector. Each sector would have projected population and housing unit limits, and each planning area would develop a plan for providing all necessary facilities, including parks, drainage, roads, open space, schools, sewers, and water. The Castleton city planning department describes this plan in a brochure: "It links residential, commercial, and industrial development directly to the availability of public services and facilities. It sets limits on the total number of housing units to be built and increases the total amount of open space to be preserved in the city."[40]

The brochure doesn't mention that this plan was Castleton's alternative to the popular growth-control initiative that imposed a limit of 500 to 750 new units per year. Similarly, it does not explain that developers would pay the bulk of the expense of implementing this program in those largely undeveloped areas where large master-plan communities had been approved or were awaiting approval. The developer of the thousand-acre Camelot agreed to pay over $10 million to provide such facilities, after it had already provided the expert staff required to develop the facilities-management plan in 1987. As Harry, a private-sector planning consultant, explained, "In 1986 to 1992 developers thought that money could solve any problem. Developers were ready to pay anything. They would put in the facilities."

Castleton managed to preempt citizen-initiated growth control at the height of the building boom in 1986 by co-opting big development companies. During the depression of 1989–1992, however, it was time to go back to the drawing board and renegotiate a plan for future development. The savings-and-loan crash, the elaborate alternative to growth limits, and the continuing economic depression all but halted new housing approvals between 1987 and 1992. In fact, approvals dropped from over 3,000 in 1986 to forty-nine in 1992.[41] As the city attempted to revise its housing element in 1991 as mandated by state law, it was clear that the world had changed since the previous revision, in 1985.

Castleton had proposed to add over 11,000 new housing units between 1985 and 1990, but fewer than 7,000 had been constructed, and although the city had expected to offer housing assistance to nearly 700 households in 1985, it managed to assist barely more than 100, which was far below its fair-share goal.[42]

In 1990 SANDAG recommended that between 1991 and 1996 Castleton should add over 6,000 new housing units, including over 2,500 that would be affordable for low- and very low-income households. Also, the city should provide subsidies for over 1,000 additional households.[43] This time, however, the city was less optimistic. Planners asserted in their preliminary draft of a new housing element the city's intention to provide fewer than half the affordable housing units that SANDAG had recommended. "The goal [over 2,500 units] indicated in the regional housing needs statement is impractical. The more modest 'Fairshare' goal [of] approximately [1,100] new housing units for low-income households [was adopted]. This is 18% of the approximately [6,000] units needed for Castleton in the next five years."[44]

Castleton city planners went on to detail how this goal would be achieved, including a policy for inclusionary zoning requiring master-plan developments to provide the affordable housing. "A minimum of fifteen percent of all units approved for any master plan community or residential specific plan shall be affordable to lower income households."[45] This was the plan that was to accommodate the demands for affordable housing within the constraints imposed by the facilities-management/growth-control plan. It was only one of the many details that were being negotiated in 1992 as part of the general-plan revision that was ongoing during the bust phase of 1989–1992.

Once Castleton had a reasonable goal for meeting its regional and fair-share responsibilities in compliance with state law, in 1991 the city turned to the developers. The challenge was to create an affordable housing plan that could be incorporated into the revised general plan without violating the terms of the facilities-management/growth-control program. While the city negotiated with the developers, an ad hoc committee produced a report on the economics of affordable housing. Armed with this report, the city then called a public work-shop meeting where the plan was presented to the planning commission, the city council, and the interested public. Once the major concerns were duly noted, the city entered into private negotiations with individual developers and their attorneys and hammered out agreements to provide affordable housing.

The ad hoc committee concluded that there was a substantial affordability gap, which developers and the government would have to cover between what the housing would cost to build and what people could afford to pay. The public- and private-sector planners who produced the report contended that con-tinuing cooperation between local government and developers would be neces-sary to bridge this gap:

> The cost of constructing and operating new housing units (not including developer profit) in Castleton are high, ranging from $134,200 to $156,600. There exists a significant gap, ranging from $75,000 to nearly $120,000, between [production costs] and what a lower-income household can afford to pay. . . . The financial burden of the affordability gap is too great for only one segment of the community to bear. . . . With all members of the community working creatively, cooperatively, and aggressively it is possible to overcome the affordability gap.[46]

At the affordable housing public workshop early in 1992, Castleton city planners presented their plan for overcoming the affordability gap. The meet-ing was held in a large auditorium that was set up in two sections. In the main section the planning commission, city council, mayor, and workshop facilitator sat at tables that were arranged perpendicularly along the front and side walls. In front of these officials, the city planning and human development staff sat at a long table facing a microphone from which individual staff members made their reports. In the adjoining section there were tables in front with coffee and cookies, and rows of chairs available for the general public. These chairs were physically distant—between twenty and fifty feet away—from the city officials and were facing the cookies and coffee rather than the microphone. When reporting on their proposals, the staff turned toward the city officials and away from the public, contributing to the impression that the general public was neither an audience nor a participant but merely an outside observer.

In this manner the Castleton city planning staff reported the broad outline of the affordable housing proposal: "In new residential developments a minimum 15 percent of the units should be low income affordable. . . . In-Lieu fees [would] be applied to approved projects without building permits as well as projects with applications completed prior to October 22, 1991." After a break the public was invited to comment. There was no microphone available to them, so speakers were obliged to stand at their seats, turn toward the city officials, and shout at them from across the room. The minutes report the public comment as follows: "[A developer] stated that the in-lieu fee is just another form of taxation. [An attorney for a developer] referenced the Government Code Section 65961 which prohibits a city from imposing new conditions at a later date. . . . [Another developer] agreed with staff that 100 percent low income projects in master plan areas will become part of the community, and should be considered."[47]

Much of the flavor of the meeting is lost in the minutes, but the general thrust of the discussion is clear. Developers virtually monopolized the public comments, and they opposed in-lieu fees for previously approved projects. The Patterson Company paid its attorney to come and explain that while "we don't like rattling legal sabers," this was clearly illegal. Others offered complaints about taxing the children for the sins of their fathers, while Pete, representing the Peterson Company, agreed with the city staff that "we can't make every eighth house affordable" and that flexibility was required. All of this posturing, including the discussion among council and commission members, was an attempt to set some ground rules for the serious negotiations that were to follow.

Clearly this meeting was not set up to accommodate serious discussion between public and private interests. In fact, although the workshop allowed grassroots participation, it certainly did not facilitate it. Everyone was free to attend and free to speak. In contrast to city council meetings there were no time limits on public comments and it was not necessary to sign up beforehand to speak on an issue that was not on the agenda. Nevertheless, there was very little citizen participation at the workshop. The workshop minutes and my field notes report the concerns of only one person not representing an organization, and he was identified only as a Castleton resident. He was concerned that the

negotiations between staff and developers would not be subject to public scrutiny. The citizen "expressed concern that staff would be given too much authority in processing projects, and suggested that at least one member of the
Council, as an elected official, should be aware of all projects in process at any
given time."

Unfortunately, the negotiations with individual developers did not occur in
public meetings. Even my favorite private-sector planner, Tom, who was
involved in the negotiations for Patterson Company's Project Camelot, told me
that I would not be allowed to attend. He also explained, when discussing the
negotiations with a consultant, that the city had asked that the developer not
report the details of the discussions to anyone—particularly to other developers, he implied. Tom was concerned and perplexed, however, by the negotiations with the city on affordable housing. They seemed too easy. The numbers
were wrong—there were not enough units in the agreement to meet the city's
policy, let alone its fair-share goal.

> Tom: [There is] not enough blood on the table. I think the city believes that
> this agreement is hurting the project.
>
> Harry: They might be afraid of you.
>
> Tom: Our lawyer's meeting with the city attorney might have been critical.
>
> Harry: The state hasn't given the city a letter of compliance yet. I think the
> state has put the city on probation. The city doesn't have a density bonus
> program in place. They don't have any means to implement affordable
> housing. The city is on the [verge] of violating its own [growth manage-
> ment] plans.

Tom and Harry continued to consider the legal aspects of the agreement.

> Tom: Approved units should not have legal/moral obligation to pay for
> affordable housing.

When Tom told this to the city, the response was that that would mess up the
city's numbers.

> Harry: The city is ready to cut a deal, and Camelot is first in line. They're
> mad that the project got a good deal.
>
> Tom: The city wants us not to tell the others.

Although it seemed that Patterson was getting a great deal in negotiating
Camelot's affordable housing burden, Harry was not convinced. There was
something strange about this deal. He advised Tom to be careful.

You need to make sure that development plans go ahead despite what happens with affordable housing. This is a mystery deal.

Something is wrong; something is missing. What's wrong with this picture?

There were two things wrong with the picture. First, as the project attorney had noted, it was illegal because it required affordable housing or in-lieu fees for previously approved planning areas. Second, it was inadequate because even if Project Camelot provided the housing that the city requested, the total would fall far short of the state mandate. The city was clearly ready to cut a deal but wanted to maintain the fiction that the project was providing 15 percent affordable housing, including 15 percent of already constructed homes. This fiction could then be used as a bargaining chip, or at least as an example, in subsequent negotiations with other developers. Castleton could say to Peterson, for instance, "Hey, look, Patterson paid up; what's wrong with you?"

Ultimately the Patterson Company, represented by Bill and Tom, settled on an agreement to build 344 apartments off-site, not within the thousand-acre Camelot development. Patterson would be allowed to sell 177 of these units to other developers, such as Peterson, so the other developers might thereby meet their affordable housing obligations without having to find a builder who could actually build the homes. Ultimately, then, Castleton managed to get at least 344 affordable units between 1991 and 1996. Perhaps if other developers cooperated and the citizens didn't oppose the building boom in cheap apartments, the city might avoid a lawsuit and appease state authorities.

Here is a classic illustration of the irony of popular participation. The grassroots movement to control growth exacerbated the planning problem and thereby forced the city into the arms of the developer, the only actor that was willing and able to provide the big-picture solution. The developer first provided the staff to develop the big-picture alternative to building caps. Next, the developer joined the city in the electoral campaign to preempt the citizen initiative with the preferred alternative. Then, the developer negotiated with the city to determine its share of the affordable housing burden, which the developer ultimately provided. The city was having problems with both its citizens and its more enlightened developers, however, in efforts to accommodate the demands of state and federal actors promoting big-picture habitat conservation plans.

Chapter Four
Development and Habitat Conservation

> The entire sea front would be in public ownership—given to the people of
> the city, of all classes, to live near and to enjoy.
>
> Donald Appleyard and Kevin Lynch, 1974

Particularly on the subject of coastal zone preservation, big-picture planning proposals sometimes sound radical in the extreme.[1] Nevertheless, big-picture planning as it emerged in San Diego County between 1970 and 1992 incorporated the
conflicting interests of liberal environmentalists and conservative developers and
attempted to accommodate reactionary no-growth interests while ignoring radical deep-ecology advocates. The goal was to establish a progressive coalition of
environmentalists and developers who are willing to concede the necessity of new
development, on the one hand, and government regulation, on the other.
Progressive planners realized by 1970 that environmentalism posed problems but
also offered possibilities. Just as early-twentieth-century industrialists had learned
of "good" and "bad" unions, late-twentieth-century financiers learned of "good"
and "bad" environmentalism.[2]

There are two types of environmental regulation. Procedural regulation,
exemplified in the National Environmental Policy Act of 1970 (NEPA) and the
California Environmental Quality Act of 1970 (CEQA), does not impose specific restrictions on development projects but imposes requirements for public
notification and consideration of environmental impact. For projects deemed
by local authorities to have significant environmental impact, an elaborate public spectacle is mandated in the course of developing and approving an
Environmental Impact Report (EIR). If the local authorities fail to follow the
federal (NEPA) or state (CEQA) guidelines, they might be liable for civil suits.
Beyond the required procedures, however, there are no statutory limitations on
what might be considered a tolerable degree of environmental destruction.
Ultimately whatever the public approves is acceptable.

Substantive regulation, as exemplified by the Endangered Species Act of
1973 (ESA) and the California Coastal Act of 1972, imposes a new layer of
bureaucracy. Federal or state officials impose a set of prohibitions or prescrip-
tions above and beyond limitations local authorities and their constituents
might call for. Thus the ESA imposes restrictions on development projects that
might harm endangered or threatened plant and animal species. Similarly, the
California Coastal Commission routinely rejects project proposals that local
governments have approved but that do not, in the opinion of the commission,

adequately protect coastal resources and provide for public access to the beach.[3]

Procedural regulation is more malleable, since local government is able to preempt state and federal law by establishing local procedures that parallel the state and federal mandates and thereby incorporate the interested public. Lacking state or federal restrictions on what is locally accepted environmental degradation, local officials need only consider local opposition, which can be co-opted or preempted fairly easily. Specifically, organized interests are co-opted by being placed on citizen advisory committees. Emerging interests are preempted by concessions offered as mitigation for the potentially adverse impacts of proposed development projects.

Substantive regulation is more problematic for professional planners, municipal officials, and developers. They cannot co-opt state and federal government officials, so big-picture plans must accommodate the substance of state and federal law, just as state and local officials must accommodate the concerns of the Army Corps of Engineers when dealing with wetlands. Such efforts are plagued by the problem of bureaucratic irrationality—in this case, the tendency for state and federal officials to enforce blind obedience to the letter of the law, even when the law gets in the way of achieving its own stated goal.

In general, big-picture planning compounds the problems that environmental regulation aggravates. The increasingly complex legal maze of environmental regulation provides the benefits of overregulation to large corporate developers, who are able to take advantage of opportunities for overcompliance or for playing one authority against another. At the same time, small property owners, particularly in the coastal zone, may find the bureaucratic maze to be prohibitive. Longtime coastal residents, for example, discovered that they could not replace deteriorating beachfront patios and stairs without providing public access to what they had enjoyed as a private beach.[4]

The frustration of property owners and neighbors compound the problem of popular participation. As the complexity of the planning process increases, particularly with the incorporation of environmental regulation and the increasingly comprehensive and regional approach associated with big-picture planning, local residents are incapable of initiating planning policies. To the extent that local residents and grassroots movements become involved in the planning process, they tend to aggravate the complexity of the planning problem. Ultimately the irony of popular participation in big-picture planning is that it tends to increase local government's dependence on private-sector developers, the only actors who are willing and able to develop creative solutions to the increasingly complex planning problems.

The irony of popular participation in big-picture planning is particularly striking in the coastal zone because the radical assault upon property rights in the battle for the beach was in some sense successful. The people—or, more accurately, the radicals—won the battle but lost the war. The Coastal Act of 1972 guaranteed public access to the beach. Once the people's right to the beach was institutionalized in legal, bureaucratic procedures, however, the war was all but lost.

The struggle between public use and private ownership extended, between 1970 and 1992, from the beach toward the coastal hills and mesas until it encompassed all undeveloped land in southern California. As the scale and scope of the conflict increased, however, the radicals were increasingly ineffective. They had won the initial skirmish, but the cooperation of liberal environmentalists and planners with conservative developers and politicians ultimately defeated the radicals. Thus comprehensive regional plans for habitat conservation and development marked the ultimate triumph of the progressive coalition in its effort to finesse regulation and manage popular participation. Such a decisive victory was certainly not a foregone conclusion, though, in the early years of the battle for the beach.

The Battle for the Beach

The battle for the beach was rooted in conflicts that predated the Coastal Act of 1972 and the environmentalist movement. In San Diego hippies were taking over the beaches in the 1960s, particularly in the less affluent southern communities of Ocean Beach, Mission Beach, and Pacific Beach. Ultimately, however, the battle for the beach reached its climax in the wealthy northern community of La Jolla, where students and East County hippies effectively challenged exclusive rights to the beach.[5]

In the 1960s there were two large beaches in La Jolla, a wealthy community in the northern section of the City of San Diego. La Jolla Shores was public, with free parking, lifeguard service, and picnic tables. Blacks Beach was private. It was used for research and teaching by the University of California, San Diego (UCSD). The university maintained the access road, which was kept locked and chained. Blacks was also connected by tramway to a home in La Jolla Farms, an exclusive residential neighborhood nestled between the cliffs above Blacks Beach and below UCSD. In the 1960s the privilege of private access to Blacks Beach was shared by the university and the wealthy residents of the La Jolla neighborhood that extended from UCSD to the private access road. By the summer of 1969, however, the beach was invaded by East County hippies, who would park in the exclusive residential community and walk to the beach via the private access road or park at La Jolla Shores and travel north by land or sea. They settled at Blacks and declared it to be the people's beach.

That a group of California hippies should entertain such a radical notion—that the beach belongs to the people—might seem plausible. In the context of the 1960s it even seems plausible that these hippies should defy the law of private property in exercising the people's right to liberate the beach. What is remarkable, however, is that the voters of California collectively declared their commitment to this principle in the Coastal Act of 1972. The Coastal Act defends public access at the expense of private ownership. For all intents and purposes, it outlaws private beaches and demands that coastal property owners provide public access. Thus Blacks Beach was liberated by the Coastal Act of 1972.

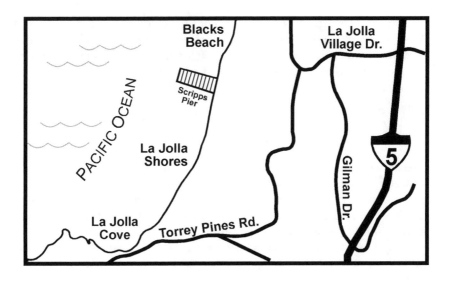

Figure 10. La Jolla Beaches
Base map provided by SanGIS

Unfortunately, Blacks was ruined in the process of its liberation. What in the 1960s had been a secluded beach shared by the marine biologists of UCSD, the friends and neighbors of the beach house owner, and the hippies from the eastern suburbs, was officially proclaimed a nude beach in the 1970s. The city even posted a sign: "Bathing Suits Optional North of This Sign." As a designated nude beach, Blacks became a tourist and media attraction, a parody of its former self. It was a postmodern, post-secluded beach where people could come to look at the nudists.

By 1992 the problem of public access to Blacks Beach had been more or less resolved. The media had lost interest in the nudists. Gradually, adolescents came to the beach to enjoy the privacy they lacked at La Jolla Shores. They tended to gather north of the access road. Aging hippies and their children, UCSD students, and a few exotic dancers who needed a total body tan congregated south of road, maintaining a limited version of the nude beach even though the sign was gone. UCSD continued to use the beach for research and teaching, and the beach house even attracted some guests. Thus, after the storm of political conflict, the beach returned to its previous state. Because it is not accessible by car except by permission of the regents of the University of California, it remains a relatively private beach. In fact, if one did not know the history of Blacks Beach, one would be reluctant to conclude that it had been ruined.

Developers might argue that the beach could be more profitably developed. Environmentalists might contend that the cliffs and the beach are not being adequately protected. Nevertheless, although Blacks was ruined in the seventies, it is gradually returning to its natural state. Thus far at least there are no plans for new development or habitat conservation projects at Blacks Beach, so it might still survive as a relatively private public beach where bathing suits are optional. Whether other coastal attractions will survive big-picture plans for habitat conservation and development remains to be seen.

Protecting the Lagoons

The coastal lagoons of northern San Diego County are one of the most environmentally threatened and politically challenged natural areas of the California coast. Agriculture and commercial, industrial, and residential development has contributed to pollution and erosion, which has resulted in serious threats to wildlife. Even where pollution has been controlled, erosion and seasonal variations in rainfall and tides create cycles of flooding and drought. When the lagoons are at flood stage, the coastal highway is impassable and the California Coastal Commission must grant municipal officials the right to remove the berm, the natural barrier that impedes the flow of lagoon waters into the ocean.[6] In drought stage the lagoons are reduced to swampy mudflats that become a haven for mosquitoes and other pests. Aside from the mud and the insects, the stench is overpowering. Thus motorists, developers, and local residents all suffer from the effects of cycles of flooding and drought on lagoons that have suffered significant erosion.

Castleton Lagoon is routinely creating these types of problems for all concerned parties. Mr. Patterson, who owns a thousand acres just north of the lagoon, donated the body of water to the city and provided public access and recreational facilities as part of a master plan for developing Camelot. The big-picture plan for preserving the lagoon includes a dredging operation that has been offered as mitigation by another developer in another county for a port revitalization project that will involve partial filling of wetlands. The port revitalization and the thousand-acre Camelot project were both approved by the interested city governments and by the coastal commission in the late 1980s, and environmental procedures per NEPA and CEQA were followed, but the Sierra Club continued to oppose the dredging. Consequently, in 1992 the Army Corps of Engineers had yet to approve the project because it was waiting until the California appeals court heard the suit prepared by the Sierra Club. Mr. Patterson, the City of Castleton, and the Friends of the Castleton Lagoon all suffered while awaiting the results of the lawsuit.

Every year if the coastal highway flooded, Castleton city planners petitioned the coastal commission for permission to "blow out the berm" to reduce the flooding. Then the lagoon would be reduced to a stagnant swamp by summer unless there was unusually late and abundant rainfall. One summer Bill, the local Patterson CEO, was so frustrated that he rebuilt the berm with cinder blocks to prevent the lagoon from draining. For this impetuous act Bill was cited by the coastal commission, fined, and ordered to remove the blocks.

Ultimately, however, the ocean tide beat the developer to it. The blocks were swept out to sea, the lagoon reverted to its summer swamp cycle, and all interested parties in Castleton continued to suffer the seasonally variable distress associated with the condition of the lagoon.

In the spring of 1992 local citizens, state and local government officials, and local agents representing Mr. Patterson cooperated in providing a temporary solution to the flooding problem. The fact that the parties were able to find even a temporary solution is remarkable. Aside from the contradictory interests involved, there were the constraints imposed by federal and state regulation by the Army Corps of Engineers and the California Coastal Commission. Finally, the delaying tactics of the Sierra Club mitigated against success.

The story began early one morning in the spring of 1992. Fred, a California Fish and Game official, had called a meeting at the edge of the Castleton Lagoon to deal with the problem of flooding. Camelot's head planner, Tom, was there, as was Dick, a good friend of Tom's who was a planning consultant and had recently been elected as an officer of the Castleton Lagoon Foundation. Another lagoon foundation officer, Len, and Castleton's assistant city planning director, Paul were also there. Observers included a reporter from the local newspaper and myself. The highway was not in danger this time, but the islands on which a bird called the least tern nests in the spring were partially submerged. Fred was concerned that the endangered bird might not be able to nest, so he wanted to bulldoze the berm to protect the nests. The questions that needed to be resolved included the need for a coastal permit or other permits and the possibility of an appeal if someone, like the Sierra Club, opposed the action.

Tom asked Fred about options. Project Camelot really needed to find a big-picture alternative to blowing out the berm and draining the lagoon. Already in 1992 hotel investors had backed out and new investors were slow to appear. Overlooking the ecological disaster of the Castleton Lagoon, the empty shell of the luxury hotel stood vacant, its construction crew idle. Eventually, Tom hoped, the Sierra Club would lose its lawsuit and the lagoon would be dredged. Meanwhile, however, he wanted to avoid turning the lagoon into a summer swampland. Tom proposed to Fred that they could bulldoze a gradual seep ("shave the berm") or put in pumps. He estimated that they could lower the lagoon by one foot in four days with one pump. If that was not enough, they could put in more pumps.

> Fred: I don't know how much lower we need to go, but a pump would be more controlled. One problem is Memorial Day weekend and coastal commission opposition to pumps on the beach over the holiday.

> Tom: We could put in sand.

> Fred: The Army Corps of Engineers would not accept that—filling in wetlands.

> Tom: But this is not for development. It's for endangered species.

Fred: It doesn't matter. You can't fill in wetlands. Maybe we better make a few phone calls before we celebrate this great idea. . . . I will call Fish and Wildlife.

Fred and Tom arranged for the Patterson Company to provide the pumps and the state and local government to negotiate with the federal authorities for whatever permits might be required.

Tom: I'll line up the pumps.

Paul: We need Coastal Commission permission.

Fred: No, it would be better to call them after the fact.

Paul: Army Corps of Engineers? Who?

Fred: [names officer] He said he just needs to be contacted.

Thus the public and private sector were prepared to cooperate in managing state and federal authorities and attempting to implement a big-picture alternative to business as usual. They all realized that this would not be easy. As Fred suggested, even the Fish and Game officials had to be very careful in their efforts to protect endangered species, particularly as nesting season approached.

Fred: I hope they are not nesting. This is a very sensitive issue. We tried to protect the area one time and some people thought we were too late. They accused us of harassing terns that we were trying to protect

Len: This should be good press. It lets people know that we've made a creative decision. Draining the lagoon usually sneaks up on the people of Castleton.

In fact, the local paper reported the "innovative plan" the following day. "The state Department of Fish and Game had planned to drain the lagoon, . . . [but Camelot staff and lagoon foundation officials] argued against completely draining the lagoon because it leaves stinking mud flats and is traumatic to wildlife that rely on the lagoon waters." The report noted that this big-picture plan was a more expensive and more time-consuming alternative to the usual remedy of blowing out the berm. Since the Camelot project was picking up the tab, however, the Castleton city planning department was happy to cooperate. "Pumping the lagoon could take up to a week and cost between $10,000 and $12,000, while opening the berm would cost only between $1,000 and $2,000. . . . Patterson agreed to pay for the pumping. 'It makes sense to us,' said the Castleton assistant planning director, 'It sounds like a win-win situation.'"[7]

In fact, the innovative strategy took weeks to complete. The negotiations with the Army Corps of Engineers and the U.S. Fish and Wildlife Service finally produced a compromise in which pumps would be used only to begin the process of siphoning water from the lagoon. Then the pumps would be removed. As Tom explained, they successfully lowered the water level until the water was below the pipes. They finally dredged a little with laborers and opened, or shaved, the berm, but they still couldn't expose enough nesting areas. Ultimately the City of Castleton and the regional city that is now dredging the lagoon as mitigation for another project constructed least tern "condos," or bird houses, that allowed the birds to nest in relative comfort despite the flooded lagoon conditions.

In this temporary solution, government agents negotiated for permits and the developer provided the money and the equipment, and their efforts were supplemented when all else failed by municipal investment in birdhouses. This big-picture alternative to business as usual maintained the lagoon and the nesting terns for two years, 1992–1994. Then the Sierra Club finally surrendered and the Army Corps of Engineers approved the lagoon-dredging project, which began in 1994. Fortunately, the Castleton Lagoon Foundation, with its newly elected officers, who seemed willing to negotiate big-picture solutions, did not attempt to oppose either the interim or the ultimate solution. Perhaps the fact that Camelot was already approved and partially built undermined local support for saving the lagoon from the developer. It appears, in any case, that local attention had shifted from saving the lagoon and saving open space toward habitat conservation. There was, at the same time, a corresponding shift of public interest from the lagoon to the surrounding hillsides, and from the least tern to the California gnatcatcher.

The Castleton Lagoon case is a good example of the irrationality of rational government. It illustrates the legal constraints of state and federal regulation and the confounding efforts of environmentalists that create problems for government officials who are trying to do their jobs—in this case, protecting endangered species—without violating the law. The story also illustrates the irony of popular participation. The public, represented by the Sierra Club and the Castleton Lagoon Foundation, was creating problems that drove government officials into the arms of the developers, the only actors with the ability and interest to provide a creative solution.

Preserving Gnatcatchers and Coastal Sage Scrub

In 1991 Governor Wilson offered Californians Natural Community Conservation Planning (NCCP) as a big-picture plan for habitat conservation that would accommodate the concerns of environmentalists and developers. The 1991 annual report of the Resources Agency of California explains the origins of the NCCP as follows: "On April 22, 1991, Governor Wilson used the occasion of Earth Day to outline a far-reaching plan. . . . In the spirit of preventative government, Resourceful California is designed to protect our natural and cultural treasures for future generations through action now, before it is too late."[8] Particularly in San Diego, the plan was sold to developers as a major improvement over the possibility that either state or federal authorities would list the California gnatcatcher as an endangered species.

The gnatcatcher lives in coastal sage scrub habitats on the hillsides near the coast that are prime development sites. Thus fear of a gnatcatcher listing and general opposition to the ESA inspired developers to take a chance on something different. When asked about the NCCP, Bill, CEO for the Camelot project, explained that he was hesitant to publicly support the program for fear that the environmentalists would take his support as evidence of the conspiracy of government and developer: "Once they [the biologists and the politicians] work it out we complain but cooperate. It will hurt, but it will become the market [condition]. If the rules are known and universally applied, then the developer can work. The ESA listing is crazy and unpredictable—a wild card."

Bill is not alone is recognizing the problems associated with the ESA and the possibility that the NCCP might be an improvement. Environmentalists often recognize the limitations of the ESA and are, in some cases prepared to negotiate for big-picture plans that might be more effective.[9] Where they tend to differ from the developer, however, is in their commitment to maintain the ESA at any cost. Much of the conflict between environmentalists and big-picture planners (including both public- and private-sector planners) comes down to the conflict between developers, particularly in San Diego, who promote the NCCP as an alternative to the ESA and environmentalists who promote the NCCP as a supplement. Environmentalists cling desperately to the ESA, at least partly for what it represents. Steve, the leader of the Southern California Habitat Defenders, explained this position: "We need to keep the Endangered Species Act. It is a line in the sand that the American people drew: a line between big money and the national heritage. It doesn't work [but] it's amazing that we got it [and] we won't get anything else."

Thus environmentalists defend the ESA even though the ESA provisions are not satisfactory. Dan, a conservation biologist and a state NCCP official, explained, however, that the ESA has been roundly criticized on all sides and that it is in need at least of supplementation or reform. The official NCCP position is: "Both federal and state Endangered Species Acts have been subject to increasing criticism from all quarters. Development interests complain of undue and unfair costs. Agency biologists complain that political pressure and limited resources compromise implementation. Environmental critics complain that species continue to decline precipitously. Thus the time seems ripe for a new approach to conservation."[10]

In California the ecological diversity of the state and the building boom of the 1970s and 1980s had placed developers and environmentalists on a collision course with one another. The listing of the Stevens kangaroo rat in 1989 was a wake up call for Orange County and San Diego County developers. The Coalition for Habitat Conservation was organized, uniting the major development interests in Orange County, and the Alliance for Habitat Conservation was organized in San Diego County. From the outset the Orange County group was much more effective because a relatively small number of large developers owned most of the coastal sage scrub habitat and because the Orange County habitat conservation program was, from the outset, well integrated with state and federal efforts.

Federal interest in creative alternatives to the ESA were undoubtedly inspired by the so-called train wreck associated with the 1989 listing of the spotted owl and the ensuing political and legal battles, which included guerrilla warfare as Earth First! spiked trees and destroyed logging equipment while lawyers, judges, and even the president attempted to litigate the issue or negotiate between logging and conservation interests.[11]

The Nature Conservancy, a private, nonprofit conservation organization that attempts to arrange for purchase or donation of land for conservation, was a critical actor in bringing together state, federal, and local interests, including environmentalists and developers. These negotiations produced the alternative approach that was then institutionalized in the NCCP. James, a Nature Conservancy official, explained how the interests of developers and the problems of due process combined with Governor Pete Wilson's leadership to foster the emergence of the NCCP. "Large development companies wanted to get pre-need [pre-listing] planning and to get assurances that this would have lasting value for subsequent listings. . . . Wilson and the Orange County developers cooperated." James went on to explain that California's Brown Act severely limited the opportunities for government to cooperate with the private sector without making meetings open to the general public. Of course, open meetings would make it all the more difficult to achieve consensus. "The election of Pete Wilson was the critical juncture. That created the possibility of doing this. . . . The Nature Conservancy formulated the scientific basis for the plan—natural community based, rather than species based."

The Kelley Bill (AB 2172), introduced to the California State Assembly in March 1991 as an amendment to the Fish and Game code, created the legal basis for the NCCP. It provides for local conservation plans that establish habitat preserves and allow development on lands outside the preserves. Thus the incidental taking of endangered or threatened species could occur without the necessity of a federal or state Habitat Conservation Plan (HCP) as required by the ESA, so long as the development was outside the boundaries of the local preserve. "Natural community conservation planning promotes coordination and cooperation among public agencies, landowners, and other private interests . . . [and] will support the fish and wildlife management activities of the Department of Fish and Game. . . . The department may permit the taking, as provided in this code, of any identified species."[12]

On the basis of this promise of progress toward preemptive conservation, Michael Mantrell, undersecretary of the Resources Agency of California, convinced the Fish and Game Commission in the fall of 1991 to reject its staff's recommendation for advancing the California gnatcatcher to candidacy as a threatened or endangered species. On December 4, 1991, the secretary of the

Resources Agency, the directors of the U.S. Fish and Wildlife Service and the California Department of Fish and Game, and the regional director of Fish and Wildlife signed a memorandum of understanding (MOU), agreeing, in principle, to support the NCCP. The memorandum describes the nature and extent of the agreement: "The agencies will work together to assure that NCCPs are designed to facilitate compliance with the Federal Endangered Species Act Section 10(a) permit requirements [for a HCP] and the California Endangered Species Act Section 2801 permit requirements [for taking species]."[13]

The legislation and the MOU were sufficiently vague to sustain competing interpretations of the relationship between the NCCP and ESA listings. On the one hand, the NCCP might preclude the necessity of a listing or might meet the requirements of ESA for an HCP (an incidental taking of an endangered or threatened species, in accordance with the ESA amendment of 1982). On the other hand, it might be seen as an alternative to listing—a better way to preserve while still allowing development. This confusion was the source of considerable controversy, but NCCP proponents were hesitant to reject the latter, ESA-alternative, interpretation because it facilitated the mobilization of developer support, particularly in San Diego. At the same time, however, they would not reject the former, ESA-supplement, interpretation, which was critical in mobilizing environmentalist and growth-control support.

James, the Nature Conservancy official, explained the confusion: "The intent was to supplement the Endangered Species Act, but there were different ways of seeing this. Some saw this as an alternative to a listing. Others saw listing as an important component." The problem, as James explained, was that California law does not allow for any taking of endangered species candidates. Thus Fish and Game had to reject the staff recommendation for candidacy of the gnatcatcher in order to implement the habitat conservation program. At the same time, the federal law, as amended in 1982, allowed for incidental taking of endangered species, under the terms of an approved HCP. Thus a state listing would make the NCCP impossible but a federal listing was not a serious problem, so long as the U.S. Fish and Wildlife Service agreed to accept the local NCCP as an HCP. James explained that the California Fish and Game decision to delay listing "created a storm in a teacup. The issue was whether the gnatcatcher should be a candidate for listing, but under California law there can be no take of candidates. That was not popular with developers. Plus, it created legal problems. California Fish and Game seemed to think that the NCCP would replace listing, but NCCP had no regulatory authority."

The environmentalists rejected the NCCP when it came to be viewed as an effort by Governor Wilson and the developers to avoid listing the gnatcatcher. Particularly important was the lack of interim protection. Environmentalists who came to the NCCP meeting in Irvine on April 23, 1992, were openly hostile to the NCCP staff.

> Environmentalist: Why are there not more [preserve] areas in the Riverside Mountains. In 1987 ten areas were identified as habitat to be preserved.

Now only three remain.

Staff: Good question. Please put it in writing. We will want to consider it.

Environmentalist: Will developers continue to develop?

The environmentalists continued to harass the NCCP staff, claiming that the developers were grading with impunity while the NCCP process dragged on. After a representative of U.S. Fish and Wildlife was introduced, the hostile questioning continued.

Environmentalist: Since NCCP has started San Bernardino County coastal sage scrub is being graded, demolished. I've been coming here since January. Why is this happening? How long does it take before the feds act?

U.S. Fish and Wildlife: We need a listing to act—

Environmentalist: [Can we establish] an eighteen-month moratorium?

The Fish and Wildlife officer explained that owners of enrolled lands had agreed to an eighteen-month moratorium and that enrolled local governments had agreed to treat sage scrub as critical in their CEQA reviews. Nevertheless, a developer with an HCP had the right to take the gnatcatcher.

Environmentalist: Straight answer please! We need a grading moratorium. We are concerned that reports of grading coastal sage scrub are always dismissed as small and insignificant. It is important to realize that these areas are being destroyed daily.

NCCP and USF&WL staff attempted to defuse the opposition by explaining that this was not the appropriate forum for telling horror stories about how developers or farmers are grading all the remaining habitat.

Staff: This [NCCP] project is not an attempt to deal with projects, grading or whatever. There is a list of grading loss. Many of these [projects] have an approved HCP or CEQA mitigation—

Environmentalist: Not all coastal sage scrub is created equal. Only some supports gnatcatchers. The assumption that local government is influenced by the people is not true. Council turns a deaf ear [but is] extremely influenced by the developer.

By March 1992 many of the environmentalists had abandoned the NCCP as a developer plot to avoid the listing of the gnatcatcher. Viewed from this perspective, while the NCCP delayed the listing with the ploy of promised conservation, developers and local governments were busy destroying habitat, scraping the hill-sides clean so that once the bird was listed there would be nothing left to preserve. "The Natural Resources Defense Council walked out [on the NCCP] in December because of the interim control issue. 'I felt that was a violation of the understanding that we went into the process with,' said Mary Nichols, director of the NRDC's L.A. office."[14]

Even after the no-growth/local environmentalist/NIMBY coalition abandoned the NCCP and focused on lobbying for a federal listing, the NCCP might have moved forward if it could have offered carrots and sticks to entice or coerce local government and developer cooperation. This was not a problem in Orange County, where the big developers cooperated with local government and agreed to pay the cost of surveying and establishing preserves. They were not concerned with "free riders"—the small developers who would reap the benefits without paying the costs of compliance.[15] A handful of companies owned most of the habitat, and they were willing to establish preserves in order to gain develop-ment rights. Bob, an Orange County NCCP official, explained their success: "The Fish and Wildlife staff working with me in Orange County are great. . . . They support NCCP [and] they came on board early. We established working groups that included Fish and Game and Fish and Wildlife and major landown-ers who are funding us." Bob went on to explain that the Orange County NCCP managed to avoid the sunshine laws governing public notification by not includ-ing local government officials in their group. "We . . . don't have public meet-ings [and our group discussions] are not a consensus process. We can move ahead even if we disagree, but there is a complete exchange of information. We have meetings before the CEQA process begins." Bob explained how big capi-tal and big environmental social-movement organizations were able to cooper-ate and how the environmentalists came to appreciate the perspective of the developers after they became involved in establishing a preserve system. "The Nature Conservancy and Audubon actually become developers [when they have conservation and preservation projects], and there is a real awakening. They become effective players. When they take on a project they come to realize that they are developers. They have to go through the tortures. They don't get any breaks and may even get tougher treatment."

Of course the very success of the caucus of Orange County development and conservation interests contributed to the perception that the NCCP was a con-spiracy between big capital and big government—neither of which can be trusted, from the perspective of the no-growth/local environmentalist/NIMBY coalition. In return, the Orange County and state NCCPs tended to view the local regulator, or anti-development, interests with suspicion. As Bob explained, attempting to regu-late development generally does not work. You need to offer carrots as well as sticks. "After years of saying no, you have to have a solution. Without incentives to bring landowners in, you get people who hold out and refuse to participate. You can't force anybody to do what they don't want to do."

As much as the Orange County NCCP contributed to the sense of conspir-acy, it was able to make progress toward establishing a preserve system. San

Diego had much more serious problems. Bob explained: "Fragmented owner-ship and municipal infighting [are major problems]. None of the cities trust each other. SANDAG has [illusions] of grandeur and nobody trusts them. San Diego City dominates the region and nobody trusts them." Bob contended that the problem in San Diego was "small subregions and lack of coopera-tion."

If Orange County follows the caucus model for private negotiation between environment, government, and the more enlightened representatives of devel-opment, San Diego's is the carnival model, with multiple authorities anxiously currying favor with constituents through endless meetings and an endless strug-gle toward consensus.[16] Steve, a vocal critic of the Orange County caucus, described the San Diego NCCPs: "There are four overlapping programs. All are multiple habitat in scope. . . . All programs have working groups or advisory committees consisting of interested parties, and a consensus-building approach using issue papers, and a facilitator is employed."

A closer look at one of these San Diego County programs should indicate the problems and possibilities in this effort to incorporate the interested public in a version of trilateral negotiation that includes neighbors, developers, and local government, as well as environmental and no-growth interests.[17]

Habitat Conservation in Castleton

Castleton developed an elaborate system of citizen advisory committees, public workshops, and private negotiations with developers as part of a revision of the city's general plan for development. When I was in the field in the winter of 1992, the open-space advisory committee was completing its work while the habitat protection committee was still struggling toward a map that could be used as a basis for negotiating with property owners.

The open-space committee produced a trail system by negotiating with developers, who allocated part of their projects' dedicated open space to form the trail. The city promised that it would assume legal liability for the trails and that trails would follow project boundary lines to the extent possible. Furthermore, the trail system would be considered as part of the 15 percent open space that all master-plan communities were expected to maintain. Thus the major developers, notably Patterson and Peterson, were on board. In fact, as is frequently the case, planning commission's approval of the open-space committee's proposal was anticlimactic. There were a few complaints, especial-ly from one particular citizen group, but open space was no longer a very con-troversial issue in Castleton. The only question was who would pay for the trail system. In 1999 the city still had not held an election to approve the bond issue that would provide the funds. Perhaps they would do so once the other ele-ments of the general plan had been approved, but my private-sector contacts were skeptical. Pete, local representative for the Peterson Company, owner of the four-thousand-acre Brigadoon project, had asked the open-space committee in 1992 who was going to pay for the trail system. The chair had replied jok-ingly, "Did you bring your checkbook?"

Much more controversial than the open-space committee was the habitat protection committee, which was to produce a preserve system that would be folded into the trail system. The Habitat Protection Plan (HPP) was built around a Habitat Conservation Plan (HCP) that Castleton and the Peterson Company were negotiating with the U.S. Fish and Wildlife Service and California Fish and Game. Carl, Castleton's representative from the Audubon Society, and Steve, the leader of a regional environmental organization, were also involved in negotiating the EIR that would serve as the foundation for the HCP. In the interest of completing Project Brigadoon and as mitigation in the EIR and HCP agreements, Pete was prepared to donate on behalf of the Peterson Company a large chuck of the land that would constitute the preserve system. Castleton officials found the proposition attractive because, beyond their interest in the HPP, they wanted to improve one of their major local thor-oughfares, which ran through Brigadoon and through the coastal sage scrub habitat that housed forty-eight pairs of gnatcatchers. This was to be the core of the HPP, and if it were accepted as an NCCP it would preclude the necessity of additional HCPs and allow the city to draw lines and grant development rights.

The city planning department and habitat protection committee in Castleton approached the NCCP with suspicion, however. Castleton officials generally echoed the concerns of environmentalists and no-growth advocates who viewed the NCCP as a developer plan to avoid the listing of the gnatcatcher. Lou, the HPP facilitator, evaluated the NCCP by explaining that it began as an "effort by an Orange County developer to enlist San Diego developers to pre-vent the listing of the gnatcatchers. . . . The state and the developers have played with dynamite to prevent a listing [but you] can't [just] talk to the pres-ident and the secretary of the interior." Lou argued that the old ways were rap-idly changing and that the developers who had initially attempted to use the NCCP to avoid a listing needed to wake up and smell the coffee. "The old-boy system won't work. NCCP, to be successful, must be as effective as if the bird were listed. [We] need comprehensive planning."

Lou framed the problem in terms of local control and the stormy relations between local and state government. "Relations between the State of California and local government have always been rotten. The state designs regulations without local input [and] mandates without [providing] state funds. [Regarding the NCCP] the city asks, 'Why should we do the state a favor?' The greatest concern is that this is like the coastal zone. The state says that localities can't do this so the state will do it. NCCP people are old coastal zone people."

Doug, the city's representative to the HPP, was not much more enthusiastic about enrollment in the NCCP, suggesting in April of 1992 that "it is not clear that there is any benefit to the city or to the species." Castleton officials were convinced that they had a better plan for habitat conservation and were far ahead of the state in this regard. Lou described local efforts: "Eighteen months ago, the city envisioned the listing of the gnatcatcher. The Peterson Company deserves credit for realizing the problem. The HPP is to evolve into a general-plan conservation section [through which Castleton] will set aside a preserve system for mitigation in future projects." Lou went on to explain how Castleton had picked the road improvement project from among a series of projects that had been identified in the memorandum of understanding through which the Fish and Wildlife Service and California Fish and Game had launched the NCCP. Castleton had chosen the project because it was the most important and most ambitious. It would provide the basis for the habitat conservation program and would offer a model for big-picture planning in the future. "The HCP [is] the city, Fish and Wildlife, Fish and Game, and the Peterson Company [working in an] effort to address the problems of gnatcatcher and coastal sage scrub in a *better* preservation plan. The alternative? The gnatcatcher is not protected. The city is not required to do more than CEQA/EIR." Lou explained that the Castleton Habitat Protection Plan was a major innovation in big-picture planning. "The HPP is a landmark because the city and the developer did not say, 'How can we prevent the listing?' but 'That's not our business.' The developer didn't just want to beat the listing. Business as usual is dead. [We] need to get out ahead of the new business climate."

The HPP is a critical piece of the Castleton general-plan review, and quite apart from its ability to establish a viable preserve, it is a mechanism for co-opting or cooling out local opposition to the city's plan for future development. Among the constituents are not only no-growth and environmental interests, but also property owners, whom Lou described as follows: "Property owners want to protect their economic interest. [Some have] global vision and [take] environmental responsibility. [Others have] narrow vision. Pete was willing to give up a lot and preserve a lot to get development rights." Lou recognized, however, that the Peterson Company could afford to be enlightened, whereas smaller property owners, such as a local man named Ben, were quite limited in their ability to accommodate increased demands for preservation. "Small landowners are in a tough position because they don't know what will happen to their property. Ben's family has always used their land to make a living—through livestock, agriculture, now housing. Now people are drawing maps and coloring his squares red—how will that affect his vision?" Lou was optimistic, however, that the HPP might provide for a win-win solution for both larger and smaller property owners. This was most critical for the small property owners, like Ben.

Needless to say, the HPP meetings offer evidence of conflicting interests. In the January and February meetings, Carl, the Castleton representative of the local Audubon Society, focused attention on illegal grading, inspiring the city to report proposals for changes in the municipal code. Here attempts to accommodate the conflicting interests of the Audubon Society and the developer were confounded by concerns of local government, particularly the Castleton Engineering Department.

> Doug: [In the] revisions to the municipal code the major goals are deterrence and punishment that fits the crime.

Pete: There is a potential problem between the city and the developer and their ongoing relations if the city is going to be punitive. I suggest putting a commission together.

Will (Castleton city engineer): The engineering department would not want a commission to determine [the disposition of grading cases].

Carl: There should be a public hearing to deal with flagrant violations—what about intent?

Aside from the debates between developers and environmentalists, there were also debates between property owners and state and federal regulators. Ben, a Castleton property owner, was clearly annoyed by the insensitivity of the U.S. Fish and Wildlife Service and local environmentalists to what he perceived to be an intolerable situation.

Ben:I own 250 acres. . . . If the gnatcatcher is listed, what can I do with this land? [Turning toward the U.S. Fish and Wildlife representative] What would you do if I put cows on it?

Fish and Wildlife: It's hard to say if that would constitute a taking. That's the problem.

Carl:Most property owners underestimate the value of riparian woodlands.

Ben: But if I can't do anything with my property I can't take advantage of this.

Lou: You might be able to gain development rights through the HPP. The city might be able to broker an agreement for payment as mitigation.

Lou and Doug, the facilitator and the city's representative, managed to push the process along. While Doug and his expert panel prepared a map of habitat and outlined a preserve system, Lou dealt with the contradictory concerns of environmental, no-growth, and development interests. At the May meeting Tim, a biological consultant, presented a habitat map and a sketch of a preserve system. Lou announced that the Castleton City Council was meeting to approve the EIR for the HCP that would provide the basis for constructing the preserve system. At that point the HPP would be prepared to move into the third phase—negotiating with property owners and the city on what could be included within the preserve. Although Ben was still worried about what would happen to his land, and local no-growth and environmental interests continued to express concerns, the apparent success of the HCP negotiations suggested that the HPP committee might finally establish a preserve. The city council meeting at which the Environmental Impact Report (EIR) was approved for the Habitat Conservation Plan (HCP) was almost the epitome of the public face of private government—the carnival of popular participation. Consequently, it is instructive to look at these proceedings in some detail before returning to the work of the HPP citizen advisory committee.

The Castleton City Council Meeting

At the Castleton City Council meeting to approve the EIR for the HCP, the room was packed. The meeting opened with a prayer from a local rabbi, who offered a note of thanks to the mayor, followed by the Pledge of Allegiance, a report on a closed session about a lawsuit, a proclamation that this was Buckle Up America Week, and the approval of minutes. As usual, there was a series of pressing issues that had to be discussed before the public hearing on the EIR began. After a spirited exercise of local government authority and local resident influence, the EIR was finally on the table.[18]

Chuck, the Castleton city planning director, introduced a member of his staff, who proceeded to describe the details of the EIR that the various interested parties had collectively produced. The agreement was that just over 450 of the total of 750 acres would be graded.

> Staff: We have met the CEQA requirement (draft, comments, response). There are six alternatives to the proposed project: realign the road, widening without mass grading, etc., plus "no project." There are several reasons not to choose these alternatives. The mitigation program seems adequate [for gnatcatcher considerations] according to biological consultants. It is in compliance with the general plan and zoning. CEQA air-quality requirements require a statement of overriding considerations.

This is all fairly standard for an EIR, except for the magnitude of the acreage that would be preserved. The planning director explained that this was due to the fact that there would be significant loss of coastal sage scrub, the prime gnatcatcher habitat.

> Chuck: The draft EIR found coastal sage scrub impact significant. The mitigation plan follows the draft EIR recommendations: 100-plus acres of open space—more than half of the gnatcatcher habitat—plus 400 acres off site. The city has started an HCP process treating the gnatcatcher as already listed. An agreement has been reached.

The planning director went on to explain that the city and the developer had made a number of concessions in the course of the negotiations and that they agreed that they would continue negotiations for an HCP, which they hoped to conclude within sixty days.

Chuck: We also request two additional conditions. If the HCP is completed and approved prior to implementation, that could be implemented as an alternative. [Second, since] all interested parties are desirous of completing the HCP, no grading permits for sixty days.

The city council members raised a few questions about increases in housing-unit density and the extent to which the HCP would be more restrictive than the EIR. Everyone seemed to be supportive, and the mayor gave a rousing speech.

Mayor: [This] proactive approach is an asset to Castleton and all of southern California. Steve endorsed [this EIR]. I commend staff, Peterson, all participants. This road alignment—we have been besieged by complaints on the hazard—we have had deaths—on the southern section. It has been a difficult process since 1983.

Councilor C: [This was] one of the first issues I had to deal with.

Councilor B: We are on the cutting edge again, preserving human and animal habitat.

Pete then gave his speech. He began with a joke: "I'd like to introduce all the little Petersons." He was speaking of the corporate executives, who usually did not attend these meetings in Castleton. He continued somewhat sarcastically.

Pete: It is wonderful to be here preserving human and animal habitat. This is the longest and most expensive EIR ever done. As the gnatcatcher became more of a media item and less of a biological concern we realized that we had a problem, [so we] bought more property.

Pete continued in a more sympathetic vein, offering an olive branch to the environmentalists and the government officials with whom he had negotiated the EIR. He said that it had been a "long, painful process" and offered a "public apology to [a staff member] of Fish and Game. That was the first time I lost my temper in fifteen years." Pete concluded on a positive note, suggesting that the "HCP will be the cornerstone of HPP." Clearly this was an agreement to celebrate. It was the first giant step toward a regional preserve system.

After Pete finished his speech, a couple of the local environmentalists and no-growth folks who were regulars at these types of events gave their speeches. First Ruby read a letter from Carl, the local Audubon representative.

Ruby: [quoting Carl] "This proves that construction and conservation can work." Finally, I would like to personally thank the U.S. Fish and Wildlife staff.

Then Emma took the microphone.

> Emma: Wonderful things [have been] done here. [I] fully support the HCP participants for mitigation in the city, corridors, [and] multispecies protection. Nevertheless, as usual, I have concerns.

There was an audible groan. People had come here to celebrate the agreement, and they had little patience for Emma, who didn't even live in the city. Nevertheless, she continued to complain about the lack of public input and prior knowledge of the negotiations.

> Emma: This is the first written evidence of the HCP. Now we are approving an EIR that includes the HCP. I am also concerned about how quickly we're moving with the EIR, open space, HCP. There will be a loss of fifteen birds.

There was very little sympathy for Emma's concerns. Everyone seemed to agree that the negotiations have been going on far too long already. One Castleton resident, a neighbor of the Brigadoon project, expressed this sentiment succinctly.

> Neighbor: For ten years people of the neighborhood have been working [on this]. Now sixty days. How long will this take?

A variety of brief comments followed. One person asked, regarding air pollution, "How can you accept degradation?" Another asked how corridors could be preserved without any preserve regions. Still another commented that for six years Pete had been great and suggested moving forward.

> Pete: This is the first time that Ruby and I have publicly agreed. To Emma— we are working on the HCP. There is nothing hidden here. The HCP needs to go through the CEQA/NEPA process. It will get another crack at the public, or the reverse is probably more accurate.

Councilor A asked about grading, the length and width of corridors, and the possibility of leaving the land in its current state for years while negotiations on the HCP continued.

> Pete: The HCP will postpone grading, hopefully not for ten years, but if so it will remain in a natural state.

At this point the proceedings were interrupted when three men with banners came in and marched up the aisle and around the room, shouting "Earth first, profits last. Peterson is lying." Then they marched out the door. Some members of the audience, children of the sixties, were amused by the demonstration, but others shouted things like "Get a job!" and "Take a bath!" It was just like the good old days, but not quite. The mayor announced a recess and called the police. But he did not sound the alarm. Two officers wearing shorts arrived on bicycles long after the demonstrators were gone. Obviously the mayor did not want to give the demonstrators a stage. Outside I asked the demonstrators about their organization. "Earth First! It's not an organization," they replied.

The council meeting reconvened.

> Mayor: [jokingly] Pete, next time if you bring guests please let us know.
>
> Councilman C: Move to accept EIR with conditions 1 and 2.
>
> [The EIR is unanimously approved.]
>
> Mayor: Thanks . . . adjourned.

Thus even Earth First! entered into the carnival of public participation. Their opposition was evidence that only people on the fringes opposed the efforts of enlightened developers, federal regulators, and local environmentalists. Although the no-growth interests were concerned that the project was moving forward too quickly, the fact that this had been a long and painful process was apparent to all. Even the environmentalists who were most actively involved in petitioning for a gnatcatcher listing endorsed the HPP as evidence that developers can work with the ESA. At this point, in 1992, it appeared that if the bird were listed the HCP would still be valid, since it conformed to the ESA regulations pertaining to conservation as mitigation for taking a listed species. Although there were still concerns, now that Pete had provided a substantial chunk of the preserve system as mitigation for the HCP, the HPP citizen advisory committee was prepared to move forward with negotiations with developers and with small property owners such as Ben.

Ratification of the HCP

At the next meeting of the Habitat Protection Plan citizen advisory committee the big news was that the EIR for the HCP had been approved and that the vegetation map was ready. The experts had finished the biological survey work, and the private negotiations between landowners and local, state, and federal authorities could begin.

> Lou [citizen advisory group facilitator]: We circulated a draft [of the vegetation map] and asked for comments. We have received a few. We would like to open up for comments now.
>
> Len [Castleton Lagoon Foundation official]: This is a fine, clear, straightforward [document], better than all the presentations you made previously.

League of Women Voters: You should use landmarks on maps [so people can find things; it becomes increasingly clear that many lay people cannot read the vegetation map].

Ben: It is very well-written. We need to keep this process moving with publication of this report. Many landowners can now do nothing with their land. We need to move forward. We need to put landownership on the preserve map [he can't read the map either].

Just when it seemed like everyone was happy, Carl, of the Audubon Society, raised concerns about the adequacy of the preserve. It became quite clear that Carl and Pete had very different perspectives on the proposition.

Carl: We haven't discussed the viability of the preserve. Saving fifteen gnat-catchers is inadequate in a 500-year plan. Also we would like to see a stronger statement on the need for connectivity.

Pete: What we learned in the HCP [was that] after preserving everything that was necessary there was little left to develop. The city needs to be flexible to allow development in areas [they] might not otherwise allow. Without allowing [for] development there is no money for preserves.

Carl: We are concerned that there are no teeth. This is not legally binding. Even the HCP does not make a commitment to the HPP.

Pete: There is this idea that this is a myth and that in thirty days [we] will start grading. That is not our intention. We have no ability to get a grading permit.

Gradually, Pete and Carl began to come to an understanding. Carl was concerned about how he could present the plan to his constituents. He needed to be able to claim a victory and justify his participation in the planning process.

Pete: We are pretty much willing to do whatever the community wants short of going bankrupt, if that is the goal.

Carl: We are out on a limb. We've been sitting at the table but have no guarantee to take to our constituents. We're concerned that we might lose the CEQA rights to protest after thirty days [actually, 180 days].[19] We don't have any guarantee.

Pete: Neither do we. We didn't have to do this. Fish and Wildlife told us that getting a grading permit would undermine the HPP. We could have obtained a permit but agreed to participate. We are in a worse position than we were before the hearing. We now have grading restrictions and need to make HPP work or we will never get a grading permit.

Carl: We have concerned constituents.

Lou: When doing something new you must take a leap of faith.

Carl: We would like something in writing.

Pete: I understand. Listen to what I say. I went to financiers and asked them to accept the grading restriction, even though we could have had a grading permit. It was difficult to convince them. [They] now refer to this as "Pete put us in jail." I don't mind, but I hope that we can continue to make progress. If I back out, the city will say I acted in bad faith. You will probably be there to remind them.

The uncertainties and suspicions of the environmentalist and no-growth interests were not resolved until the gnatcatcher was listed in March of 1993. The city and the developer had prepared for that. They had managed to wear down the opposition. As soon as the state and federal regulators were able to work out the details with the city and the developer, the HCP would be approved and the CEQA and California Coastal Commission (CCC) review would proceed, hopefully without a hitch.

Finessing Regulation

Tom watched the NCCP and HPP nervously but tried not to get involved. He was interested in the big-picture planning involved in the NCCP, but his boss, Bill, was not prepared to put Camelot on hold as Peterson had done with Brigadoon while they negotiated for the rights to develop what was left of sections two and three of their master-planned project. In section two there was only one planning area that had coastal sage scrub and gnatcatchers that had not been rough-graded by February of 1992. The short-term plan was to grade that immediately, before the gnatcatcher was listed or the HPP decided that they wanted to include the area in a preserve system.

The problem was that the tentative map that had been approved by the city and the coastal commission had conditions on winter grading (December through March) and on grading during gnatcatcher nesting season (March through May). Winter grading required a permit from the coastal commission staff—it did not require a coastal commission hearing—and had to meet strict standards for drainage and erosion control. Generally the Castleton city planners deferred to the coastal commission staff on winter grading. More problematic was grading during nesting season, since it required a biological survey to ensure that there were no nesting birds that might be disturbed by the activity.

The coastal commission staff was routinely imposing these conditions, and Tom and Bill, as part of their damage control efforts, were prepared to challenge the conditions at the February meeting of the California Coastal Commission, which was to be held in San Diego. At the meeting sympathetic commissioners sent its staff a clear message. They should stop treating the gnat-catcher as an endangered or threatened species as if it were already listed. Specifically, they should be less stringent in conditioning grading permits to protect gnatcatchers during nesting season, particularly in the case of fine grading, which is done in preparation for building houses, as opposed to the rough grading that is required for building roads and sewers. This was a major coup for Camelot and a key decision in the ongoing battle over whether to list the California gnatcatcher. The commissioners publicly declared that they were unwilling to go farther than California Fish and Game officials, who had refused to advance the gnatcatcher to candidacy.

Although this was a particularly important decision, CCC meetings are usually media events in which issues of great consequence are discussed, if not resolved. The commissioners are celebrities, or at least regionally prominent political figures. Some of them dress like movie stars and take long breaks to provide photo opportunities. Others appear to be running for higher office and never miss an opportunity to offer an impassioned plea. This is big-time professional politics. City council meetings are dwarfed by the scale and scope of the California Coastal Commission meetings.

The meetings last for two or three days and are held at fancy hotels and country clubs up and down the coast. The meeting in San Diego was at Hotel Circle, in a huge exhibition hall at a luxury hotel. CCC proceedings are extremely formal and bureaucratic, and the rules sometimes get in the way, but the commissioners give passionate speeches and fight among themselves. After I attended a few sessions, it became clear that some commissioners represented environmentalists and others represented business, or development, interests. They all were acutely aware of the fact that they were on the public stage. This morning they had a busy session.[20]

In the afternoon session following lunch, the commissioners heard two requests for grading permits in which Project Camelot was the applicant. Both were routine. There were no neighbors, environmentalists, or no-growth people who wished to complain about the grading. The staff report was typical, with the usual conditions for winter and nesting-season grading. Bill, Tom's boss, was present, and he accepted the staff recommendations. Although there was no public comment, Commissioner A offered an opening salvo in what became an attack on the nesting-season grading condition.

> Commissioner A: The rules are not consistent regarding winter grading and the gnatcatcher. They are not so tough in L.A. Grading would stop if a single gnatcatcher is found?

> Staff: Yes

> Commissioner A: Didn't California refuse to list the gnatcatcher and [didn't] the federal government say they might?

Although the commissioner believed that the conditions regarding gnat-catchers were extreme—one little bird could stop the entire project—the permit was approved with the grading condition. Nevertheless, Commissioner A had provided Bill with an indication that he would support a reconsideration of the condition. Thus, in the hearing for the second grading permit later that afternoon, Bill took advantage of the opportunity to challenge the grading condition. As the hearing began, Commissioner A set the tone.

Commissioner A [in a stage whisper]: It deals with gnatcatchers again.

Bill: I object to the grading condition. The bird has not been listed, [but] many areas that might have gnatcatchers are being treated as [if the bird were] endangered. Yes, we do disagree, but in the interest of moving on we will accept it.

Commissioner B: Are there really gnatcatchers there? In Marin people carry little mice around to stop development.

Commissioner A: [to Bill] Has this condition been imposed before?

Bill: No.

Commissioner A: The habitat areas have already been protected. Staff doesn't see the difference between fine grading and mass grading.

Staff: Yes, but we are concerned about dirt, noise, etc.

Commissioner A: State Fish and Game has already decided not to list the bird. Why are we going further than the state? I'm concerned about the precedent. I propose that we withdraw the condition.

The amendment was adopted in a roll call vote of eight to two, and the permit was approved unanimously. This was clearly a victory for Tom and Bill. By February 1992 the CCC seemed to be defining a policy of not conditioning fine grading even if there were gnatcatchers in the adjacent open space.

This was an important decision. The commissioners had told their staff to be less gung ho on protecting the gnatcatcher, at least for fine-grading permits. The staff were visibly disturbed by this retreat from defending the gnatcatcher, but as good bureaucrats they accepted the letter of the law as interpreted by the commissioners. To Tom's delight, he could now expect less stringent regulation on his future planning-area permits, at least until the gnatcatcher was listed, the NCCP was approved, or the rules changed again for some other reason.

Tom was doubly delighted because, ironically, the gung-ho coastal commission staff had already issued a rough-grading permit for Tom's project just eight days before this meeting in which they were fighting the commissioners to protect gnatcatchers nesting in open space during fine-grading operations. It is also ironic that the city was engaged in fighting illegal grading, putting teeth into its local ordinance to punish farmers and property owners who were grading small sections of coastal sage scrub. At the same time, however, they approved the grading of roughly fifty-five acres that housed a considerable number of gnat-catchers—perhaps two dozen—that were presumably preparing to nest.

This is a classic example of the benefits of overregulation. The city and the coastal commission staff were fighting separate battles to regulate grading. It is instructive to consider how Tom managed to finesse the regulators and gain a winter-grading permit even before the coastal commission staff were checked in their efforts to protect gnatcatchers.

The problem in early February 1992 was that Tom wanted to rough grade a planning area where gnatcatchers were present. The grading would take six weeks, which meant that it would not be finished before nesting season. Tom already had a winter-grading permit from the city, but he still needed to meet a set of conditions established by the coastal commission staff. These included a deed restriction for the designated open space, the development and approval of grading and drainage/erosion plans, and a bond to cover costs in case the developer could not finish grading and the city needed to revegetate or repair the site. All of this was in process and was almost finished and ready to sign in the first week of February 1992.

Tom also needed to meet with the coastal commission staff for a coastal permit to grade. This was a session that I could not attend, because Tom wanted the meeting to be as routine as possible. The staff might ask if grading would be complete before nesting season, but Tom hoped they would not ask that. In order for grading to be done during nesting season, a biologist would have to conduct a survey to see if there were any nesting birds. Tom didn't want a survey because he knew there were gnatcatchers on the site, but he didn't want to wait because the bird might be listed before the end of nesting season. Tom was worried because the project could lose six million dollars if this planning area could not be developed because the coastal sage scrub had to be preserved.

Tom met with consultants Dick and Stan, who had surveyed the planning area and found plenty of gnatcatchers. Before the meeting started, Tom told a horror story about premature grading. The moral was that you shouldn't grade until you are ready to build, but this, of course, was exactly what Tom was intending to do. Clearly this was bad planning, but fears of the impending listing and the local HPP called for desperate measures. Dick reported that he had spotted about twenty-three gnatcatchers that morning.

Tom: I don't pay people to find gnatcatchers on my property.

Dick: You pay us not to call [the city or the coastal commission] and tell them.

All of this joking suggests the seriousness of the problem and the mixed emotions that these friends had about rough grading an area that was not ready for construction and willfully disturbing birds before they can nest so the developer wouldn't lose development rights. In the best of all worlds, they would have waited until after nesting season and attempted to grade with minimal disturbance of the habitat that sustained birds. Of course, this is not the best of all worlds, and nobody was very happy about what they were planning to do.

Two years later Tom later told me that he and the city now laugh about this planning area, which merely confirms my conclusions. Planners tend to laugh about the crazy things they do because of the lack of good-planning alternatives. Clearly at the time Tom was nervous about the planning area. He told me in the context of a "you know too much" discussion that he had not even told his wife about the premature grading. When I joked that the grading permit was our little secret, Larry, the Camelot engineer, remarked, "You do know too much."

In any case, Tom described the options to Dick and Stan and developed his strategy.

> Tom: We either convince the coastal commission staff that we can grade now or we will be requested to have a biologist do [a site survey]. We won't bother to hire a biologist. We'll just wait until June and sweat the listing.

> Dick: What's the city's problem?

> Tom: No problem. It says in the tentative map that winter grading is okay.

Tom and Dick recognized that both the state and the local government were concerned with coastal sage scrub habitat destruction. Fortunately, however, government officials possessed limited knowledge of where such habitat was located, and so far they had no plan regarding what should be preserved and what might be sacrificed.

> Dick: Fish and Wildlife is concerned that cities will give permits prematurely. They may pressure the city to refuse grading permits.

> Tom: The city is ignorant—nobody knows what is on that land. [The coastal commission staff member] has said nothing. He is just waiting for the landscape plans. Section two was the same scenario.

The depth of public ignorance was a resource that these planners could exploit strategically. Intellectually, however, they were curious about the status of the gnatcatcher and the prospects for sustaining the species.

> Dick: It would be interesting to have a biologist study gnatcatchers.

> Tom: They seem to be making a comeback.

> Dick: How much habitat do they need? If undisturbed, how many would there be next year? Where will they nest?

These were, of course, exactly the questions that the biologists who were running the NCCP and the HPP would have liked to answer, but in San Diego County, unlike Orange County, developers were not cooperating with the NCCP because they didn't control and didn't trust the regional planning authorities. Ironically, a biologist had asked Tom for permission to do a gnat-catcher survey on the Camelot site, but the request was denied. Thus the data that might have answered the questions posed by these private-sector planners was not likely to be forthcoming. The planners and biologists continued to speculate about the effects of development on gnatcatchers.

The frustration of professional planners who must exploit collective igno-rance despite their professional judgment and personal curiosity is sometimes expressed in humor. Tom joked that the gnatcatchers were not in the designat-ed open space on the hillsides where they belonged. "Don't they have copies of the plans?" he asked. "We need to let them know where they are supposed to be nesting." At the same time, however, Tom continued to be curious—and frustrated at how little the biologists, and by extension the planners, knew about the gnatcatcher and its habitat. Dick and Stan's report indicated that there were more gnatcatchers on the site than had been identified in the EIR. "It's a miraculous comeback," Tom exclaimed, "Or else they are moving from across the road." Tom and Dick considered the possibility that rough grading on adjacent sites was driving gnatcatchers onto this ungraded site. "The biolo-gists have said that they can't cross the road," Tom stated.

Tom instructed Dick and Stan that no written report was necessary, imply-ing that the discovery of the gnatcatchers would be officially forgotten. Still, Tom couldn't help but wonder about the significance of the discovery in the larger picture of efforts to preserve habitat. "I wonder if they really are endan-gered," Tom mused. But "at this point, numbers don't matter." What mattered, in practice, was how to obtain permission to destroy the habitat on which the newly discovered gnatcatchers might be preparing to nest. Clear on that mis-sion, Tom left his consultants and got to work on obtaining the grading permit.

Tom and Larry met with CCC staff, who asked about sending a biologist out for a site survey of gnatcatchers. Tom said that his interpretation of the condition was different. The staff hemmed and hawed. Tom agreed to have a biologist come out on the first day of March and to follow the biologist's recommendations. He would even halt grading if that were the recommendation. The staff seemed to think that was okay, but they could not give the grading permit yet. They need-ed to talk to a lawyer and deal with some minor details.

Later the CCC staffer called, expressing concern about drainage and runoff, which had been designated in the winter-grading condition. Tom was delighted that the CCC staff was distracted by the erosion and drainage problems. Those issues were technical in nature and could be resolved by Larry, the project engi-neer. The call implied that the legal problems associated with interpretation of the nesting-season grading condition were being ignored. The permit was delayed by the details, but Larry walked the plans through, and the permit was issued one week after Tom's meeting with his consultants and eight days before the coastal commission hearing reported above. After a delay due to rain, grading began. Tom drove by and looked at the grading operation, making sure that every visible speck of coastal sage scrub was gone, except on the hillsides, which were being preserved as open space.

The Benefits of Enlightenment

In March of 1993 the U.S. Fish and Wildlife Service listed the California gnatcatcher as a threatened species. The no-growth/environmentalist coalition had won, and the rules were changed.[21] By 1994 Tom had still not obtained a tentative map for section three of his project, and he was still engaged in negotiations with the city for a permit that would allow for a 5 percent interim take of coastal sage scrub habitat while the city developed its NCCP. Of course, the planning area that was graded in February of 1992 had to be regraded several times in the interim, but they never did that in the winter or during nesting season, so they managed to keep the area clean until they could sell it to a builder. By 1994 houses were being built on that site.

Meanwhile, Pete's HCP was revisited and the Castleton HPP was placed on hold until the approval of a new regional plan reflecting the increased bargaining power of the regulators after the bird was listed. The environmentalist interests, most notably the Southern California Habitat Defenders, had changed their tune. In June 1992 Steve, the leader of the umbrella organization, had said that Pete was "way ahead of the others" on the path to enlightenment. In August 1994 Steve reported that "at least Pete and [an Orange County developer] are willing to talk." He went on, however, to explain that he no longer supported the HCP and the HPP.

> [I became] disenchanted with Pete when I realized that the HCP/HPP wasn't going to fit into the regional picture. They get credit for trying to get out in front, but there are many reasons why it won't work. We and Pete can't work together [anymore].

> They played a high-pressure game—if you don't make a decision we're going to grade because the road has to be built. I felt misled because those constraints were not really there.

Whether Pete and the City of Castleton were misleading the environmentalists and no-growth folks is subject to debate, as is the question of who was in a better position after the listing—Pete or Tom. Clearly, the preemptive strike was more effective in the short term. One might argue, however, that Pete had won enough trust to be in a stronger bargaining position under the new rules. It is clear that the path of enlightenment requires deep pockets and a timeline that seems unlimited. As Dan, an environmental biologist and NCCP official, explained, "It is hard to be enlightened when you've got ten acres." In a similar vein, Bob, an Orange County NCCP official, said in relation to enlightened developers, "If there is a horizon that is far enough into the future I can work with them. Most projects have five-to-thirty-five-year time horizons." Perhaps in the long-run enlightened developers are rewarded; in the short run, however, enlightenment did not pay in this San Diego County suburb.

In Orange County, however, it seems that the enlightened developers were rewarded. Because the NCCP was not promoted in Orange County as alternative to the gnatcatcher listing, the listing did not affect progress on the NCCP. Matt, a Nature Conservancy official, explained in 1994 that "after the federal listing and the exemption for the NCCP, then people got to work." Bob explained, however, that this really was not true for the Orange County NCCP, which was hard at work before the listing. The listing was most important in providing carrots and sticks for reluctant cities and less enlightened landowners in the San Diego County region. In 1994 Bob explained the problem: "San Diego has spent years developing a plan for a plan. Now they are actually talking about drawing lines and establishing preserves. That's how we started in Orange County—drawing lines. Inside is preserved; outside can be developed."

Since 1994 San Diego County cities have attempted to draw lines on maps and to decide which projects can be permitted as an interim take, assuming that the NCCP will eventually be approved. Meanwhile, the financial backing for Pete's development collapsed when the bank recalled the loan, so Castleton had to go back to the drawing board. Tom's project, Camelot, has received federal, state, and city approval, with appropriate conditions, of course, and is proceeding more or less according to plan. Ben, the property owner who had attended the HPP meetings and complained that he was losing the use of his acreage, has since sold his property to the Patterson Company. The purchase price was $2 million, considerably less than the $10 million he had been offered a few years earlier, before the listing of the California gnatcatcher and the clear and present danger that Ben's property would be in the middle of a habitat preserve.

It may be that good things come to those who wait, but it appears that deep pockets, as well as an indefinite timeline, are required for those who wish to benefit from overregulation. Of course, it is also important that the investor not be particularly interested in what is to become of the land. Perhaps Ben was too attached to his family estate to exploit it effectively, but he was arguably wise to sell it to a disinterested investor who viewed land as a commodity—something to buy cheap and sell dear, without regard to its utility or replacement cost. As for our enlightened developer, it is hard to know. More than one city planning official identified Pete as an example of the enlightened developer. Now that his project has gone bankrupt, what lesson has Pete learned? Maybe he has learned the costs of cooperation in big-picture planning as opposed to the benefits of overregulation that accrue to the developer who is willing to finesse, if not manipulate, regulation and regulators.

Chapter Five
Planning the Postmodern Community

> I'm a third-generation San Diegan, and I think that the way San Diego has
> grown is good—scenic, and the zoning is generally good.
>   Bill, vice president of Patterson Company and local CEO for Camelot, 1992

When I left San Diego in 1975 all my friends were asking, "When are you going
to move back?" Now when I tell them that I walk or ride my bike to work—I
live in a small Midwestern city—they are jealous. Life in San Diego is crazy. Its
people live in the best climate in the world, with beaches, mountains, desert—
whatever the nature lover might want. What is crazy, however, is that they live
in their cars. They drive their cars to a health club to get exercise after work,
or they mount their bikes on their cars and drive for an hour so that they can
take a half-hour bike ride. When people find that most of their social encoun-
ters take place in an automobile, there is a problem. It is enough to make people antisocial. Behind the wheel of a car is the worst way to meet people. No
wonder road rage is rampant in southern California. I think the quality of day-
to-day work and home life is far better in the Midwest.

Obviously there are divergent opinions on the extent to which the paradise
of 1960s San Diego has been lost. Some, including Bill of the Patterson
Company, see the changes as major improvements. Others, including no-
growth reactionaries and deep-ecology radicals, are convinced that paradise
has been lost to corporate greed and government corruption. These value judg-
ments reflect different perspectives on established institutions and human
nature. Ultimately, however, these essentially partisan positions sustain very different explanations of how and why the form and content of land-use policy
has changed and what we should do about it.

Not surprisingly then, when in 1999 I spoke with some of the major players
about how the world had changed since 1992, the interviewees offered different
versions of the same story of San Diego County land-use politics. These versions
of the story provide the basis for various morality plays. Each account of what
happened supports an account of what went wrong from 1970 to 1990, and what
should be done to improve the planning process for the twenty-first century.

San Diego County Update: 1992–1999

Between 1992 and 1999, planning in San Diego County shifted from a
growth management strategy to a smart-growth approach. This shift marks the

institutionalization of big-picture planning through the cooperation of big capital, big government, and big environmentalists.

When we left San Diego in 1992, Peter Navarro was running for mayor on a no-growth platform. The Natural Community Conservation Plan (NCCP) was in limbo. San Diego County and various San Diego suburban cities continued to work on a variety of local and regional plans for habitat conservation without any assurance that these would be acceptable or even feasible in the context of federal, state, and regional programs and policies. The building industry was in the doldrums, still reeling from the savings-and-loan crash of 1989 and the series of growth-control measures, general-plan updates, and other attempts to limit growth that were multiplying after 1985. Nobody was building houses, and everyone was waiting to see what would happen next.

Bill Clinton and the Democrats, who won the national elections in November, supported big-picture planning in California, the poster child for what would become smart growth. Locally Navarro lost the mayoral election, and SANDAG effectively preempted the suburban growth-control movement by instituting growth management as a regional plan, in keeping with the countywide electoral mandate. The NCCP collapsed in 1992 but then recovered after the federal government listed the gnatcatcher as a threatened species in 1993.

From that point forward, local governments encouraged development within the limits of the state and federal allowance for a 5 percent interim take of local land that was not yet part of an approved NCCP. Because the building slump continued through 1996, the 5 percent interim take was more than enough to keep developers happy between 1993 and 1997. Thus large master-plan projects, like Camelot, negotiated with U.S. Fish and Wildlife and California Fish and Game officials for a series of Habitat Conservation Plan (HCP) agreements. In 1997 the building boom returned, particularly in suburbs like Castleton, where complex facility-planning programs and the presence of vast tracts of vacant land increased the cost of development far beyond the ridiculous regional inflation rate and into the realm of the unbelievable. Dick, a planning consultant based in Castleton, described the inflation of local land prices to me when we spoke in the summer of 1999: "You are looking at $240,000 for a finished lot . . . a 7,000-square-foot lot. If you had asked me three years ago if this was possible, I would have said no. [But] people are buying $800,000 tract houses here. And they are selling like hotcakes."

The high stakes, high risk land-office business was booming once again in 1999. Local governments were inspired to cooperate with the three regional NCCP programs in the county to the extent that developers had already exhausted the interim take and were still willing to pay any price for building permits in the city. Particularly in Castleton it almost looked like déjà vu all over again. There was no limit to efforts to facilitate quality development. Doug and Dave from the Castleton city planning department confirmed my impression that the 1999 boom was on the same order of magnitude as the boom of the Reagan years. Dave explained: "Here are a couple of numbers to give you a perspective. In 1992 the total number of dwelling units that were constructed in that entire year was fifty two. . . . In 1999 in the month of April alone we did 438. [That was] just in Castleton. So we are approaching the same magnitude as we experienced back in '85 and '86, which was the highest growth rate hitherto seen."

Census figures indicate that Castleton entered a boom phase in 1997. Fewer than 700 new housing permits were issued in 1995 and 1996, but in 1997 that increased to over 1,200. That growth was projected to continue: new permits for 1998 were projected at 1,426. Dave suggested that the figure might almost double again in 1999. "Based on the first four months of this year, we will be hitting somewhere around 2,500 to 2,800 dwelling units. That is comparable to the peaks that we had back in '85 and '86." U.S. census data tend to support Dave's impression. In 1985 over 2,400 units were approved, and in 1986 over 3,100. This was at the height of the boom, just prior to the initiation of growth-control and facilities-management programs.[1]

By 1999, in Castleton at least, the city and the developers were approaching the same level of speculative frenzy they had achieved in the Reagan years. Dave reported, "We are all working very hard on completing additional new master plans and subdivision maps. So there is plenty of subdivided land that will carry this through over the next couple of years, provided that the economy allows it to continue. . . . That is the big question. I was at a conference on Friday, on grading, and people were speculating that maybe we are over the peak on this economic cycle, and the developers are now in a rush to get as much on the ground and sold as they can." With 20/20 hindsight we can appreciate the perspicacity of these planners. Although nobody could predict in 1999 when the crash would come, everyone was taking advantage of the favorable conditions.

The unexpectedly good news was both economic and political. Politically the contradictory demands of the suburban no-growth movement and state and national affordable housing programs were much less problematic than had been anticipated in 1992. The protracted depression of 1990 to 1996 had solved that problem to some extent. Having achieved de facto (and de jure) growth control, local residents had moved on to other concerns—to habitat conservation in 1992, and more recently to traffic control. At the same time, state and federal authorities backed off of affordable housing goals, in part because of the depressed housing market.

Pete, who had been the local representative for the Peterson Company and its Project Brigadoon, had told Castleton citizens in 1992 that without development there would be no big-picture planning solutions. By 1999 it was clear that this was as true for affordable housing as it was for habitat conservation. The regional housing needs survey that had been scheduled for 1995 was postponed year by year until 1999. Meanwhile, state and federal pressure for affordable housing diminished to the point that inclusionary ordinances were viewed as constraints on efforts to achieve general-plan housing element goals. It appears that even affordable housing goals were preempted by the new regional plan for managing growth.

Thus, from a planning perspective things were not nearly so bad in 1999 as we might have expected they would be from the vantage point of 1992. The major threat to big-picture planning posed by the prospect of citizen-imposed—or mayor-imposed—growth control was effectively preempted by SANDAG. The reactionary no-growth coalition was all but abandoned by politicians and liberal environmentalists. The new governing coalition, which combined big capital, big government, and big environmentalists, marked the triumph of comprehensive regional planning.[2]

This change is evident in the linguistic shift from the discussion of "no growth" or "growth control" to the more recent focus on "smart growth." It is equally apparent in the ultimate success of the NCCP in establishing habitat conservation programs not only in Orange and in San Diego Counties, but finally in Riverside County as well. Of course, the return of prosperity since 1997, particularly in Castleton, is both a cause and an effect of the triumph of comprehensive regional planning.

Big-picture planning has not, however, resolved the fundamental problems that have plagued planning efforts since 1908. The contradictory interests of residents and investors are no less real, even if they were less apparent in 1999 than in 1992. The fact that the state backed off of affordable housing and that growth control was a victim of its own success merely indicates the critical importance of economics as the base from which political struggle is organized. The enduring depression in the building trades created fewer opportunities for either local residents or the state to demand concessions. Nevertheless, the conflicts and contradictions of big-picture planning continued to impede progress.

Castleton, the suburban city that faced the most serious challenge in 1992, had finished its general-plan revision by 1999, but none of the more controversial projects had been completed. The road-widening project that was to be sustained by the Brigadoon HCP was still on hold. Since that was the cornerstone for the Castleton Habitat Protection Plan (HPP), Castleton's piece of the NCCP habitat preserve was still the missing link in the county plan. The big environmentalists seemed unconcerned, however, since they were focusing on saving big pieces of less valuable land in the rest of San Diego County. The adjacent suburban cities and the small, local and regional, environmentalists were complaining, however, that the Brigadoon HCP was a sweetheart deal that never would have been made in the post-listing environment.

That is probably true. However, the City of Castleton was cooperating not with adjacent suburbs, but with the California Bank, which had foreclosed on the Peterson Company and was managing the still-undeveloped sections of Brigadoon in 1999. The bank and the city defended the HCP that state and federal officials had approved in 1995 and the EIR approved by the Castleton City Council in 1992, which represented the Castleton contribution to the regional NCCP. California Bank and the City of Castleton were like two 600-pound guerillas. They had negotiated their sweetheart deal with state and local authorities and were insisting that others would have to preserve more to meet the more rigorous standards of the current development and conservation world.

Meanwhile, the Castleton highway project that was to begin after the EIR approval in 1992 was still awaiting approval in 1999.

In a similar vein, the open-space/trail system that was approved by the city council in 1992 had still not been implemented, in part because of the lack of funding. The idea that a bond issue would provide the funding was even less popular in 1999 than it had been in 1992. Nevertheless, developers continued to support the plan for allocating designated open space on the basis of the assumption that Castleton would eventually administer that open space as a trail system. Of course, the bank had foreclosed on Peterson, the biggest local developer, which was to have provided the biggest chunk of that trail. Thus until the NCCP and road-widening problems are resolved, the designated open space will not become a trail system, and the undeveloped land will not become a preserve.

In 1999 traffic was the major grassroots concern in Castleton, and it was clear that this local problem would require a regional solution. With the ongoing struggle over the regional NCCP, however, regional planning solutions were elusive. At the municipal level there was already discussion of a building moratorium until city planning could deal with the traffic problems associated with regional growth and tourism. There was also a brewing conflict between local and regional planners over the incompatible assumptions of smart growth and growth management. Castleton planners were willing to facilitate growth in the short run but refused to exceed the long-term limits on growth at build-out that are part of the city's general plan. Thus Castleton planners expressed what appeared to be a general pattern of conflict between local growth management programs and SANDAG's regional plan for smart growth.

Smart Growth versus Growth Management

Along with the subtle change in the governing coalition, which now included big environmentalists, big capital, and big government, there was a less subtle change in the rhetoric of land-use policy in the twenty-first century. In the 1990s big-picture planning was an alternative to ballot-box planning by citizen initiative. Growth management was big picture. It included long-term population and housing projections and complex systems for ensuring that the private sector provided local facilities as the price for local development. No growth was the popular alternative, usually associated with annual building caps.

In the rapidly growing San Diego suburbs of the 1980s, planners and developers attempted to preempt no growth with growth management. Then, after the collapse of the building industry in the wake of the savings-and-loan crash of 1989, planners and developers attempted to co-opt no-growth interests by involving them in habitat conservation efforts. Through the mid-1990s, while the building depression lingered, developers and city planning departments negotiated for future development rights, co-opting interested parties into general-plan updates and other such big-picture planning mechanisms aimed at

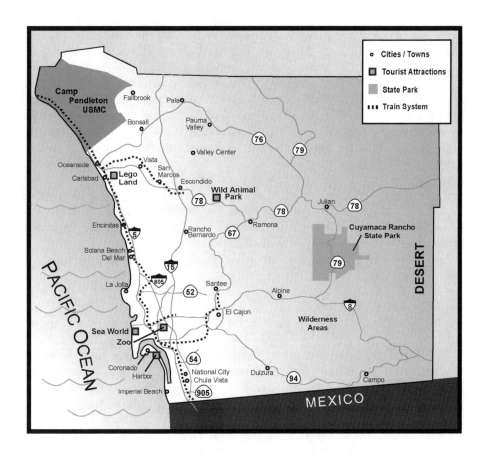

Figure 11. Yuppie Heaven, 2001, with Railroads Indicated
Base map provided by SANDAG

solving the problems of uncontrolled growth that had plagued the region in the 1970s and 1980s.

By 1999 the building industry had recovered. Developers and planners had worn down local opposition to growth and had outlasted the state and federal enthusiasm for affordable housing, which diminished sharply as the building depression continued. Along with economic recovery, which arrived just in time for the presidential election in 1996, came the latest and greatest version of big-picture planning, known as smart growth. This was the environmentalist vision of the 1970s, which called for concentrating development within the urban area, and particularly within the transportation corridors.

With enough population growth within these transportation corridors some version of mass transit might be feasible. In other words, aside from the Tijuana Trolley, which was, primarily for tourists and senior citizens, commuters might actually get a light-rail system that would be a viable alternative to sixteen-lane freeway gridlock. Ultimately, smart growth might bring the monorail to Yuppie Heaven, connecting Lego Land, on the north coast at Carlsbad; the Wild Animal Park, north central near Escondido; Julian, North Mountain; Cuyamaca, Central Mountain; the San Diego Zoo, downtown; and Sea World, at Mission Bay. This would be the most spectacular theme park ever built.

Unless cities are willing to accept high-density housing along transportation routes, however, smart growth is an illusion. The plans for light-rail construction—the monorail for Yuppie Heaven—will only come to fruition if suburban cities are willing to face the united opposition of constituents and developers. Suburbanites tend to support estate lots and single-family dwelling units as the epitome of the suburban lifestyle. Developers seem to be unwilling to propose high-density developments with less expensive homes. Thus, unless the suburban cities push for a different vision, it is just a matter of time before the smart-growth coalition faces another critical challenge.

In other words, until suburban city planners are willing to challenge the mass market that offers housing, policies, and politicians for sale to the highest bidder, the clash of contradictory interests will remain. The conflict that lay in abeyance during the depression in the housing market will emerge in a different form, gaining strength as the market for new housing permits heats up again.

Meanwhile, the benefits of overregulation have become more apparent as the recovery from the doldrums of the savings-and-loan crash was supervised by fewer yet larger developers, who were subject to increasing demands from a growing array of federal, state, and local regulatory and administrative bodies. Since the gnatcatcher was listed in 1993, the federal presence has also become more apparent. The U.S. Fish and Wildlife Service became the guardian of the highlands, much as the Army Corps of Engineers had earlier become the guardian of the wetlands, including the coastal lagoons.

As the federal government added a new layer of bureaucratic administration, the professional private-sector planners and their corporate employers and clients were increasingly able to reap the benefits of overregulation. The federal government is the party least familiar with what actually exists on the development site. Also it is in many ways the most predictable and the most easily manipulated party, simply because it is a bigger bureaucracy that is distant from the concerns of the grass roots and from the developers who attempt to finesse regulation.

However, the federal government was increasingly leading the negotiations and providing successful negotiators with the means to avoid making further concessions. Regulation was becoming increasingly federal, which augmented the benefits of overregulation, which accrued to the largest corporate development companies. In the NCCP negotiations, for example, Castleton and the California Bank, which had assumed control of Brigadoon, were particularly advantaged in the NCCP negotiations of 1999. Brigadoon had negotiated for an HCP in 1992, which the state and federal authorities approved in 1995. Consequently, the project and the city now have a legally binding agreement that regional habitat conservation plans must accommodate.

This same advantage extended to the Patterson Company. Tom and his boss, Bill, on behalf of Project Camelot, were able to negotiate with the wildlife agencies for building permits issued under the terms of the 5 percent interim take. These negotiations occurred between the 1993 listing and the depletion of the interim take, for the most part during the doldrums of 1993–1996. The big-money developers claimed the choicest morsels and thus depleted the interim take in the most desirable locations prior to the building boom of 1997.

On the basis of prior agreements with federal and state officials, the two largest developers, California Bank and Patterson, in the most prime location, Castleton, were effectively exempted from additional demands associated with the adoption of a regional NCCP. The biggest master-plan communities in Castleton, the wealthiest, most exclusive, and still fastest-growing coastal city, did not need to negotiate for development rights under the terms of the NCCP. They already had federal and state approval—the equivalent of the HCP, the Reagan-era escape clause for the ESA.

As the regulatory net expands, it becomes increasingly difficult for small-scale developers, or even homeowners wishing to improve their property, to navigate the complex approval process. At the same time, the large corporate developers, armed with their private-sector planners, are increasingly effective in gaining approval for large-scale, master-plan development projects. One private-sector planner, our old friend Tom, who now works as a consultant, explained in 1999 how his work had changed since 1992: "I spend far more of my time processing permits through the Army Corps of Engineers because they reinterpreted what are considered 'waters of the U.S.' Originally it was navigable waters. Now it is any waters. That means any drainage channel one foot wide." Tom went on to explain that even the State of California authorities were becoming more of a burden. They would be deterred only by the effective use of attorneys and private-sector planners. "Since there is now a Democrat in the governor's mansion in California, and the Democrats hold both houses of the state legislature, the Coastal Commission is 100 percent environmentalists now. And the threat of lawsuit really is the only thing that allows anything to be developed in the coastal zone anymore."

Dick, another private-sector planner, offered a similar assessment. In 1999 city officials were deferring to California Fish and Game and U.S. Fish and Wildlife Service officials, just as they had deferred to the coastal commission in the 1970s. "It gives them a way to say that it is not [their] fault. And that is exactly what is happening." As the scale and scope of regulation has increased, the cost and complexity of gaining building permit approvals has risen astronomically. Accordingly, a smaller and smaller number of larger and larger investors have been able to play the game. As Dick explained, "It just gets more and more complex. There are fewer and fewer people who are familiar with the process who really want to jump in. So this creates a fairly hard core of developers that understand the drill and are willing to function within that and take the risks associated with that."

Of course, the benefits of overregulation have always accrued to the large corporate developers, who have always been more successful in finessing regulation and negotiating with regulators. That is, in part, why Orange County was more successful than San Diego and Riverside Counties in developing an NCCP program in the first place. Camelot and Brigadoon, the largest projects in Castleton, are largely exempt from the NCCP negotiations. This suggests that Castleton will have to redouble its efforts to attract even larger developers or investors who will be willing to pay any price to gain development rights in the city. Dick suggests that this is becoming increasingly difficult. Developers are an endangered species in Castleton. Now banks and other financial institutions are eliminating the middlemen and acting as property owners as well as financiers, and are using local consultants, such as Dick and Tom and even Bill, who is also now a private consultant, rather than financing development projects for other companies. Thus the circle of corporate actors who might be enticed into big-picture planning in Castleton is continuing to shrink. It is not clear who will be persuaded to pay for the Castleton habitat preserve.

Equally important, neighboring suburbs will have to absorb an inordinate share of the regional preserve to accommodate the relatively small share that Castleton will provide in keeping with its previously negotiated HCP. Clearly not every suburban city will be able to attract big capital. Some are already built out. Others are in less desirable locations. Even for the most desirable locations, however, the ability to attract capital investment will not resolve the problems of planning. In fact, the cooperation of big capital and big government during the building boom is likely to generate serious challenges from the grass roots, especially in these wealthy coastal suburbs. The support of liberal environmentalist organizations is not enough. The fact that the big environmentalists have bought into smart growth and essentially abandoned their no-growth and growth-control allies suggests that there will be a new wave of protest once the implications of smart growth become apparent.

Castleton, which in many ways was most successful at managing the coalition of environmental and no-growth interests, still faces serious problems in managing popular participation in the twenty-first century. The most controversial and most integral components of the revised general plan (open space and habitat conservation, housing, and traffic) continued to defy simple solution in 1999. Given the interdependent nature of these proposed programs, the fact that grassroots opposition might be focused on only one issue, such as traffic, will not allow the city to negotiate the less controversial issues in efforts to avoid public confrontations.

Furthermore, Chuck, the city planning director, was moving away from the trilateral-negotiation model of policy making. The guiding vision was that the city had already endured the carnival of government by citizen advisory committee. It had paid its dues in the process of cooling out opposition to the general-plan revisions. Thus the city was prepared to operate as an executive committee, according to the caucus model, implementing the policies and programs that, in theory, the citizens had already endorsed in their advisory committee meetings and public workshops. The people had spoken. The multimedia theatre of city council and planning commission policy making, which proved so entertaining in 1992, was over. Doug and Dave described the plan of attack in 1999 as follows.

> Doug: The citizen advisory committee was disbanded because they finished their work.

> Dave: The [new] committee is Doug and the planning director.

> Doug: At one time we did have a citizen committee, but one of the things that I personally learned from this experience was that citizen committees, while they might be the right thing to do democratically, often do not really help advance your planning process.

Doug had come to the conclusion that citizen committees had outlived their usefulness. "We have given up on using citizen committees, and [are] just negotiating directly with the wildlife agencies." I asked Doug what had happened to Carl, Ruby, Emma, and all the people who routinely attended City Council meetings in 1992. "Well," he replied, "We wore them out."

Thus the new direction for progressive planning in 1999 was a move away from managing popular participation through co-optation. That may be a result partly of fatigue and partly of a lag in the mobilization of grassroots opposition to the latest version of big-picture planning. Generally the city tends to preempt opposition during the boom phase, when developers are prepared to pay any price and can be convinced to make concessions. Co-optation is characteristic of the bust-phase approach to managing the general public. When no one was building, it was an excellent time to spend months in prolonged discussion, making plans for a plan.

In 1999 Castleton was back in the boom phase, so the city could not waste time managing the public. Generally the grass roots will be ignored until they are able to mount effective resistance, as they did in 1986, and thereby increase the complexity of an already difficult planning problem. The irony of popular participation is that even when it is effective, it merely drives the government into the arms of the private sector. Of course, should the grassroots struggle ever unite the politically excluded, particularly labor, women, and poor people in general, and members of racial and ethnic minorities in particular, there might be enough power to undermine the progressive coalition of liberals and conservatives. As illustrated recently in Seattle, such a coalition would be much more effective in street fighting than in attempting to work within the established political system.[3] Ultimately the coalition would have to reject the liberal compromise position and dedicate itself to a sustained struggle, not simply to reform the system but to change it fundamentally.

The first step in this direction is a frontal assault on free-market conservatism and the corresponding liberal efforts to channel discontent into consumer cooperatives or social democratic reform parties, which are essentially the political expression of this consumer (status) interest. In the terms of the U.S. presidential electoral options for the year 2000, this would have meant not simply that the forced choice between George W. Bush and Al Gore should be rejected, but that the Social-Democratic consumer advocate, Ralph Nader, should be rejected as well. Even in progressive states like California the revolution will not be achieved by citizen initiative. There will be no quiet revolution. That is, of course, one of the reasons that liberals and conservatives close ranks in efforts to prevent radical change.

Ultimately, this revolution will be rooted not in some philosopher's vision of a better world but in a better understanding of the world that exists. Once the disenfranchised are prepared to fight against the free market in food, clothing, housing, policies, and politicians, and against the commodification of the earth, they will not be looking for a friendly philosophy. Instead, they will be looking for their enemies: the liberals and conservatives who defend existing institutions and might continue to defend them with their lives. Thus it is with these liberals and conservative that we should begin in our quest for an alternative to big-picture planning.

Divergent Perspectives on Land-Use Policy

Free-market conservatives argue that the market ultimately dictates what can be built. From this perspective, land-use policy is simply the political expression of consumer demand. Both public policy and private industry respond to consumer preferences. Thus big-picture planning emerged when consumer preferences changed between 1970 and 1990 and voters and prospective homebuyers demanded that something closer to big-picture planning be instituted. Of course, this change produced chaos in the short run. The passions of citizens and the enthusiasms of regulators threatened to undermine orderly development with radical notions. Ultimately, however, after the market correction of 1989 more practical interests came to govern big-picture planning, accommodating citizen concerns, but also recognizing that without development there can be no planning.

As Tom explained, the people, as consumers and voters, demand improvements, but they depend on the private sector to provide them. "As people become better educated and wealthier, the demand for a quality environment increases dramatically. Environmental and planning improvements really require innovations by profit-making entrepreneurs." This faith in entrepreneurs is even more enthusiastically expressed in a report commissioned by the U.S. Small Business Administration, which argues that entrepreneurs have saved the San Diego region from the devastation that the federal government caused when it cut defense spending after the end of the Cold War. "San Diego in the late 1980s and early 1990s was hard hit by defense cutbacks. . . . But less than one decade later, all of the lost jobs were replaced, mainly by new jobs in business services, high technology clusters, and tourism. Small firms [in] service and high technology [sectors] grew at unprecedented rates during the

1990s."[4] Even the Small Business Administration report admits that wages are lower in the high-tech firms, but they tend to minimize this fact by focusing on the industrial sectors where wages are relatively good. Thus they virtually ignore the bulk of the new jobs, which are in business services, where wages dropped more rapidly than in any other sector except for medical services.

Despite the obvious gaps and leaps of faith that are evident in the Small Business Administration report, conservatives will probably believe it simply because they want to believe that entrepreneurial capitalism can reinvent America. Twenty-first-century conservatives celebrate the American frontier legacy, World War II veterans, and more recently police, fire, and military heroes of the war on terrorism. As the United States stumbles into a period of unbridled nationalism and unblushing imperialism, liberals are reeling in the waves of patriotism. Their fears have paralyzed their efforts to articulate even a liberal domestic policy that will not elicit the wrath of the nationalists, including Homeland Security officials who proclaim, "you are either with us or with the terrorists."

Despite the impression that is offered in the mass media, particularly in the feeding frenzy in the wake of September 11, 2001, the liberals and the conservatives are not very far apart philosophically, particularly with regard to faith in U.S. institutions. They share substantial confidence in self-correcting economic and political systems and tend to view disturbances such as economic recessions or international wars as temporary problems that the system will ultimately overcome. Thus both conservatives and liberals tend to see social change as cyclical. As Tommy, the Farmington city planning director, explained in 1992, "People vote from the rice bowl—good times bring stringent legislation, environmentalism, and quality of life [concerns], but bad times bring pressure to reduce standards. Hence, we have enterprise zones to entice business. It's a pendulum. Cities are either in slow-growth or booster phases." Chuck, the Castleton city planning director, was even more explicit on the cyclical nature of change. "The pendulum swings. In the 1980s staff facilitated growth. That has slowed based on citizen concerns; it is now swinging back to facilitate— 'helping out' [but] not compromising on standards." Harold, the Waterton city planning director, explained in 1992 how negotiations with developers follow the cycle of economic boom and bust. "During the boom years [of the 1980s, developers] were willing to modify design to get approval. Now they negotiate for months and delay the process because they are not rushed" when the builders are not buying.

Thus liberals and conservatives agree that social change is cyclical and that systemic changes such as big-picture planning represent adjustments or adaptation to changes in consumer or constituent demands. In this regard, both view big-picture planning as a response to the environmentalist and no-growth interests that waxed and waned in the 1970s and 1980s, interspersed with booster phases. In the early 1970s environmentalism was the watchword, but that subsided in the economic depression of the early 1980s. When the boosterism of the early 1980s brought a return to prosperity and growth, this inspired the growth-control movement.

Liberals and conservatives part company on their faith in people versus institutions and, accordingly, in political versus market solutions to problems that
might impede prosperity and growth. Conservative developers and private-sector
planners argue that the housing market tends to adapt to changing demand and
to produce what the consumer wants. The economy is the leading edge of social
change, and politics must ultimately accommodate changes that originate in the
economy. At times, however, politics gets in the way of attempts to respond to
consumer demand. Grassroots environmentalism, growth control, and state-
sponsored affordable housing requirements are several cases in point. These were
political responses to the increasing demand for suburban housing that had
inspired the construction of large-scale housing developments, such as Mira
Mesa, that had provided relatively affordable housing in the form of traditional
suburban ranch houses.

The boom in consumer demand had led to a short-run expansion of the
housing stock that outstripped the ability of local government and private
investors to provide the necessary infrastructure. Eventually, the conservative
argument goes, that problem would have been resolved by a decline in consumer demand until commercial and public services were able to catch up.
Unfortunately, however, this sort of market adjustment was preempted by the
overreaction of political extremists—in other words, liberals.

The growth of these middle-class suburbs provoked a liberal hue and cry,
with old, Great Society liberals demanding that the government provide housing for poor people in the inner city and new, environmental liberals demanding that the government preserve the land in its natural state. This led to a series
of frequently contradictory policies and procedures that effectively hamstrung
private-sector builders and created the need for a creative solution, which the
private sector ultimately provided in the form of big-picture, or comprehensive
regional, planning.

In short, conservative developers and their private-sector planners tell us that
politics in general and government regulation in particular interfered with the
natural laws of supply and demand, undermining efforts to find an optimal
market solution. Fortunately, however, now that the dust has cleared, it is back
to business as usual.

The liberal public-sector planners, as might be expected, defend the need for
government intervention. They argue that government mediates between developers and residents, attempting to balance the competing interests of the buyers and sellers of local property and to serve the collective interests of local residents. From this perspective, the tragedy of Mira Mesa, or of uncontrolled
growth between 1970 and 1989 more generally, was due to insufficient government regulation.

The developer's selfish interest in speculative profits and the consumer's
equally selfish demand for suburban housing combined in the 1970s and early
1980s to produce a crisis of overbuilding. The cookie-cutter suburban ranch
projects were built in the interstitial spaces of municipal government authority
and thus managed to get approval despite the lack of public services, such as

schools, fire departments, and so on. By 1986 the public outcry was deafening. Fortunately, however, the City of San Diego had already sponsored an evaluation of planning and development problems and possibilities that laid the groundwork for comprehensive regional planning.

Despite their mutual recriminations, public- and private-sector planners are able to cooperate on the basis of a general consensus on how and why big-picture planning developed and how they might use it to serve their common and competing interests. They agree on the general nature of economic and political cycles and the tendency toward equilibrium. In fact, both public- and private-sector planners attempt to anticipate and to preempt or co-opt interests that might disturb the equilibrium.

Private-sector planners and their employers tend to stress consumer choice and free-market solutions. Public-sector planners and their employers tend to stress voter choice and political solutions. Similarly, the private sector tends to stress growth, change, and the demands of future residents. Thus it defends inclusive interests. The public sector, on the other hand, tends to stress stability and the exclusive demands of current residents. These differences are negotiated within a general agreement on the rules of the game and with a common desire to manage uncertainty and conflict.

Big-picture planning facilitates efforts to manage uncertainty and conflict. This serves the developer's interest in predictable profits and consumer support and the politician's interest in predictable partisan support. In addition to serving the otherwise competing class and party interests of capitalists and politicians, big-picture planning serves the professional interests of the planners, who defend comprehensive regional planning not simply as a useful means to achieve the goals of capitalists and politicians, but as an end in itself. Planning is, in short, the interest of planners. Big-picture planning is—or was in 1992— the cutting edge of the planners' efforts to promote their profession.

A professional interest in big-picture planning unites public- and private-sector planners and facilitates their efforts to serve the economic and political interests of their employers. Nevertheless, the conflict between public- and private-sector interests and between liberals and conservatives more generally remains. This is most apparent in the conflict between environmentalists and developers.

Liberals in general and liberal environmentalists in particular view popular participation as essential to counterbalance the incredible influence of the landowners, who, viewed from this perspective, dominate land-use decisions. The lack of public knowledge and public interest is a critical problem, according to the liberal environmentalists. As Steve, leader of Southern California Habitat Defenders explains, "The landowners tend to be politically very powerful, and they tend to get what they want. So we have a system where land-use decisions are really dominated by a very narrow set of people. The general public does not get involved that much even though it affects their quality of life— affects the whole nature of their community. Most people do not know what a general plan is."

These liberal environmentalists clash with conservative developers and private-sector planners on the role of the state, or public sector, and the role of
the market, or private sector. Most liberal environmentalists, like liberals more
generally, support state regulation. Steve expressed this perspective: "My own
personal view is that there needs to be a larger state role in things like infrastructure and what sort of infrastructure gets paid for, because transportation
infrastructure is what really drives development patterns."

Liberal and left-leaning sociologists and other students of community politics who defend a power-elite perspective share the environmentalists' concern
with grassroots political struggle, but frequently argue that the impact of progressive reform movements, and especially of regulation, is blunted by elites
who co-opt the policy-implementation process.[5] Thus, radical ideas about public ownership and egalitarianism are reduced to private ownership and public
display—for example, limiting access to "public" spaces so that only paying
customers and motorists can enjoy them. In the effort to accommodate both
liberals and conservatives, big-picture planning became a complex process of
producing upscale development along freeway arteries with preservation and
affordable housing in the interstitial spaces. But the goal of the big-picture plan
was undermined by the effort to accommodate both the liberal environmentalists and affordable housing advocates who demanded that local government
extract mitigation in the form of development fees or services and the conservative free-market devotees who wanted to limit intrusion on the prerogatives
of property owners. The progressive vision was lost in the process of developing the big-picture planning procedure.

The radical argues that progressivism is an attempt to use first aid, or at best
cosmetic surgery, to treat a malignancy. Free-market consumerism in republican capitalism is plagued by crises of overproduction. We overproduce houses,
politicians, regulators, and regulations. To save ourselves as we face the
prospect of drowning in our overabundance, we need to make fundamental
institutional changes, reorienting life and work toward collective well-being.
We need to focus on the survival of the planet and attempt to sustain and ame-
liorate our collective life in a child-centered, life-centered effort. We must recognize that all are not equal in need or capacity, and we must be prepared to
sacrifice equality and even liberty to life.

The progressive vision of Donald Appleyard and Kevin Lynch's report
Temporary Paradise? was rooted in egalitarian principles of public access and
public use and in an environmentalist commitment to public transportation and
pedestrian and bicycle routes that would ultimately displace the automobile-
centered development that had been firmly established since 1950.[6] Whether
this vision is better than the Yuppie Heaven motif is, of course, a matter of
opinion. The critical point is that big-picture planning did not produce the city
or county that was envisioned by Appleyard and Lynch.

The failure of planning in San Diego from 1974 to the present is more
instructive than the failure of planning in Los Angeles from 1930 to the present, because in Los Angeles the Chamber of Commerce effectively opposed the

big-picture plan.[7] In San Diego it appears that the business community was more supportive, and the big-picture plan of 1974 was, in a sense, adopted. At least the path suggested in the plan was followed to a large extent in the development and promotion of comprehensive regional planning. This progressive vision also seems to have guided the more recent efforts to promote smart growth. Nevertheless, though the plan did not fall on deaf ears, it failed to redeem the paradise of 1960s San Diego.

Why San Diego developed as it did instead of how it might have is a complex story of collective choice and structural constraint. With regard to choices made, it is clear that regional planning was going to accommodate the interests of property owners and voters and attempt to balance conservative fears of regulation against liberal demands for reform. Ultimately the marriage that produced Yuppie Heaven was a compromise that facilitated development that would attract tourists and their dollars but discouraged development that might accommodate permanent residents, whether they be wealthy or not. This is, of course, the Disneyland, not the Hotel California, model.[8]

Clearly this vision accommodates the conservative interest in protecting free trade and the use of land for income generation, that is the inclusive interest of capital, as well as the exclusive, no-growth, interest of voters. To the extent that private development, such as Horton Plaza, also provides affordable housing, the inclusionary liberal interests of state and federal government are also accommodated. In fact, only the most radical interests—such as Earth First! and other interests prepared to use any means necessary to stop development of natural areas—are contested or repressed in the big-picture planning effort. Liberal environmentalists make it clear that they are prepared to work within the system. When asked to consider the radical argument against private property rights, Steve, the leader of Southern California Habitat Defenders, responded, "Environmental factors, despite the protest of the extremists, are being recognized as a very legitimate basis for the regulation of land. We have all the tools we need. It's just that we don't use them. I don't think we really need to change the system. The [free-market] system of land use really is not broken."

Matt, the San Diego representative of the Nature Conservancy that was actively involved in the NCCP, was likewise committed to working within the system and was concerned that the extremists were unrealistic. "Anyone who sits in southern California and says my goal is to stop growth is emotionally fine but in reality they are just . . . I don't know where they are, because we have got 7 million more people coming into southern California in the next thirty years. Where are we going to put them? What are we going to do with them? It is easy to say, 'No. We're just not going to let them in.' Well, good luck." The extremists Matt was referring to were not radicals, however, but reactionaries. It appears that the coalition of no-growth reactionaries and conservationist liberals is breaking down. The reactionary interests that were tolerated, if not accommodated, in big-picture planning may be left out of the smart-growth coalition.

Ideologically, reactionary political attitudes are rooted in general pessimism about common people, who are viewed as selfish and lazy, and about established institutions, which are believed to foster selfishness and sloth by providing elites with opportunities to gain power and nonelites with social services— the proverbial free lunch. The historical referent is the farmer who believed that a good plow and a good shotgun were all that were needed for the good life in the antebellum Northwest. In the 1830s Tocqueville identified these rugged individualists as follows: "Individualism is a novel expression, to which a novel idea has given birth. Individualism is a mature and calm feeling, which disposes each member of the community to sever himself from the mass of his fellows, and to draw apart with his family and friends; so that, after he has thus formed a little circle of his own, he willingly leaves society at large to itself."[9]

Reactionaries as an organized interest, as opposed to individuals with a reactionary attitude, are best represented by citizen militias and other vigilante organizations, including the Ku Klux Klan. In local land-use politics the reactionary is represented by the landowner and the neighborhood association that continue to struggle against liberal court decisions that have outlawed restrictive covenants. We might consider these reactionary interests as fighters for a lost cause. Neighbors do not have the legal right to keep undesired people or land uses out of their neighborhood. Conservatives defend the free market in real estate. Liberals defend equal rights or antidiscrimination. Each of these interests precludes reactionary exclusion. Nevertheless, neighborhood associations are routinely organized to harass and intimidate unwanted neighbors.[10]

In San Diego reactionaries routinely proclaim their interests in opposition to legally mandated public access to the coast. In La Jolla, for example, the Cove is maintained as a public beach with a seaside sidewalk that provides an extended walking tour of the rocky coast. Across the street pre–Coastal Act owners of single-family dwelling units defy the intent of public access with signs that state simply, "Armed Response." Here is the quintessential contemporary reactionary, protecting private property rights at the point of a gun. More subtle forms of reactionary politics are apparent in the exclusionary claims of the open-space and no-growth movements, as well as in tax reform measures, such as Proposition 13, that privilege the established residents at the expense of the newcomers. All of these movements accommodate the reactionary interests of those who proclaim, "I got mine. To hell with the rest of you."

Conservatives and liberals publicly distance themselves from reactionary attitudes and interests, but the progressive coalitions that have accommodated the conservative defense of property rights and the liberal defense of civil liberties, or individuals' rights, have routinely tolerated the reactionary strains of progressivism. Generally progressives choose to repress the violence of radicals who would forcibly seize or destroy private property and implicitly condone the violence of the reactionaries who would defend private property at gunpoint—as they readily admit and even advertise.

Conservatives and liberals seem to be more frightened by the radical call for violent struggle than by the reactionary defense of sustained violence. Perhaps it is the fear of the unknown that maintains their allegiance to the devil they know.

The undiscover'd country from whose bourn
No traveller returns, puzzles the will,
And makes us rather bear those ills we have,
Than fly to others that we know not of?
Thus conscience does make cowards of us all.[11]

Nevertheless, by 1999 the smart-growth coalition had abandoned the reactionaries and was using the radicals as a threat to encourage the conservatives to cooperate with the liberals, lest they face more extreme opposition.

Four Paths to the Future

There are four paths toward planning in the twenty-first century. First, there is the conservative path of free-market private-sector planning, in which government involvement is limited to enforcing existing zoning restrictions. This is the path blazed by Herbert Hoover, which led to the economic crisis of 1929. More recently, it is path of deregulation and New Federalism, blazed by Ronald Reagan, which led to the economic crisis of 1989. This is the path followed by less progressive city planning departments, especially in the South. The extreme free-market city is Houston, Texas, but there are other examples in the frontier towns of the Dakotas, Idaho, and Montana.

One problem with this path is that the role of government is unclear. Is it a watchdog, a lapdog, a cheerleader, or a sugar daddy? Conservatives pretend that they are rugged individualists, but they generally advocate welfare for the wealthy. A more serious problem is that this path inevitably leads to financial crises that defy free-market solutions. In 1929 and 1989 the only solution to fiscal crisis was for free-market conservatives to relinquish control of the government to liberals who were prepared to offer an alternative path.[12]

A second path toward city planning is currently being promoted as smart growth. The coalition of big environmentalists, big capitalists, and big government is promoting growth within the transportation corridors of metropolitan areas while preserving undeveloped land as natural areas. This is simply the latest version of big-picture planning, but it differs from the earlier version in that the reactionary no-growth interests have been abandoned and the exclusionary interests of local, particularly suburban, actors have generally been subordinated to the inclusionary interests of state and federal actors.[13] This triumph for inclusionary interests does not extend beyond the interests of developers and environmentalists, however. Conspicuous in their absence are the poor, Latinos, blacks, labor, women, and children.

The plan for smart growth entails two sets of contradictory elements. First, there is the checkerboard of green and white spaces, where green is preserved and white is developed. Second, there is the transportation corridor, which is the target for growth, and the hinterland, which is to be preserved. Theoretically development is high-density along the transportation corridors,

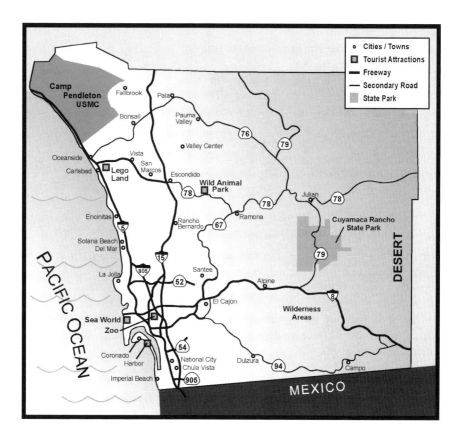

Figure 12. Yuppie Heaven, 2001, with Highways Indicated
Base map provided by SANDAG

which are white zones. Then there is limited development elsewhere: none in
the green zones and little in the adjoining rural and suburban areas. The problem, however, is that the preservation of green zones increases the cost of development in the white zones. Thus only high-priced estate lots or single-family
tract homes are profitable. In San Diego County there is no evidence that suburban cities are going to promote high-density development that neither developers nor suburban residents desire, and it seems unlikely that mass transit will
be viable so long as growth continues as suburban sprawl. It seems that the
checkerboard of upscale residential properties bordered by green zones will
ultimately prevail. In all likelihood Yuppie Heaven will never get its monorail.

More likely, the freeway and highway system will be expanded. If the 2001
projects are completed, Yuppie Heaven will still lack easy freeway access to
some of its East County attractions, such as mountain parks like Cuyamaca
Rancho and Laguna, and the Gold Rush frontier town of Julian.

A third path for city planning is the social-democratic, or state-centered
approach. This is the European path, which was state-centered in both Eastern

and Western Europe but more democratic in the west and more socialist in the east. Ideally, it would include both public ownership and grassroots democracy. Plus, it would need to accommodate local administration if applied to the United States, where it might be reduced to financing local administration with federal funds. It would depart most sharply from contemporary planning in the abolition of private property and the defense of usage rights. The problem with this path, however, is that it is impossible to dispossess the defenders of private property without a mobilized grassroots constituency, but such a constituency is the bane of the planner's existence. Professional planners are more willing and able to negotiate with government bureaucrats or private sector developers.[14]

If the problem with smart growth is economic then the problem with social democracy is political. Most generally, however, both sets of problems plague big-picture plans for better communities. The constraints of the consumer market in housing units or the voter's choice in public policy have plagued progressive planning for nearly a century. Within this institutional context, the planners must sell their plans to the private or public sector consumers. Are the consumers prepared to buy these homes? Are the voters prepared to adopt this policy? Are their economic or political representatives responsive to the demands of the grassroots? These are simply two versions of the same problem. Who will pay for or vote for the big-picture plan?[15]

Thus the social democratic and the free market alternatives bring us back to the problem of how much faith we have in republican government and capitalist economy. Do we trust elected leaders and business leaders to represent the interest of the people in negotiating with the professional planner on the big-picture plan for the future?

The only viable alternative is a truly revolutionary change, but whose revolution will it be? Whose revolutionary consciousness should we follow? We have the middle-class liberal interests: environmentalist, feminist, anti-nuclear, peace, and animal rights. We have the petty bourgeois reactionaries who promote no growth and no taxes. We have tenants unions and labor unions. What collective interest might offer a viable alternative to the status quo?

I propose that we focus on the alienation of life and work, revisiting the feminist socialism of the nineteenth century while recognizing its limits and the limits of Marx and Engels's utopian vision. We might consider, in this context, why middle-class families do not resemble factories, and we might ask what we can learn from peasants and farmers about living and working together.

All of the progressive visions of planned communities, beginning with the master plans of 1908, were based on an ecological model of community development that is rooted in the exploitation and monopolization of natural resources by the actors who are most efficient in extracting or appropriating the value of these resources.[16] Extracting value is the ultimate goal. Efficiency is the primary criterion for evaluating the means of extraction. Consequently, the form of community development is largely determined by the mode of extraction. In other words, the form of the community settlement is largely determined by the technical capacity to move people and things into and out of the community.

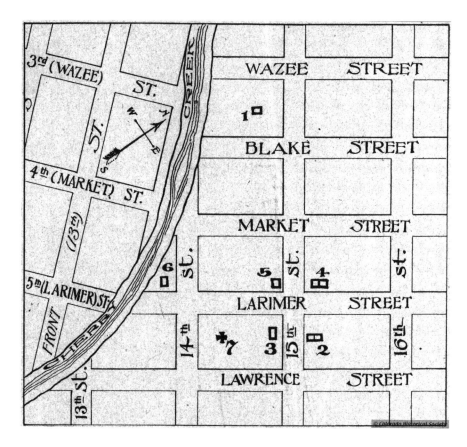

Figure 13. Denver, Colorado, Circa 1858
Denver Map #10028131 Courtesy, Colorado Historical Society

Historically we have the walking city, the streetcar and railroad city, and most recently the automobile city. Most interesting, however, is not the extent to which these cities differ but the extent to which they are similar. Long before the automobile and even before the transcontinental railroad, U.S. cities were laid out in square blocks of roads that brought people and things to and from the houses and businesses. Consider, for example, the frontier map of what later became the City of Denver, Colorado.

The development of streets and alleys, which became functionally differenti-ated in the movement of people and things, is another example of the same process. Nineteenth-century cities, which developed along railroad lines, and twentieth-century suburbs, which developed along highways, were simply two forms of the same enterprise.[17] Form follows function, and the primary function was the extraction of value, particularly labor value, which was produced and reproduced on a daily as well as generational basis in the homes that consti-tuted these communities.

Late-nineteenth- and early-twentieth-century feminists of the progressive and socialist persuasions were among the first to recognize the extent to which life within the home was subservient to the paid employment of men, which occurred outside the home. Charlotte Perkins Gilman, for example, envisioned a domestic economy that employed the efficiency of the modern factory. Thus domestic labors would be less of a burden, freeing women to work outside the home. Her version of utopia was a life-centered community, with public facilities and services at the center and private spaces at the periphery. People lived in two-room flats and ate out or picked up food to eat at home. In this child-centered feminist utopia, child bearing and child rearing were the ultimate collective responsibility. These activities were not carried out in private residences, however, and were not left to the efforts of private individuals.

In Gilman's utopia, only the best and the brightest were qualified to raise children. The rest of the women in Herland performed agricultural and industrial tasks needed to secure the future life and well-being of the generations to come. Since women in Herland somehow developed the capacity to reproduce asexually, there was no place for men in this world. Gilman leaves open the possibility of a heterosexual utopia, but it would require a very different type of man from the rugged individualist of the late-nineteenth- and early-twentieth-century United States.[18]

Such a life-centered community might use contiguous circles, rather than rectangles, as the building blocks for a community in which the public space was at the center and the private space at the periphery.[19] Imagine, for example, contiguous housing units surrounding woods, meadows, gardens, schools, eating and gathering places, libraries, and athletic fields. Not every circle of units would need to contain the same amenities, since people could easily walk from one contiguous circle to another. The goal would be to provide everything necessary within walking distance, but what was necessary would be subject to change, particularly as individuals moved through the life course.

The extent to which there is heterogeneity within and between circles is an interesting question to consider. In contrast to Gilman's utopia, I would be inclined to retain some vestige of family life in the relations between parents and children, together with a tendency for families with children to cluster around neighborhood schools. If we dispensed with private ownership and accumulation of material goods, however, we would move to a much less restrictive family life. How individuals moved into and out of families and neighborhoods and how they contributed to the well-being of each would be determined collectively, but always with sufficient flexibility to cultivate diversity in the path through the life course.

One might imagine such a community in comparison to an existing college town in the Midwest, whose street plan indicates that the university is located at the confluence of two major highways. Other highways bound the student and single-family housing districts. There is one major north-south thoroughfare (Salisbury) that runs through the residential neighborhoods and connects Highway 26 (State Street), the main street on campus, to Highway 52, which is the major commercial route.

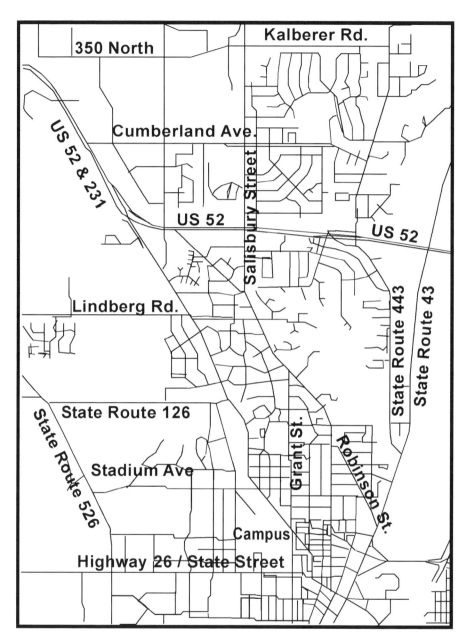

Figure 14. West Lafayette, Indiana, a Midwestern University Town
Base map provided by Tippecanoe County Area Planning

This is a very nice, relatively well-planned community. There are a variety of ways for students and athletic fans to come and go. The town has an efficient public transit system, and students and faculty can ride the buses for free. The major highways connect to freeways located outside of town. There are schools and parks and all the amenities that one might expect in a college community. Hiking trails are located along the river, and a pedestrian bridge crosses the river, connecting this town to the river town on the opposite shore. The major problem is that the community is dominated by a system of streets, roads, alleys, and highways, all designed for the extraction of resources and refuse. One can easily walk to work or school, but only along the streets and alleys.

In the utopian model of this community, the rectangular maze of streets and alleys would be eliminated. Major industries would be located in the center of each contiguous circle. Each circle would be rimmed by residences, which would be oriented toward the center of the circle, into the public area that is the center of neighborhood life. The university, high school, elementary school, and city government offices would still be in the same general locations, but they would now be connected by rail—perhaps monorail and subway. Tunnels and bicycle and pedestrian trails would cross the circles. Mass transit would be located on the edges of the circles. Golf carts would be provided for seniors and differently abled persons. Other types of public transportation could also be incorporated.

Unlike utopian dream communities, a life-centered community would face the problems of birth and death, love and hate, fear and anger, and perhaps even jealousy and envy. Hopefully, however, having mobilized the capacity to reclaim the earth for the living, with the promise to improve the quality of life for everyone, we would manage to deal with our human emotional and physical weaknesses as well as our strengths. At any rate, it seems a more promising path than continuing to sell the earth in subdivided lots.

We could eliminate real estate, finance, and insurance and decentralize and collectivize other consumer services, including the production and distribution of food and clothing. Recycling and laundering, building and land maintenance could combine neighborhood collection with municipal processing and administration. Economies of scale could also be effected with some specialization in basic industries: education, health, food, transportation, and energy. This life-centered world would be dominated by education, but the separation of the academic and the practical would not replace the alienation of life and work. We should all be students and teachers, dedicated first to teaching ourselves, then to sharing with others.

Basic human needs would be met through collective enterprise: "from each according to ability, to each according to need." The day-to-day necessities of life could be available to all within their community circles, but people certainly would chose to travel and some might even choose to work outside the circle where they live.

There still would be room for entrepreneurial efforts. A resident who wanted to bake bread, cook Vietnamese food, or establish a church or museum would need only to convince local residents to support such an endeavor. One would expect that the education, food, health, energy, and transportation industries would have suggestions and advice about what type of enterprise might work best where.

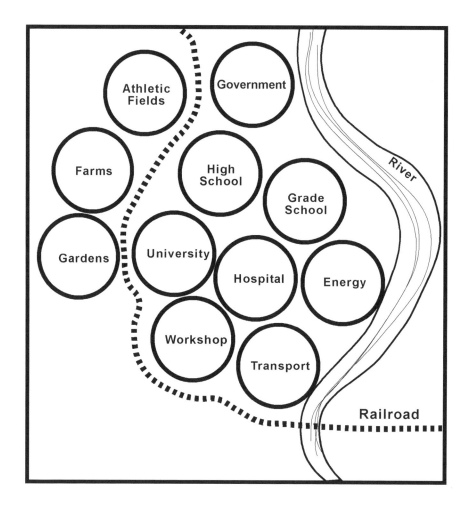

Figure 15. Utopian University Town

Generally, however, innovation would be local and small in scale, as would regulation. Before establishing a bakery, for example, one might use a local kitchen to bake some bread to see how popular fresh-baked bread might be.

Decentralizing innovation and administration to the greatest extent possible would mean sacrificing efficiency in value extraction—production and trade—for efficacy in value cultivation, enhancement, and sustenance. The goal would be to sacrifice efficiency in work to foster efficacy in life, to sacrifice quantity for quality, the individual for the collective. In short, this utopia is based on the collective determination to choose life.

Appendix A: On Method and Moral Judgment

In nonparticipant observation, as opposed to survey or archival research, the researcher is personally involved in social relations with subjects and is thus hard pressed to maintain professional claims to objectivity or disinterestedness. Consequently, the researcher faces a series of problems and possibilities associated with the lack of scientific control in the field experience or uncontrolled experiment. This tends to muddy the distinction between professional and personal judgment.

Thus methodological and moral dilemmas are compounded as the researcher is confronted with the problems of everyday life. Specifically, the researcher must negotiate reality with a set of individuals who have more-or-less established working definitions of who they are in relation to each other and of what they are doing in light of the current situation. The problem for the researcher is to establish some sort of identity in relation to the subjects and their activities in order to develop an understanding of the situation, initially as viewed through the eyes of the participants.

As is the case with anthropological fieldwork, the major practical problems are getting in and getting out. The first problem is more than a matter of physical access. It is fundamentally social: how can one gain entry into a group of individuals who collectively defend the border of their group through shared understandings to which outsiders are not privy? It goes beyond the jargon. It involves developing an identity within the group that allows the group to function normally, as if the observer were not present

The second problem is captured nicely by the anthropology idiom of "going native." Once one has gained access to the group by "becoming a marihuana [sic] user," for example, one can develop an insider's perspective on social life.[1] Once one has become an insider, the problem is how to extricate oneself—not just physically and socially, but also intellectually, or analytically. The recent experience of a graduate student who was studying homelessness provides a useful example of this problem. The student lacked an advising professor and a dissertation committee and was well beyond all possibility of financial support from the department. He faced the dilemma of getting out of the field. The most fundamental problem facing this student was the social construction of identity. Was he unemployed—in fact, unemployable—and homeless, or was he a student researcher studying homeless people?

To overcome barriers to access, the researcher usually relies on at least one personal contact who can provide background, ongoing commentary, and critical reactions as the researcher begins to struggle with a perception of what is going on in the course of field study. Equally important, this contact can introduce the researcher to others, thus legitimating the researcher's presence and participation while opening up the possibility of establishing new contacts.[2]

Ultimately routine participation in ongoing activities provides opportunities for the researcher to establish new contacts, including some with individuals who are not known to the other contacts. Ideally the researcher attempts to establish contacts with individuals from both sides of antagonistic relationships, so the researcher can get both sides of the story. For example, the student studying homelessness should establish contact with the police officers and social welfare workers who are part of the social world of homeless people. This is, however, difficult in practice, since parties to political and interpersonal disputes generally attempt to associate only with people on one side or the other. Homeless people, for example, presumably do not trust police officers and social workers. A college professor or graduate student might find it easier to establish relations with a police officer or social worker, but this might undermine the researcher's access to homeless people.

In my research I was fortunate to have two independent personal contacts with people who were essentially in an antagonistic relationship. One of these persons, Tom, is a friend from high school. We have become increasingly friendly since then, and our wives and even our children have become close friends. Without the help of this old friend my research would have been impossible. In fact, my close personal relationship with Tom has opened the door to all of the possibilities and potential problems I have faced over the past nine years in my effort to understand and analyze land-use planning in San Diego County suburbs.

Tom is a city planner who now works as a consultant. Initially he worked for the Castleton city planning department. Then, during my fieldwork, he was employed by the Patterson Company, a major development company that was negotiating with the City of Castleton on continuing efforts to complete Camelot, a one-thousand-acre master-plan community complete with hotel, country club, and upscale housing. As it happens, the city planner who had been assigned back in the 1980s to represent the city in these negotiations was Tommy, an old friend of mine from elementary school with whom I had not maintained social contact. Tommy then moved to Farmington and continued to work in the public sector, as a planning director. Tommy did not invite me into his world and introduce me to his friends and family. He was, however, more than willing to offer me Farmington's perspective once I had gained his confidence and demonstrated my professional discretion by not telling him things Tom had told me and by assuring him that I would similarly guard his anonymity and respect the confidentiality of what he told me.

In my initial fieldwork I followed Tom to public and private meetings, where I was introduced as an old friend and a college professor who was doing research on land-use politics. That frequently produced laughter in mixed (public- and private-sector planner) company, particularly at private meetings between the planning and engineering staffs of the city and the developer. At the first such meeting, in 1992, interested parties from both sides joked about how dull things must seem now, during the building depression. "You should have been here in the eighties," they said. That was when the battle lines were being drawn. The laughter indicated the extent to which these people were uncomfortable in relations with each other and, to a greater extent, in relation with me (and by extension with you, my readers). The fact that the major controversies were already been resolved made them less nervous, however, and probably helped them to justify talking freely in front of me—even though I did not get clearance from the municipal government, but instead followed the developer's planner into these private meetings.

Gradually I gained the confidence of other planners, particularly the consultants (Dick, Harry, and other private-sector professionals) whom Tom trusted. Although I met many city planning department staff members at public and private meetings, the fact that I was an old friend of Tom's limited my contacts with the city. Fortunately, after I began attending local citizen advisory group meetings and state habitat conservation meetings, my routine presence led to a series of new contacts. This solo work began with Tim, an environmental biologist who worked as a consultant and was on the expert panel that was developing the Habitat Protection Plan (HPP) in Castleton. My contact with Tim facilitated my efforts to extend my sample to include other consultants, including Lou, the HPP facilitator, and city government officials, including Doug and Dave.

These contacts led to still other contacts with biologists, environmentalists, and planners. This is what sociologists call a snowball sample, where each contact suggests someone else until these referrals begin to bring the researcher back to people already contacted, at which point the researcher can conclude that all of the major players have been identified. Generally these contacts, established independently of my relationship with Tom, were much more useful in representing the other side, specifically the environmentalist and public-sector planner perspectives.

At the same time, however, my relationships with biologists and city planners limited my access to the general public, and particularly to no-growth proponents. Many of these people saw me at the citizen advisory committee meetings and at the workshops. When I approached them on such occasions, they spoke with me informally, but they seemed to view me as part of the conspiracy of professional planners, consultants, and developers. The fact that I was a college professor did not help. Thus while I was able to observe these people and at times engage them in informal discussion, they never really confided in me and never returned my calls when I attempted to set up interviews.

Generally the farther I moved from the local suburban community where Tom's project, Camelot, was located, the less suspicion I encountered from potential contacts in the public sector and the environmentalist community. County- and state-level officials in SANDAG and the NCCP, and in the Nature Conservancy and other environmentalist organizations, did not seem to view me with suspicion, and like the biologists they seemed to be more at ease when they learned that I was a college professor.

Curiously, both the no-growth suburban residents and the pro-growth development interests seemed to become more suspicious when they learned that I was a sociology professor. Anticipating this problem, I always introduced myself as "Rich Hogan, an associate professor of sociology and American studies at Purdue University, here studying land-use politics." I hoped that the more conservative parties might find some solace in the fact that I was in American studies and that I taught at Purdue University.

Developers other than Tom's boss, Bill, were generally inclined to ignore me. I was able to engage some—particularly the smokers, who huddled outside public meeting halls—in casual conversation, but I generally didn't introduce myself as a researcher or try to interview them. Instead, I allowed them to think I was a consultant. At citizen advisory group meetings, for example, when each person made an introduction to the group, I always said, "Rich Hogan, visiting at UCSD." People probably heard "visiting from" and assumed I was a biologist, particularly after I started to hang out with Tim, the biologist who was a consultant for the HPP. I joined the HPP citizen advisory group shortly after arriving in the field and never missed a meeting from January through May of 1992. I was the most regular attendee other than Lou, the facilitator.

Only once did my failure to introduce myself produce unintended consequences. In that case I was clearly at fault because I appeared at a private meeting under what could only be considered false pretenses. Tom was meeting the local representative of the San Diego County association of developers that was supporting the statewide habitat conservation plan (the NCCP). Because Tom and I were both interested in learning more about this local organization, he had set up a meeting, and I tagged along. Tom introduced me as "Rich Hogan, who works with me." With 20/20 hindsight, it is clear that this was a mistake, but we didn't anticipate any consequences since Tom's boss, Bill, was not going to join the organization and we expected to have no further contact with its leader.

Once I started attending state-level NCCP meetings, however, our paths crossed again. At this point I was almost ready to leave the field, and I was beginning to ask questions at public meetings—particularly, at the state-level meetings where I felt secure in my anonymity. In fact, as I became more involved in the state-level meetings, asking questions but not expressing opinions, my relationship with at least one city planning official was developing. As we saw each other at these meetings, Doug and I became increasingly friendly, and he became more inclined to express himself on a variety of issues.[3]

Thus my participation in these meetings where I identified myself as "visiting at UCSD" seemed to facilitate my efforts to establish relations with public-sector planners and environmentalists. That probably increased the sense of betrayal on the part of the San Diego developer who had met me as someone who worked with Tom. He had presumed that I was a private-sector planner, Tom's assistant, since I took notes but didn't say much at our meeting. During a break at one of the NCCP meetings the developer followed me outside. "Who the hell are you?" he asked. "You are not [Tom's] flunky. Who are you, and what are you doing here?"

I apologized and explained who I was, but I had burned that bridge to San Diego County developers. We had lunch later, my treat, and the developer seemed reasonably forthcoming, but when I tried to get on the organization's mailing list it became increasingly evident that I was not trusted.[4] There is, of course, a lesson to be learned here. The professional and moral code is simple. Tell the truth. This may not open doors, but it is better than the alternative. Telling the truth is particularly important for private meetings, where misleading introductions are likely to be viewed as deceptions.

Aside from this one case, where the lapse in professional and personal judgment is embarrassingly obvious, the problem of my relationships with my contacts remains. When I left the field in May of 1992, I felt comfortable with my understanding of the actors and issues and was convinced that I would stay in touch with my contacts, particularly Tom, in the course of writing up my analysis. I was convinced that time would diminish the passions associated with some of the stories I hoped to tell. At the same time, my return to the ivory tower would help me to gain a new perspective on the information I had gathered. Thus I would be able to look at the situation first from the perspective of the participants, as preserved in my field notes, and then from the perspective of a disinterested academic.

For the past nine years I have been looking at this research from a different perspective—attempting to address issues in the academic literature, reading the secondary literature, and analyzing data found in government records.[5] In the process I have come to appreciate what I have learned and how it relates to what I observed and what I think. But it is only now, as I am sharing the fruits of these labors, that I am also beginning to appreciate the importance of my feelings in relation to how my contacts will feel about what I have published. The fact that my closest friends and favorite contacts from the field fundamentally disagree with my interpretation of the story is disturbing but not surprising.[6] It has at least alerted me to another element of the personal nature of this story. Perhaps my daughter will never marry Tom's son, but hopefully he and I will laugh about his project and mine someday, when both are finally completed.

Notes

Notes to Preface

1. "They paved paradise and put up a parking lot" is a line from "Big Yellow Taxi," a song by Joni Mitchell from the album *Ladies of the Canyon*.

2. The conspiracy of government and developer in the growth-machine coalition will be discussed in some detail in chapter 1.

3. The speculative frenzy of 1972–1989 will be discussed in detail in chapter 2.

4. See chapter 5; on Reagan see chapter 2.

5. Enlightened developers will be contrasted with more opportunistic real estate speculators in chapter 4.

6. Particularly useful was Max J. Pfeffer and Mark B. Lapping, "Farmland Preservation, Development Rights, and the Theory of the Growth Machine: The Views of Planners," *Journal of Rural Studies* 10, no. 3 (1994): 233–48. Also useful was Thomas K. Rudel, *Situations and Strategies in American Land-Use Planning* (New York: Cambridge University Press, 1989), which is discussed in some detail in chapter 1.

Notes to What Can Be Done

1. On May 6, 1968, French students, including university and high school students, with the support of the national teacher's union, declared a general strike and began a series of demonstrations that led to violent confrontations with the police. One week later (May 13, 1968) labor joined in what became a national strike that threatened to topple the de Gaulle government. The Gaullist party re-established its control of the government by winning the special election of June 30, 1968. By then the universities were open but the faculty and students were still on strike. See A. Belden Fields, "The Revolution Betrayed: The French Student Revolt of May–June 1968," in *Students in Revolt*, ed. Seymour Martin Lipset and Philip G. Altbach (Boston: Beacon Press, 1970 [1969, 1967]), 127–66; the chronology is offered on pp. 128–41.

Notes to Personal and Professional

1. Richard Hogan, "Do Citizen Initiatives Affect Growth? The Case of Five San Diego Suburbs," in *Research in Community Sociology*, ed. Dan A. Chekki (New York: JAI Press, 1997), 249–75.

Notes to Overview

1. Daniel Burnham and Edward H. Bennett, *Plan of Chicago* (Chicago: Commercial Club, 1908), 124, quoted in Zane L. Miller and Bruce Tucker, *Changing Plans for America's Inner Cities: Cincinnati's Over-the-Rhine and Twentieth Century Urbanism* (Columbus: Ohio State University Press, 1998), 5.

2. My last Sears Tower tour was in the early 1990s. They might have made a new video by now.

3. Chicago has often been designated the second city because it was for many years second only to New York. Los Angeles has since surpassed Chicago, in population if nothing else. Second City is now the name of a Chicago comedy club.

4. It is clear that Chicago was a hotbed of progressive reform both in theory and practice. On the Chicago School and Robert Park and his students, see Vernon J. Williams Jr., *From a Caste to a Minority: Changing Attitudes of American Sociologists toward Afro-Americans, 1896–1945* (New York: Greenwood, 1989), chapter 4 and especially pp. 85–90. On the Chicago School and urban ecology, see M. Gottdiener, *The Social Production of Urban Space* (Austin: University of Texas Press, 1985), 27–35. For a more sympathetic treatment of the Chicago School, see Martin Blumer, *The Chicago School of Sociology: Institutionalization, Diversity, and the Rise of Sociological Research* (Chicago: University of Chicago Press, 1984). For a sympathetic treatment of urban ecology, see W. Parker Frisbie and John D. Kasarda, "Spatial Processes," in *Handbook of Sociology*, ed. Neil J. Smelser (Beverly Hills, Calif.: Sage, 1988), 629–66. See also Zane L. Miller, "Pluralism, Chicago School Style: Louis Wirth, the Ghetto, the City, and 'Integration,'" *Journal of Urban History* 18 (May 1992): 251–79.

The dates for municipal plans, general plans, and comprehensive regional plans vary from city to city. Both Chicago and San Diego had municipal plans in 1908, but Cincinnati did not adopt a master plan until 1925. These master plans of the early twentieth century were not municipal in the present-day sense, in that they were not carried out under the auspices of a municipal government (Zane Miller, private communication). They occupied an intermediate status between the private plans of the frontier land-claim clubs and the public plans of the mid-to-late twentieth century. On San Diego, see Abraham J. Shragge, "Boosters and Bluejackets: The Civic Culture of Militarism in San Diego, California, 1900–1945" (Ph.D. diss., University of California, San Diego, 1998), 196–98; on Chicago and Cincinnati, see Miller and Tucker, *Changing Plans*, 5, 18. California cities were required to include a housing element as part of their general plans for municipal development beginning in 1967. See San Diego Association of Governments (SANDAG), *Regional Housing Needs Statement: San Diego Region* (San Diego, Calif.: Source Point, 1990), 3.

John W. Reps, *The Making of Urban America: A History of City Planning in the United States* (Princeton, N.J.: Princeton University Press, 1965), 524–25, explains how the Burnham plan for Chicago represented a major break from previous planning, which had been concerned primarily with the alignment of streets and alleys. The Chicago municipal plan was three dimensional and included public spaces and transportation. Even in Chicago in 1908, municipal planning was still a private enterprise, but cities soon assumed control of municipal land use. In New York in 1917 municipal planning became public and more comprehensive, including public regulation of private property that incorporated setbacks, building heights and widths, as well as land use. Thus modern city planning, based on zoning, was established.

This was still a far cry from the more comprehensive municipal planning circa 1968, however. Geographically, the general plan was still municipal but it encompassed, for example, plans to meet projected housing needs. Thus it was, already, more comprehensive than the municipal plans circa 1908 that had paved the way for city planning.

The change from general plans of the late sixties to comprehensive regional planning in the eighties happened on two fronts. Planning became more comprehensive, including habitat conservation plans and other such elements in addition to housing. Also, particularly in housing and in habitat conservation plans, the plans were based on assessments of regional needs with the expectation that suburbs absorb the costs of implementing metropolitan, regional, or even statewide plans.

The emergence of public planning in urban development in the first decade of the twentieth century in the United States might be explained as a "restructuring" of the "mode of development," as theorized by Manuel Castells in the first chapter of *The Informational City: Information, Technology, Economic Restructuring, and the Urban-Regional Process* (Oxford: Basil Blackwell, 1989). A speculative effort in this direction might be summarized as follows: Municipal plans emerged in the first decade of the twentieth century in cities that combined university research centers and transportation or communication centers with the ability to attract private-sector venture capital and public-sector (government) contracts. In 1908 cities like Chicago were able to attract speculative investment that paid major dividends as the market price of building futures soared, particularly during the first two decades. Public works continued to provide more security than purely speculative private ventures might otherwise offer. After the bubble burst in 1929, public ventures, and federal projects in particular, became increasingly important in efforts to revitalize urban America.

5. In chapter 1 we will consider big-picture (comprehensive regional) planning, as this term was used by San Diego County city planners in 1992 and is represented by Donald Appleyard and Kevin Lynch in *Temporary Paradise? A Look at the Special Landscape of the San Diego Region* (a 1974 report to the City of San Diego, located in the Government Documents section of the University of California, San Diego, library). In chapter 2 we will consider the history of master plans, general plans, and comprehensive regional plans, particularly in San Diego County, from 1908 to 1992. In the concluding chapter we will consider smart growth as this term was used by San Diego County city planners in 1999.

6. Jon C. Teaford, in *The Unheralded Triumph: City Government in America, 1870–1900* (Baltimore, Md.: Johns Hopkins University Press, 1984), argues for the success of nineteenth-century U.S. cities and is, in this regard, most optimistic about urban success. He seems less optimistic about suburbia and postsuburbia. See Jon C. Teaford, *Post-Suburbia: Government and Politics in the Edge Cities* (Baltimore, Md.: Johns Hopkins University Press, 1997), and *City and Suburb: The Political Fragmentation of Metropolitan America, 1850–1970* (Baltimore, Md.: Johns Hopkins University Press, 1979). On the promise of planning in general and zoning in particular see Charles M. Haar and Jerome S. Kayden, eds., *Zoning and the American Dream: Promises Still to Keep* (Chicago: Planners Press, 1989).

7. For the growth-machine perspective that municipal governments are undemocratic, see John R. Logan and Harvey Molotch, *Urban Fortunes: The Political Economy of Place* (Berkeley: University of California Press, 1987); John R. Logan and Min Zhou, "Do Suburban Growth Controls Control Growth?" *American Sociological Review* 54 (1989): 461–71; Harvey Molotch, "The City as a Growth Machine," *American Journal of Sociology* 82 (1976): 309–32; and Harvey Molotch and John R. Logan, "Tensions in the Growth Machine: Overcoming Resistance to Value-Free Development," *Social Problems* 31 (1984): 483–99. For a classic statement of the underlying theory, see C. Wright Mills, *The Power Elite* (New York: Oxford University Press, 1956). Andrew Szasz, in *EcoPopulism: Toxic Waste and the Movement for Environmental Justice* (Minneapolis: University of Minnesota Press, 1994), offers a more critical perspective on the challenge facing progressive grassroots movements.

In the planning literature, see Nico Calavita, "Growth Machines and Ballot Box Planning: The San Diego Case," *Journal of Urban Affairs* 14, no. 1 (1992): 1–24, who suggests that citizens win some short-term victories but the growth machine tends to win the war.

See the first chapter of Richard Hogan, *Class and Community in Frontier Colorado* (Lawrence: University Press of Kansas, 1990), for a review of the larger theoretical issues. If I were to revisit this debate today I would amend my earlier argument as follows: Certainly there are towns and cities that could be characterized as having public (carnival) or private (caucus) government. Nevertheless, in any particular city or town we should expect to see varying degrees of the two faces of power described in the classic paper by Peter Bachrach and Morton S. Baratz, "Two Faces of Power," *American Political Science Review* 56 (December 1962): 947–52. I would maintain, however, that we must locate these two faces of power in organized and institutionalized local economic and political relations and, equally important, in local economic and political history, viewed as an ongoing process of conflict between more or less organized and established interests.

8. William Kornhauser, in *The Politics of Mass Society* (New York: Free Press, 1959), distinguishes between two versions of mass-society theory, the aristocratic and the democratic, which are similar to the two critiques of city planning described here. For what might be considered the aristocratic critique (too much democracy) see Miller and Tucker, *Changing Plans,* 177, and, especially, Teaford, *City and Suburb* and *Post-Suburbia,* on the problem of fragmentation and local autonomy.

The literature on the NIMBY (not in my backyard) or LULU (locally unwanted land use) phenomena is vast. See, for example, Robert D. Bullard, ed., *Confronting Environmental Racism: Voices from the Grassroots* (Boston: South End Press, 1993); Laurie Graham and Richard Hogan, "Social Class and Tactics: Neighborhood Opposition to Group Homes," *The Sociological Quarterly* 31, no. 4 (1990): 513–29; M. J. Dear and S. M. Taylor, *Not on Our Street* (London: Pion, 1982); Hogan, "Do Citizen Initiatives Affect Growth?" For a classic statement on LULUs, see Frank J. Popper, "When the Development Is a LULU," *Re:Sources* (spring/summer 1981): 14–15, and *The Politics of Land-Use Reform* (Madison: University of Wisconsin Press, 1981).

9. Members of Earth First! drove spikes into trees in an effort to prevent logging that was threatening the habitat of the spotted owl and other species. In an unrelated effort the highly photogenic media darling and former model Julia Butterfly Hill occupied a tree house in a thousand-year-old redwood tree in a contested old-growth forest. This media darling, Julia Butterfly Hill, even made the *Rolling Stone* (Issue 816/817 July 8–22, 1999), 66–67.

10. For present purposes republican capitalism can be defined as a political system with elected or representative governing officials and an economic system that rests on private ownership of the means of production and a free market in labor and its products. These economic and political institutions tend to develop in tandem since republicanism is essentially the political expression of capitalist economic relations.

Republicanism mimics capitalism. Voters are the structural equivalent of consumers; politicians and policies are commodified. The modern state witnesses not only fiscal crises, but also production crises—for example, the overproduction of law and lawyers, policies and politicians. The general inefficiency, or anarchy, of the market for policies and politicians begins to restrain capitalist development. Thus it is not simply that crises of capitalism undermine republicanism, creating political or legitimation crises (see Jürgen Habermas, *Legitimation Crisis* [Boston: Beacon, 1975]). In addition, crises of republicanism undermine the development of capitalism. In this sense, republican capitalism is characterized as two dialectics in search of a synthesis. See James O'Connor, *Accumulation Crisis* (New York: Basil Blackwell), 1984; Frederick Engels, *Socialism: Utopian and Scientific, with the Essay on the Mark,* trans. Edward Averling (New York: International Publishers, 1985); and Karl Marx and Frederick Engels, "The German

Ideology," in *The German Ideology,* ed. C. J. Arthur (New York: International Publishers, 1970).

11. I will use the term *community* to refer to social relations linking people who live and work in a particular place. The extent to which communities are organized in pursuit of collective interest is problematic. It is clear that the organization of life and work and the political organization of cities, counties, and states undermine the organic community ties that potentially link people who work and live together. On this point even Durkheim and Marx could agree. See Emile Durkheim, *The Division of Labor in Society* (1893; reprint, New York: Free Press, 1933); Karl Marx, *The Economic and Philosophic Manuscripts of 1844* (New York: International Publishers, 1964 [first published in German in 1932]), especially "Estranged Labor," 106–19).

12. The argument about the irrationality of legal rationality is from Max Weber, *Economy and Society: An Outline of Interpretive Sociology,* ed. Guenther Roth and Claus Wittich (1956; reprint, Berkeley: University of California Press, 1978). See in particular chapters 10 and 11 of volume 2: "Domination and Legitimacy" and "Bureaucracy," respectively, and appendix 2, section 4, "The Political Limitations of Bureaucracy." More recently Habermas, in *Legitimation Crisis,* offers a similar critique. The "professional" versus "selfish" (lay) interests will be discussed in the chapters that follow. As will become apparent, Andrew Abbott's perspective on professions, *The System of Professions: An Essay on the Division of Expert Labor* (Chicago: University of Chicago Press, 1988), shaped my thinking on the subject in a variety of ways. Jerry Van Hoy's work on the proletarianization of professions, *Franchise Law Firms and the Transformation of Personal Legal Services* (Westport, Conn.: Quorum, 1997), might offer a nice complement to Abbott's perspective. Hopefully Abbott or Van Hoy or one of their students will write a history of the planning profession. Meanwhile, Carl Abbott, *Urban America in the Modern Age: 1920 to the Present* (Arlington Heights, Ill.: Harlan Davidson, 1987), offers a bibliographic essay for the interested reader; see in particular "Government, Planning, and Public Policy," pp. 160–63.

13. In the debate between consensus and conflict movements, I take the conflict side. See Michael Schwartz and Shuva Paul, "Resource Mobilization versus the Mobilization of People: Why Consensus Movements Cannot Be Instruments of Social Change," versus John D. McCarthy and Mark Wolfson, "Consensus Movements, Conflict Movements, and the Cooptation of Civic and State Infrastructures." Both are published in Aldon D. Morris and Carol McClurg Mueller, eds., *Frontiers in Social Movement Theory* (New Haven, Conn.: Yale University Press, 1992). In *Radical Protest and Social Structure: The Southern Farmers' Alliance and Cotton Tenancy, 1880–1890* (1976; reprint, Chicago: University of Chicago Press, 1988), Michael Schwartz argues that interests are capable of effecting institutional change only when they combat the institutional order by relying on their "structural" (positional or relational) capacity and using extra-institutional (illegitimate) means.

This is the standard position of structural Marxists and is similar to the argument offered by Manuel Castells in *The City and the Grassroots: A Cross-Cultural Theory of Urban Social Movements* (Berkeley: University of California Press, 1983), 327–29, in which he explains that urban social movements are reactionary consumer movements. Even if they are rooted in working-class neighborhoods, they are not working-class movements, and thus they are not capable of effecting significant, that is revolutionary, institutional change.

14. On the self-fulfilling prophesy, see Robert Merton, *Social Theory and Social Structure* (New York: Free Press, 1957), 421–36.

15. Unfortunately, neither Adam Smith nor Karl Marx appreciated the tendency for

capital accumulation and state making to destroy the earth. Marx at least appreciated the fact that the capitalist system was self-destructive, but he never considered the possibility that the capacity to transform material life included the capacity to destroy the earth. Thus Marx's failure as an environmentalist, much like his failure as a feminist, has plagued radical critics who can't accept the failures of the prophets.

See Marx and Engels, *German Ideology,* on what distinguishes humans from other animals: the ability to transform material life by cultivating crops, domesticating animals, and otherwise decreasing the labor power socially required to meet the fundamental human needs of food and shelter. Kevin Anderson discusses the feminist critique of Marx in some detail in "Marx on Suicide in the Context of His Other Writings on Alienation and Gender," in *Marx on Suicide,* ed. Kevin Anderson and Eric A. Plaut (Evanston, Ill.: Northwestern University Press, 1999). Anderson defends Marx as less sexist, or more feminist, than Engels, as evidenced by Marx's critique of bourgeois marriage and the exploitation of women more generally. He suggests the possibility of a Marxist feminist perspective that might be particularly enlightening. On Marx the environmentalist, see John Bellamy Foster, "Marx's Theory of Metabolic Rift: Classical Foundations for Environmental Sociology" *American Journal of Sociology* 105 (September 1999): 366–405.

The most compelling statement of a philosophy of sustainable social and environmental relations seems to be the Native American philosophy of living with, rather than off, nature. See, for example, Winona LaDuke, "Foreword," in Al Gedicks, *The News Resource Wars: Native and Environmental Struggles against Multinational Corporations* (Boston: South End Press, 1993), for a statement of this philosophy, summarized as "'you take only what you need and leave the rest'" (xi).

16. On the peculiarities of San Diego and on Pete Wilson, the growth-management mayoral candidate of 1971, see Anthony W. Corso, "San Diego: The Anti-City," in *Sunbelt Cities: Politics and Growth since World War II,* ed. Richard M. Bernard and Bradley R. Rice (Austin: University of Texas Press, 1983). Wilson was mayor until 1982, when he was elected to the U.S. Senate. In 1990 he was elected governor of California.

17. The distinction between enlightened negotiation and the operation of the free market is not always clear. The Habitat Conservation Plans (HCPs) that have been negotiated since the Endangered Species Act (ESA) was amended in 1982 combine elements of each. Similarly, Natural Community Conservation Planning (NCCP), which Bill Clinton and his Secretary of the Interior Bruce Babbitt celebrated as the future of big-picture planning and smart growth, incorporates an elaborate scheme of transferring development rights that was devised as a free-market solution to the problem of the ESA. See, for example, Todd G. Olson and Dennis M. Moser, "The Habitat Transaction Method of Conservation Planning, Land Acquisition, and Funding," unpublished discussion draft, May 27, 1992.

In chapter 4 of *City and Suburb,* Jon Teaford compares British and U.S. land-use planning. See also Harold Wolman, "Cross-National Comparisons of Urban Economic Programmes: Is Policy Transfer Possible?" in *Community Economic Development: Policy Formation in the U.S. and U.K.,* ed. David Fasenfest (Basingstoke, U.K.: Macmillan, 1993).

18. Manuel Castells, in *City and the Grassroots,* offers the model for these urban social movements, although, as he argues so persuasively, the movements he studied fell far short of revolution. Clearly these movements need to reunite the alienated components of community (life and work) if they are to achieve revolutionary consequences.

For a more optimistic perspective on urban social movements, see Stella M. Capek and John I. Gilderbloom, *Community versus Commodity: Tenants and the American City* (Albany: State University of New York Press, 1992), 240–42.

"Planting socialism" is offered, with tongue in cheek, as a parallel to Michael Burawoy's concept of "painting socialism." As he tells the story, factory workers in Hungary, under the soviet system, were preparing for an official visit by sprucing up the factory. They explained that they were not "building" socialism, but only "painting" it, thus ridiculing their efforts to impress the party bosses. Burawoy told this story at a brownbag presentation at Purdue University in 1987. Here my intention is to suggest the more positive project of planting socialism.

We might return to the tortured debates about the collectivized farms in czarist Russia and the need to replace those with soviets. See Karl Marx and Frederick Engels, "Preface to the Russian Edition of 1882, Manifesto of the Communist Party," in *The Marx-Engels Reader,* 2d edition, ed. Robert C. Tucker (New York: W. W. Norton, 1978), 472. Most generally, however, "Plant a garden" is my standard response to the question "What shall we do after the revolution?"

19. Charlotte Perkins Gilman offers a feminist perspective on gender roles in *Women and Economics: A Study of the Economic Relation between Men and Women as a Factor in Social Evolution* (Boston: Small, Maynard & Co., 1900). She offers a socialist feminist critique of the domestic economy in *The Home: Its Work and Influence* (New York: McClure, Phillips & Co., 1903). The closest Gilman comes to a model of socialist-feminist land-use policy is in her utopian novel *Herland: A Lost Feminist Utopian Novel by Charlotte Perkins Gilman, with an Introduction by Ann J. Lane* (New York: Pantheon Books, 1979). Here Gilman describes homes as "two rooms and a bath" and options for dining as "any convenient eating place" where one can dine in or order food for home delivery or take out (125). This is a critical component of Gilman's critique of Gilded Age U.S. domestic life. She wanted the kitchen removed from the home, and she proposed professional housekeeping and child rearing to free women for work outside the home. I discuss her vision of socialist-feminist community, along with the vision of Marx and Engels, in the concluding chapter.

Notes to Why San Diego Suburbs?

1. The various approaches to defining the Sunbelt are discussed in the introduction and first chapter of Carl Abbott, *The New Urban America: Growth and Politics in Sunbelt Cities* (Chapel Hill: University of North Carolina Press, 1987). San Diego is always in the heart of the Sunbelt regardless of definitions. Abbott places San Diego at the top of his list of "emerging regional centers" on the basis of its jump from the forty-eighth to the nineteenth largest U.S. metropolitan area (39). In *Urban America in the Modern Age,* Abbott reports that San Diego's metropolitan population increased from 1.4 million to 1.9 million in the 1970s (102). This net gain of 504,000 ranked fifth in the nation (behind growth in Houston, Dallas–Fort Worth, Phoenix, and Anaheim). Manuel Castells, in *The Informational City,* argues that "information-intensive" industry characterizes the cutting-edge cities. On this measure, percent of total employment that is in the information-intensive sector, San Diego ranks ninth in the nation, according to Castells (145).

Mike Davis's *City of Quartz: Excavating the Future in Los Angeles* (New York: Verso, 1990) is the quintessential poststructural treatment of the quintessential post-modern city. The University of California, Irvine campus houses what appears to be a growing cottage industry for analyses of the postmodern condition that use Orange

County as its laboratory. See, for example, Rob Kling, Spencer Olin, and Mark Poster, eds., *Postmodern California: The Transformation of Orange County since World War II* (Berkeley: University of California Press, 1991).

Jon C. Teaford, in *Post-Suburbia*, identifies Orange County as one of the postsuburban counties that has been studied intensively. He also recognizes that the contiguous San Diego County is not postsuburban (private communication). On this point we agree.

Postmodern is an overworked and ill-defined term. Here it refers to a period circa 1970–1990 that is characterized by flexible patterns of capital accumulation, and particularly, speculation, that are associated with deregulation, especially during the Reagan-Thatcher Era. See David Harvey, *The Condition of Postmodernity: An Enquiry into the Origins of Cultural Change* (Cambridge, Mass.: Blackwell, 1990).

2. The date for San Diego's first municipal plan comes from Abraham J. Shragge, "Boosters and Bluejackets," 198. He cites the primary source John Nolen, *San Diego: A Comprehensive Plan for Its Improvement* (Boston: George H. Ellis and Company, 1908). The 1997 date for San Diego's first Natural Community Conservation Plan (NCCP) comes from two independent sources who were involved in the negotiations. There is, however, some room to dispute what qualifies as an NCCP plan and what constitutes approval. One of the three pieces of the San Diego County NCCP had not yet been approved by 1999, although one piece of that plan was approved as a Habitat Conservation Plan (HCP) in 1992.

"From warfare to welfare" is a characterization of economic development facilitated by federal military support, which is an important ingredient in California's growth according to Shragge in *Boosters and Bluejackets* and Roger W. Lotchin in *Fortress California, 1910–1961: From Warfare to Welfare* (New York: Oxford University Press, 1992). The importance of federal subsidies for Sunbelt growth in general is a central concern of Joseph R. Feagin in *Free Enterprise City: Houston in Political-Economic Perspective* (New Brunswick, N.J.: Rutgers University Press, 1988) and Carl Abbott in *The Metropolitan Frontier: Cities in the Modern American West* (Tucson: University of Arizona Press, 1993). Manuel Castells refers in chapter 5 of *Informational City* to the policy shift from Great Society to Reaganomics, which Miller and Tucker also discuss in *Changing Plans,* calling it "the transition from the urban welfare state to the suburban warfare state." In this regard we can argue that San Diego has moved from warfare to welfare and back again.

3. When I studied residential segregation of Mexican-Americans in Monterrey County with Dennis McElrath at the University of California, Santa Cruz as an undergraduate, I identified this pattern in an unpublished 1973 paper titled "Residential Segregation in Monterrey County." The western pattern of segregation was evident when I was growing up in the San Diego suburbs in the 1960s. On the more typical national or northeastern segregation patterns, see Harvey Marshall, "White Flight to the Suburbs," *American Sociological Review* 44 (1979): 975–94. See also John Stahura, "Suburban Status Evolution/Persistence," *American Sociological Review* 44 (1979): 937–47.

4. San Diego County suburbs experienced speculative growth and overbuilding in the 1970s and 1980s and were able to build upon the experience of northern California cities, such as Petaluma, which had adopted growth control in the 1970s. See Richard Hogan, "Do Citizen Initiatives Affect Growth?" On learning and imitation, see Sam Cohn and Carol Conell, "Learning from Other People's Actions: Environmental Variation and Diffusion in French Coal Mining Strikes, 1890–1935," *American Journal of Sociology* 101 (1995): 366–403.

San Diego is a particularly appropriate case for the analysis of growth control and affordable housing because county voters approved a regional growth-control planning referendum in 1988 , which suggests local support for growth control. At the same time, however, San Diego was under intense pressure to provide its regional share of affordable housing, particularly after the City of San Diego lost a lawsuit (*Buena Vista Gardens Apartments Assocation v. City of San Diego Planning Department*) and its 1985 appeal. As a result of the lawsuit the city lost its authority to permit a planned residential community until the court was convinced that the city was meeting its obligation to provide affordable housing. See Hogan, "Do Citizen Initiatives Affect Growth?" 258.

San Diego was on the cutting edge of progressive planning, including growth control, as early as 1967, when it won the All-American City award. Guided by the Comprehensive Planning Organization (CPO), a 1966 countywide council of governments that presaged the San Diego Association of Governments (SANDAG) as the instrument of comprehensive regional planning, San Diego was committed to popular participation in planning. See Laura Ann Schiesl, "Problems in Paradise: Citizen Activism and Rapid Growth in San Diego, 1970–1990" (Senior Honor's Thesis, San Diego State University, Department of History, 1999), 14. See also Anthony W. Corso, "San Diego: The Anti-City." Both Corso and Schiesl document the ongoing struggle between citizens and planners in the negotiation of general plans in the 1960s and 1970s. Both view Pete Wilson's election as mayor in 1971 as a critical step in the development of comprehensive planning in general and growth management in particular. Neither seems to appreciate, however, the national context within which these events were occurring. In "'A New Federal City': San Diego during World War II," *Pacific Historical Review* 63 (1994): 333–61, Abraham Shragge is more cognizant of the national context.

None of these sources recognizes the role of national business and government coalitions in fostering the shift to comprehensive regional land-use planning in the 1970s. The Rockefeller Brothers Fund was instrumental in this regard. The first Rockefeller Brothers Task Force, which included Mayor Pete Wilson, proposed national land-use planning modeled on the procedural regulations associated with the National Environmental Policy Act (NEPA) of 1970. Clearly Natural Community Conservation Planning (NCCP), the model for comprehensive regional planning and smart growth in the closing years of the twentieth century, was the culmination of a plan that had been in the works in San Diego and in Washington, D.C., for decades. The NCCP proposed by Wilson's gubernatorial administration in 1992 was rooted in the governor's experience as a member of the task force twenty years earlier. See William K. Reilly, ed., *The Use of Land: A Citizen's Policy Guide to Urban Growth. A Task Force Report Sponsored by the Rockefeller Brothers Fund* (New York: Thomas Y. Crowell Co., 1973).

San Diego's suburbs, rather than the City of San Diego, are the focus of this analysis because the suburbs are generally more progressive in urban planning than is the central city. Thomas K. Rudel, in *Situations and Strategies in American Land-use Planning* (New York: Cambridge University Press, 1989), argues that suburbs are more progressive in facilitating the cooperation of developers and residents in trilateral negotiation. "In suburbs, developers make cooperative gestures toward interested homeowners associations; in cities . . . more frequently cooperation takes the form of collusion between developers and land-use commissioners" (28).

Jon C. Teaford, in *City and Suburb*, argues that, contrary to popular belief, suburbanites were the leaders of the progressive reform movements promoting comprehensive metropolitan planning through county councils (4, 122).

Notes to Chapter 1

1. Donald Appleyard and Kevin Lynch, *Temporary Paradise? A Look at the Special Landscape of the City of San Diego* (a 1974 report to the City of San Diego, located in the Government Documents section of the University of California, San Diego, library), 44, emphasis in original. *Regional* in this report generally means countywide or metropolitan, which is the level of planning authority that is deemed necessary. The natural community is international, however, and the proposal explicitly calls for cooperation between San Diego and Tijuana.

2. What I call progressive planning is cutting-edge planning that might once have been called modern. A more extensive discussion and a definition of the term *progressive* are offered in note 20 (below).

How and why this change toward big-picture planning occurred need not concern us here. For present purposes, it suffices to note that economic and political crises from 1970 to 1989 inspired city governments to seek creative solutions to the political and fiscal constraints associated with speculative growth and grassroots revolt. For more on this topic, see Richard Hogan, "Do Citizen Initiatives Affect Growth? The Case of Five San Diego Suburbs," in *Research in Community Sociology,* ed. Dan A. Chekki (New York: JAI Press, 1997), 249–75.

3. Zoning law specifies types of activity (e.g., industrial, commercial, residential) and, more recently, physical dimensions of the envelope within which construction is permitted. On architecture and zoning see Michael Kwartler, "Legislating Aesthetics: The Role of Zoning in Designing Cities," and on legal restrictions see Robert A. Williams Jr., "Euclid's Lochnerian Legacy," both in *Zoning and the American Dream: Promises Still to Keep,* ed. Charles M. Haar and Jerome S. Kayden (Chicago: Planners Press, 1989).

4. Appleyard and Lynch, *Temporary Paradise?* 45; emphasis in original.

5. Ibid.

6. The Natural Community Conservation Plan (NCCP) divides all undeveloped land into "preserves" (lands to be conserved as undeveloped or natural communities) and "development" (lands that might be developed). For our purposes *communities* refers to people who live and work in a geographically defined area. We could extend this concept to include plants and animals living in the area, but the distinction between *natural* and *developed* (unnatural?) is essentially arbitrary and political.

7. Appleyard and Lynch, *Temporary Paradise?* 45.

8. Ibid., 41.

To aid in the evaluation of the radical nature of these proposals, a little theory and a few definitions are in order. Political attitudes and interests are distinguished by the degree of optimism or pessimism concerning human nature, on the one hand, and the nature of established institutions, on the other. For present purposes institutions are defined as relatively enduring forms of social organization (e.g., republicanism and capitalism) that, for whatever reason, are viewed as integral components of a particular society. The following definition of political attitudes conforms to the general outline of my freshman political science professor, Thomas Ruth, from his course California Government (Grossmont College, El Cajon, California, spring 1970).

Conservatives are optimistic about established institutions—they think that republican capitalism is at least the lesser of available evils—and pessimistic about "common" people. They are inclined to think that good institutions are needed to protect us from ourselves. Liberals are similarly optimistic about established institutions but more optimistic about human nature, being inclined to think that given half a chance people will do the right thing. In contrast to conservatives, liberals are inclined to trust people more than established institutions. If people are behaving badly, liberals are inclined to blame the system and to suggest appropriate reforms.

Radicals take this liberal position to what liberals and conservatives consider the illogical, utopian extreme. Radicals are extremely optimistic about human nature and equally pessimistic about established institutions. Marx, for example, thought that people were inherently sociable and productive but were alienated from their human nature by an institutional order based on the exploitation of labor. He was so optimistic about human potential that he didn't offer a blueprint for utopian communism. He thought that the workers would figure it out for themselves. Marx's optimism regarding human nature is most apparent in his early, philosophical, writings. See Karl Marx, *The Economic and Philosophic Manuscripts of 1844* (New York: International Publishers, 1964), and "Introduction to a Critique of Political Economy," in *The German Ideology,* ed. C. J. Arthur (New York: International Publishers, 1970), especially p. 125. His pessimism regarding the instituted order is most developed in *Capital: A Critique of Political Economy,* 3 vols. (New York: International Publishers, 1967), especially in vol. 1, chapter 25. The closest Marx and Engels come to offering a blueprint is in "The German Ideology," in *The German Ideology,* ed. C. J. Arthur (New York: International Publishers, 1970), and in Marx's "Critique of the Gotha Program," in *The Marx-Engels Reader,* 2d edition, ed. Robert C. Tucker (1872; reprint, New York: W. W. Norton, 1978). Frederick Engels offers even less of a blueprint in *Socialism: Utopian and Scientific, with the Essay on the Mark,* trans. Edward Averling (New York: International Publishers, 1985). Compare this with, for example, V. I. Lenin, *What Is to Be Done? Burning Questions of Our Movement* (Peking: Foreign Languages Press, 1975).

Reactionaries are also pessimistic about the instituted order but are equally pessimistic about human nature. They are inclined to think that a good shotgun and a good plow are all that are really needed. The good life is menaced equally by people, who are inherently selfish and greedy, and by established systems, which tend to facilitate selfishness and greed.

9. See the previous note for a definition of *radical.* The assertion that big-picture planning is not radical enough is rooted in a radical perspective on the internal contradictions of republican capitalism. In a nutshell, the argument is that the proposed reform is too little, too late. See Harry Targ, *Strategy of an Empire in Decline* (Minneapolis: MEP, 1986).

On the California Coastal Act of 1972, see Paul Sabatier and David Mazmamian, "Regulating Coastal Land Use in California, 1973–1975," *Policy Studies Journal* 11, no. 1 (1982): 88–102. See also Richard G. Hildreth and Ralph W. Johnson, "CZM in California, Oregon, and Washington," *Natural Resources Journal* 25, no. 1 (1985): 103–165.

10. Thomas K. Rudel, in *Situations and Strategies in American Land-Use Planning* (New York: Cambridge University Press, 1989), 23–28, distinguishes among "bilateralism, legalism, and trilateralism," which he associates with slow-growth rural areas, the rapidly developing urban fringe, and slow-growth suburban settings, respectively. The argument about the development of legalism is essentially Rudel's (24).

Rudel thus associates different forms of land-use planning with different geographic settings that are distinguished by their relationship to the metropolitan center and to the regional market for land. His point is well taken. I would add only three qualifications. First, the difference between rural and suburban is socially constructed and historically situated. Second, these forms of land-use planning represent something of a historical progression: from prezoning (bilateral) to zoning (legal) to contemporary (trilateral) planning. Third, and finally, each form of planning incorporates elements of the previous forms. Thus, big-picture planning incorporates elements of all three earlier forms of land-use planning.

The contradictory interests in a community have been presented in a somewhat different form by John R. Logan and Harvey Molotch, who in *Urban Fortunes: The Political Economy of Place* (Berkeley: University of California Press, 1987) associate the contradiction with the "use values" embraced by residents and the "market values" pursued by investors. Sidney Plotkin, in *Keep Out: The Struggle for Land Use Control* (Berkeley: University of California Press, 1987), associates the contradiction with "exclusive" (resident) and "inclusive" (investor) interests. The contradictory interests that plague U.S. communities are, in fact, rooted in the more general alienation of life and work, which is experienced by both residents and investors. Historically, the alienation of life and work can be traced to the late nineteenth century.

11. For the irrationality of legal rationality see Max Weber, *Economy and Society: An Outline of Interpretive Sociology,* ed. Guenther Roth and Claus Wittich (1956; reprint, Berkeley: University of California Press, 1978), on bureaucracy (223–31) and capitalism (63–107). See also Jürgen Habermas, *Lifeworld and System: A Critique of Functionalist Reason,* trans. Thomas McCarthy, vol. 2 of *The Theory of Communicative Action* (Boston: Beacon Press, 1987), particularly with regard to politics and communication. The professional interest of lawyers is not unlike professional interest in general which is, simply stated, the interest in promoting the profession and the professional approach (i.e., legalism).

12. The National Environmental Policy Act (NEPA) of 1970 marks the beginning of procedural environmental regulation, as exemplified by the Environmental Impact Report (EIR). This regulation specifies a process of public notification and, if deemed necessary, extensive analysis, in the form of an EIR, of the potential environmental impact of any proposed land-use project. There are no substantive guidelines—no particular uses, structures, or impacts that are required or prohibited. The procedures simply facilitate the mobilization of opposition and impose a complex set of legally mandated steps that must be followed in evaluating the environmental impact of a project. On NEPA passage, see Sherry Cable and Charles Cable, *Environmental Problems, Grassroots Solutions: The Politics of Grassroots Environmental Conflict* (New York: St. Martin's Press, 1995), x. See also State of California, *The California EIR Monitor* 14, no. 4 (Sacramento: Secretary for Resources, 1988); and on NEPA, see William K. Reilly, ed., *The Use of Land: A Citizen's Policy Guide to Urban Growth. A Task Force Report Sponsored by the Rockefeller Brothers Fund* (New York: Thomas Y. Crowell Co., 1973), 71–73.

13. The State of California has mandated general plans for future development since 1967, but such plans were considered, at least initially, as recommendations rather than requirements. General plans that include a housing element explaining how the city will meet its housing needs have been required since 1971 and have become increasingly important and more comprehensive since then. As California's attorney general explained in 1975, "It is apparent that the [general] plan is, in short, a constitution for all future development within the city" (McCutchen, Doyle, Brown & Enersen, "Shaping Future Development in a Slow-Growth Era, A McCutchen Land Use Seminar" (San Francisco: McCutchen, Doyle, Brown & Enersen, 1989), 5.

Master plans are elaborate proposals for large-scale development projects in areas that are zoned as planned communities. In rapidly growing suburban cities in San Diego these master-plan communities are instrumental in implementing the goals of the general plan. In neighboring Orange County the bulk of new development is in planned communities, particularly in the projects of the Irvine Company and, more recently, in Mission Viejo.

14. For our purposes a profession can be defined as an organization that defend a particular expert (disciplinary or paradigmatic) approach. Professionals are members who are educated or trained in this approach, which is promoted among members of the profession as an end in itself—as an inherently valuable approach, or a calling—and among potential consumers or employers as an effective means toward a variety of ends, such as the provision of a useful or indispensable service or tool.

In this sense, the professional is disinterested—not motivated by ulterior class or status interests (like the biologist who doesn't live or work in southern California but consults on the Natural Community Conservation Plan). At the same time, however, the profession is interested in promoting its professional approach, as Andrew Abbott has indicated in *The System of Professions: An Essay on the Division of Expert Labor* (Chicago: University of Chicago Press, 1988). This is, essentially, the definition of professional interest.

15. Comprehensive regional planning was routinely praised as an ideal, at least, by all of the professional planners, including public- and private-sector planners, whom I met in 1992. *Big-picture planning* was the term that they used to represent this ideal.
The San Diego Association of Governments (SANDAG) became the effective regional planning authority, gradually assuming control of planning for transportation, housing, and growth control, and habitat conservation. In 1966 the Comprehensive Planning Organization (CPO) was formed. In the course of the 1970s, CPO was designated by the State of California as the regional transportation planning agency (1971) and was charged with implementation of federal and state clean-air acts (1978) and preparation of regional housing needs statements (1979). In 1980 the CPO was renamed SANDAG. The following year SANDAG released its first regional housing needs statement (Agenda Report R-36, November 16, 1981; dates above from SANDAG's website: <www.sandag.cog.ca.us>).

A variety of federal, state, and local interests were promoting comprehensive regional planning in the 1970s. The Rockefeller Brothers Fund sponsored a Task Force on Land Use and Urban Growth, which published its report in 1973 (William K. Reilly, ed., *The Use of Land*). Here was a national call for comprehensive planning. The task force reported that "the small scale of most development remains a major obstacle to quality development" (28) and recommended a federal land-use law that would enable states "to regulate all large-scale development" (72).

Pete Wilson, the mayor of San Diego, was a member of this task force and clearly supported comprehensive regional planning in his city. Toward that end, the San Diego city planning department commissioned the analysis that produced *Temporary Paradise?* in 1974. In the technical appendix, "An Environmental Planning Process for San Diego," report authors Appleyard and Lynch stress the extent to which environmental planning "is a *regional* problem" (2) and point toward the lack of regional planning authority. "The CPO, which might be the ideal location for an environmental design effort, is primarily an advisory body" (2). The CPO also recognized this problem and recommended, in 1972, that a regional authority be established to develop and administer plans to meet regional housing needs. See Comprehensive Planning Organization of the San Diego Region, "Housing Needs of the San Diego Region" (unpublished report located in the Government Documents section of the University of California, San Diego, library, December 1972.

In this regard, the expressed interests of professional planners, as represented by the San Diego city planning department, the consultants that they hired (Appleyard and Lynch), and the Comprehensive Planning Organization (CPO) is clear. All were promoting comprehensive regional (big-picture) planning between 1972 and 1974.

16. Comprehensive regional affordable housing plans were promoted by the Comprehensive Planning Organization in its December 1972 report, "Housing Needs of the San Diego Region." Comprehensive regional habitat conservation was essentially what Appleyard and Lynch were proposing in *Temporary Paradise?* In both cases professional planners were promoting big-picture planning.

17. *Class* refers to a position in the social relations of producing and reproducing the necessities of life, which are, of course, socially and culturally defined. This includes the relationship to the socially necessary means of production and reproduction, the product that is produced or reproduced, and other classes. Class interest, most generally, is focused on the goal of securing the basis for class-based control—specifically, control of the means of production, the product, and other classes.

Status refers to lifestyle or consumer behavior. To the extent that status provides the basis for collective action, its collective interest is to secure the basis, or means, for achieving the necessities or luxuries associated with a particular lifestyle.

Party refers to power, the ability to get what you want despite resistance. Party interests are organized to secure the basis for exercising power, specifically, the office, the access to office holders, the resources (primarily labor and capital), and the organization that provide the partisan with power.

Weber's class, status, and party interests (926–940 in *Economy and Society*) have been used as a basis for developing a pluralist perspective on political partisanship. See, for example, Robert A. Dahl, *Who Governs?* (New Haven, Conn.: Yale University Press, 1961).

The economic and political interest in reform is routinely debated by conservatives and liberals, who attempt to associate reform with the interests of the people (Dahl, *Who Governs?*) or the power elite (C. Wright Mills, *The Power Elite* [New York: Oxford University Press, 1956]; G. William Domhoff, *Who Rules America Now?* [Englewood Cliffs, N.J.: Prentice Hall, 1983]). In these debates both parties accept the Weberian concept of multidimensional—class, status, and party—interests. They disagree, primarily, on the extent to which these interests are crosscutting or superimposed, shifting or stable.

Weber, in *Economy and Society,* clearly viewed these interests as crosscutting (relatively independent) and shifting. As Weber explains, "When the bases of acquisition and distribution of goods are relatively stable, stratification by status is favored. Every technological repercussion and economic transformation threatens stratification by status and pushes the class situation into the foreground" (938).

Although I think that Weber was correct in recognizing the relationship between class struggle and social change, I would suggest that the implied causes and consequences are problematic. Specifically, class, status, and party interests diverge in the process of capital accumulation and state building as life, work, and politics become increasingly alienated activities. They converge, however, in the process of political struggle, becoming essentially indistinguishable in revolutionary situations.

In revolutionary situations, such as France of 1789, the struggle for control of commodities—in France's case, food riots—might escalate to encompass production and entitlement. In such a status conflict, the alienation of life and work, reproduction and production, are contested. Thus the class-status distinctions dissolve as both class and status conflicts escalate. Aside from such revolutionary situations, however—in normal, nonrevolutionary republican capitalist politics—the distinctive struggles of status and class interests are apparent.

Environmentalists who oppose development in natural communities, or undeveloped wilderness areas, are challenging not just the sale or rent of nature but the means of producing community. In some sense the no-growth movement also shifts from value and price to means of production, although no-growth advocates generally oppose the production of housing rather than the means of producing it. Neither environmentalists nor no-growth advocates appear to be interested in considering the problem of entitlement, however, with the exception of the radical environmentalists, who challenge private property rights, or individual legal entitlements, in their defense of environmental rights, or collective moral entitlements. The extent to which those concerned with status, particularly the environmentalists, challenge the legal rights of property and of capitalist enterprise may be the best predictor of where political challenges in the United States are heading in the twenty-first century.

18. See Hogan, "Do Citizen Initiatives Affect Growth?" on the building depression of the early 1990s. The irony of carpenters who need homes clearly indicates the alienation of life and work and the corresponding independence of status interests (homeownership) from class interests (employment in building homes). If carpenters need homes they should, perhaps, build them: "from each according to ability, to each according to need" (Karl Marx, "Critique of the Gotha Program"). That would, however, be socialism. Instead, Habitat for Humanity provides homes to the dependent population, relying on voluntary, often unskilled labor rather than promoting independent proprietorships in which people build their own houses to meet their own needs. See the discussion in the previous note on status versus class interests.

19. People tend to associate the conservative perspective with developers. Some developers, however, particularly the more enlightened ones, are more liberal in attitude and even interests. Some Fortune 500 developers tend toward corporate liberalism. Private-sector planners, aside from having a professional interest in big-picture planning and espousing whatever personal attitudes and interests they might possess, represent, as a condition of employment or as a result of class circumstance, the interests of developers.

The extent to which planners, as a class rather than as a profession, are organized in opposition to their employers (as a class "for themselves") appears to be quite limited. My impression is that the cleavage between public-sector and private-sector planners is a major barrier to the organization of planners—as a profession or a class.

To the extent that private-sector planners face larger but less reliable income, they share with other small capitalists and self-employed workers an aversion to anything that might upset their slender margin of profit. Thus, the class circumstance or experience of private-sector planners may influence their attitudes, producing a tendency for them to be more conservative. Class circumstance may also create a tendency for conservatives to be attracted to private-sector planning.

There is no doubt that cohort and previous life experience can affect class attitudes or the subjective evaluation of class interests. People who were hippies in the 1960s may continue to espouse more radical attitudes and interests than others, for example, although it seems that life experience in the movement and at work matters more than birth cohort. See Barbara Epstein, *Political Protest and Cultural Revolution: Nonviolent Direct Action in the 1970s and 1980s* (Berkeley: University of California Press, 1991);

Doug McAdam, "Gender As a Mediator of the Activist Experience: The Case of Freedom Summer," *American Journal of Sociology* 97 (1992): 1211–40.

In a personal letter to me, Tom, who graduated from high school with me, wrote, "I considered myself a socialist in college, but over the intervening years, the utter failure of communist and socialist countries has blunted my early enthusiasm for such political structure. I am now absolutely convinced that the fundamental problem with such structure is that human nature (Mother Theresa notwithstanding) [is] self-centered, and that there is nothing that we can do about this."

Clearly, those of us who continue to work in the public sector can more easily accommodate the radicalism of our youth in the class circumstance of our present professional lives. This seems to be true even for those of us who have achieved fame and glory, including some who claim six-figure family incomes. Such deviant cases undermine the simple correlation between left-leaning political attitudes and family income.

Most of my respondents distinguished no-growth interests from environmental interests, which clearly differ in their perception of good development. Dan, an environmental biologist, explained, "Good development means a small footprint. Build up, not out. Build inside the urban area." Steve, an environmentalist who is not a biologist, offered a similar characterization of good development, describing it as "in-fill, transit-oriented, greater density." In contrasting this view with the perspectives of other partisans, he explained that "local government is pro-growth/pro-sprawl [and the] general public sees higher density as evil."

There is, however, tremendous variety in the environmental movement. Established social-movement organizations, such as World Wildlife, sell stuffed animals and pieces of the rain forest to middle-class liberals, and challenging groups, such as Earth First!, engage in industrial sabotage and guerrilla theater.

Most important for present concerns is that environmentalists, who advocate the inclusive principle of sharing the earth, are cooperating with the exclusionary no-growth movement, which, like tax revolt, coastal protection, and growth-control movements, for example—tends to create problems that progressive planners and enlightened developers attempt to accommodate. In this regard a liberal critique would argue that the environmentalists are on the wrong side. From a radical perspective, however, the coalition with no-growth interests might facilitate a revolutionary break within environmentalist and liberal interests: they must choose whether to accommodate reactionaries and repress radicals or accommodate radicals and fight reactionaries. Of course, the radicals support the liberals only when the liberals are prepared to fight the reactionaries, not when they cooperate with the conservatives in defending public order.

20. I differ with Robert H. Wiebe, *Businessmen and Reform: A Study of the Progressive Movement* (Cambridge, Mass.: Harvard University Press, 1962; reprint, Chicago: Ivan R. Dee, 1989), in identifying professionals as a new class. We agree, however, on their interest in progressive reform. For our purposes, changes in established institutions that are promoted and defended as necessary or desirable might be considered progress. Those who promote and defend such changes might be considered progressives.

More generally, in American history the term *progressive* refers to a social movement, a political party, and an era of political reform in the United States between 1900 and 1929. Although I use the term more generally to include big-picture planning in the late twentieth century, my definition seems to cover both early- and late-twentieth-century progressivism. In fact, early and late progressivism are sufficiently similar that one might argue that they represent an ongoing social movement, despite the wax and wane of progressive challenges. See Verta Taylor, "Social Movement Continuity: The Women's

Movement in Abeyance," *American Sociological Review* 54 (1989): 761–75, on continuity in the women's movement; and Sidney Tarrow, *Power in Movement: Social Movements, Collective Action, and Politics* (New York: Cambridge University Press, 1994), chapter 9, on cycles.

Wiebe, in *Businessmen and Reform,* describes the Progressive issues and interests of the early twentieth century as follows.

> The many voices of the progressives concerned themselves with three general issues: regulation of the economy to harness its leaders and to distribute more widely its benefits; modifications in government to make elected representatives more responsive to the wishes of the voters; and assistance for the dispossessed to open before them a richer life in America. The first issue cast the widest net. Among those prominent in the movements for a regulated economy were businessmen and farmers after greater profits, politicians in need of an issue, journalists in search of a story, a new class of economic and administrative specialists looking for ways to utilize their knowledge, and clergymen hoping to re-establish morality in industrial America. (6–7)

The issues that united progressives of the early twentieth century are quite similar to the issues that unite the proponents of big-picture planning. First and foremost they call for regulation. At the same time, however, they are concerned with government accountability and issues of social justice, which are, now as then, more controversial.

21. If we consider political interests in general as expedients or mechanisms for defending class or status, then the organized interests that support progressive reform in both national and local, early- and late-twentieth-century U.S. political struggles can be reduced to the following class, status, and party interests: Classes support reform to the extent that they are organized in defense of their control of the means of production, the products, and their relations with other classes, and they view reform as a means to achieve these goals. Similarly, status interests that are organized to secure their control of the production, value and price, and distribution of the necessities and luxuries of life, and of the entitlement to those goods, support reform to the extent that it appears to advance these goals. Established political parties—which are, by definition, organized in pursuit of power—support reform in order to increase or sustain their control of offices and access to officials, as well as their organization, membership, contributions, and other such political resources.

To these, class, status, and party interests I would add professional interests, particularly the interests of the professional planners.

22. On ballot-box planning, see William Fulton, *Guide to California Planning* (Point Arena, Calif.: Solano Press, 1991). Generally progressive reform accommodates liberal and conservative interests in maintaining the established institutional order. At the same time, progressive interests that promote reform routinely clash with radical interests that promote revolution.

23. See Fred P. Bosselman and David Callies, *The Quiet Revolution in Land Use Control* (Washington, D.C.: U.S. Government Printing Office, 1972).

24. Charles Tilly, *The Contentious French: Four Centuries of Popular Struggle* (Cambridge, Mass.: Harvard University Press, 1986), chapter 12, especially pp. 395–98, explains four centuries of struggle in France in relation to state-making and capital-accumulation processes.

25. On the California Coastal Act of 1972, see Sabatier and Mazmamian, "Regulating

Coastal Land Use"; and Hildreth and Johnson, "CZM in California, Oregon, and Washington." On SANDAG see note 15 (above).

26. See William A. Fischel, *Regulatory Takings: Law, Economics, and Politics* (Cambridge, Mass.: Harvard University Press, 1995), for an opposing view. Fischel argues that it was the California courts that hindered development. Also, on SANDAG's involvement in regional growth control since 1988, see SANDAG, "Protecting Region's Quality of Life is Growth Strategy Aim," *Association News* (spring/summer 1991): 2.

27. On habitat conservation, see California, State of, Assembly Bill 2172 (the Kelly Bill establishing the NCCP) (Sacramento: Legislative Council, March 1991). See also other California state documents published by the secretary for resources in Sacramento: "Memorandum of Understanding by and between the California Department of Fish and Game and the United States Fish and Wildlife Service Regarding Coastal Sage Scrub Natural Community Conservation Planning in Southern California" (December 1991); *The Resources Agency of California Annual Report* (January 1992); "NCCP Special Report No. 1" (February 1992); and the "Natural Community Conservation Plan Draft Process Guidelines" (April 1992).

28. See "Why San Diego Suburbs" in the introduction for a discussion of why I selected San Diego's suburbs for this study.

29. This argument is developed in Richard Hogan, *Class and Community in Frontier Colorado* (Lawrence: University Press of Kansas, 1990), chapter 1, especially 14–16.

30. On the demise of independent households, see Christopher Clark, *The Roots of Rural Capitalism: Western Massachusetts, 1780–1860* (Ithaca, N.Y.: Cornell University Press, 1990). The decline of "subsistence plus" production by yeomen farmers is described by Allan Kulikoff, "The Transition to Capitalism in Rural America," *William and Mary Quarterly,* 3d series, 46 (January 1989): 120–44. On the demise of artisans, particularly miners, see Hogan, *Class and Community in Frontier Colorado.* All of these changes might be considered as elements in the general process of proletarianization or capital accumulation.

Capital accumulation and the alienation of life and work proceeded in tandem in the course of the nineteenth century. In the twentieth-century United States the alienation of life and work is manifested in the distinctive class and status interests of the home-owning employee. See Kenneth T. Jackson, *Crabgrass Frontier: The Suburbanization of the United States* (New York: Oxford University Press, 1985), and David Harvey, "Labor, Capital, and Class Struggle around the Built Environment," *Politics and Society* 6 (1976): 265–95.

31. See Jackson, *Crabgrass Frontier,* chapter 8. On the conflict between the home world and the work world, see Habermas, *Lifeworld and System.*

32. Plotkin, *Keep Out,* 74.

33. Even at the neighborhood level the apparent social-class difference in exclusionary interests is probably only true of expressed interests. Such apparent social-class differences seem to reflect differences in access to public-policy decisions rather than differences in the interests of wealthy and poor residents. See Laurie Graham and Richard Hogan, "Social Class and Tactics: Neighborhood Opposition to Group Homes," *Sociological Quarterly* 31, no. 4 (1990): 513–29.

On the tax revolt of 1978, see Clarence Y. H. Lo, *Small Property versus Big Government: The Social Origins of the Property Tax Revolt* (Berkeley: University of California Press, 1990). On growth control, see Hogan, "Do Citizen Initiatives Affect Growth?"

Growth-control and, particularly, no-growth movements are clearly exclusionary. The tax revolt, which resulted in relief only for those who owned property in 1978, was also clearly exclusionary. The California Coastal Act of 1972, which preserved the coast for the general public, was in theory, and to some extent in practice, inclusionary. The extent to which inclusive coastal and environmental protection interests have come to be allied with exclusive no-growth interests is considered in more depth in chapters 4 and 5 and in the discussion of "The Problem of Popular Participation" (below).

34. Quoted in Jackson, *Crabgrass Frontier,* 151.

35. One critic of capitalism who viewed private property as a fetter on capital accumulation—or efficient land use—was Marx (*Capital,* 3:748–72). On use value and exchange value, see Logan and Molotch, *Urban Fortunes;* on farmers and speculators, see Allan Bogue, "Social Theory and the Pioneer," *Agricultural History* 34 (1960): 21–34.

36. Pluralists, such as Dahl (*Who Governs?*), argue that the government represents the people. Proponents of the growth-machine perspective, such as Logan and Molotch, (*Urban Fortunes*), contend that city governments are essentially servants of speculative interests. Hogan, in *Class and Community in Frontier Colorado,* argues that both are, in some sense, right.

37. Rudel argues, in *Situations and Strategies in American Land-Use Planning,* that legal formalism characterizes land-use planning in rapidly growing exurban regions at the perimeter of metropolitan areas, but that trilateral negotiation involving government, developers, and local residents characterizes the planning process in established suburban communities. While it is not apparent that legal formalism has been abandoned in the suburbs, it is clearly true that elaborate public relations efforts that diverge sharply from the legal-formal model have been incorporated into the planning process, particularly in efforts to develop or modify the city's general plan for development.

Sociologists offer various opinions about the potency of grassroots opposition to the growth machine. Growth-machine theorists tend to be skeptical about the potential for grassroots influence, suggesting that even "successful" growth-control movements do not affect growth. See, for example, John R. Logan and Min Zhou, "Do Suburban Growth Controls Control Growth?" *American Sociological Review* 54 (1989): 461–71. Others, including Hogan, in "Do Citizen Initiatives Affect Growth?" suggest that citizen-initiated growth control does have some effect in inspiring certain types of legislation. Still others have argued that effective grassroots movements must encompass interclass coalitions. Roger V. Gould, in *Insurgent Identities: Class, Community, and Protest in Paris from 1848 to the Commune* (Chicago: University of Chicago Press, 1995), has focused on the interclass, neighborhood-based coalitions in the Paris Commune of 1871. Lo, in *Small Property versus Big Government,* has indicated that suburban property owners could not have effectively mounted the tax revolt of 1978 without the support of shopkeepers and business owners who also sought tax relief.

38. Sociologists from Weber (*Economy and Society*) to Habermas (*Lifeworld and System*) have developed the critique of legal formalism suggested by the private-sector planners.

39. This master-plan community will be considered in more detail in the next chapter (chapter 2).

40. The problem of the lagoon will be considered in more detail in the discussion of development and habitat conservation (in chapter 4).

41. Hogan, "Do Citizen Initiatives Affect Growth?"

42. Kitty Calavita and Henry N. Pontell, "The Savings and Loan Crisis," in *Corporate and Governmental Deviance,* ed. M. David Erman and Richard J. Lundman (New York: Oxford University Press, 1992).

43. Weber, *Economy and Society*, 223. Weber was convinced that this was equally true of communist or socialist systems. We could certainly extend this criticism of republican capitalism to Soviet state socialism, but that would take us far beyond our current concerns.

Regarding the iron cage, Max Weber, in *The Protestant Ethic and the Spirit of Capitalism* (1958; reprint, New York: Charles Scribner's Sons, 1976, 181), said of the spirit of capitalism, "The Puritan wanted to work in a calling; we are forced to do so."

44. On commitment to popular participation, see Appleyard and Lynch, *Temporary Paradise?*, 45. The vast literature on Locally Unwanted Land Uses (LULUs) and exclusionary, not-on-my-backyard (NIMBY) neighborhood sentiments suggests that potential neighborhood opposition is the rule rather than the exception, regardless of the location or the nature of the proposed project. See Graham and Hogan, "Social Class and Tactics: Neighborhood Opposition to Group Homes." On racial and class discrimination in siting unwanted facilities, see Robert D. Bullard, *Dumping in Dixie: Race, Class, and Environmental Quality* (Boulder, Colo.: Westview Press, 1990); on the importance of neighborhood organization in opposition, see Richard Hogan, "Community Opposition to Group Homes," *Social Science Quarterly* 67 (1986): 442–49.

45. See State of California, *State CEQA Guidelines* (Sacramento: Secretary for Resources, 1989). See also, Michael H. Remy, Tina A. Thomas, and James G. Moose, *Guide to the California Environmental Quality Act (CEQA)* (Point Arena, Calif.: Solano Press Books, 1991). The 1986 Castleton Environmental Impact Report runs well over five hundred pages, more than half of which are in unnumbered appendices. This 1986 EIR for a master-plan community is quite a bit longer and more detailed than the 1990 general plan for the neighboring city of Farmington, which is substantially larger than Castleton.

46. The Sierra Club is another example of a social movement organization. See John Lofland, *Social Movement Organizations: Guide to Research on Insurgent Realities* (New York: Aldine de Gruyter, 1996). On neighborhood opposition, more generally, see Graham and Hogan, "Social Class and Tactics"; Robert D. Bullard, *Dumping in Dixie*; Hogan, "Community Opposition to Group Homes."

47. William A. Gamson, in *The Strategy of Social Protest* (Chicago: Dorsey Press, 1975), chapter 3, defines *co-optation* as recognizing interest groups as legitimate without granting them any other advantages. He defines *preemption* as granting new advantages but not recognition. Aside from a tendency to co-opt the organized and preempt the unorganized, there appears to be a pattern of preemption when times are good and thus political opportunity is greater and co-optation when times are bad and there is less political opportunity.

48. On issue attention or focus, see Christian Joppke, "Social Movements during Cycles of Issue Attention: The Decline of the Anti-Nuclear Energy Movements in West Germany and the USA," *British Journal of Sociology* 42 (1991): 43–60.

For a different perspective on popular opinion and political frames, see William A. Gamson and Andre Modigliani, "Media Discourse and Public Opinion on Nuclear Power," *American Journal of Sociology* 95 (1989): 1–37, and William A. Gamson, *Talking Politics* (New York: Cambridge University Press, 1992). My fieldwork in San Diego County in 1992 tended to support this social constructionist perspective on popular versus official frames. Specifically, what politicians and planners view as the critical issues facing the city are frequently not the issues that are the focus of public opinion or the media. In one suburban community the government sponsored a huge public relations effort to inspire public interest in a general plan revision that incorporated growth control, affordable housing, open space, and habitat conservation programs. Nevertheless, the local newspaper and the general public seemed to be most agitated about a sculpture in a city park. One private-sector planner offered this as evidence that the general public is irrational and given to enthusiasms. From my perspective, this simply indicates the extent to which popular political frames are not simply imposed by governments as a hegemonic meaning system but are, instead, developed in opposition to official frames.

49. On contradictory exclusionary versus inclusionary interests, see Plotkin, *Keep Out*.

Political parties and consensus movements, like "liberal" environmentalism and "conservative" opposition to drunk drivers, are able to gain considerable popular support because they can accommodate contradictory class, status, and party interests. They do this by appealing to political icons—natural resources, mothers, and children, for example—that are so politically charged that no one except wild-eyed radicals dares to challenge them. For this reason even builders and developers present themselves as environmentalists. On icons, see Andrew Szasz, *EcoPopulism: Toxic Waste and the Movement for Environmental Justice* (Minneapolis: University of Minnesota Press, 1994), 62–63.

There is a debate on whether these consensus movements are capable of producing social change. John D. McCarthy and Mark Wolfson, in "Consensus Movements, Conflict Movements, and the Co-optation of Civic and State Structures," argue for the efficacy of consensus movements, while Michael Schwartz and Shuva Paul, in "Resource Mobilization versus the Mobilization of People: Why Consensus Movements Cannot Be Instruments of Social Change," argue against this proposition. Both of these essays are published in Aldon D. Morris and Carol McClurg Mueller, eds., *Frontiers in Social Movement Theory* (New Haven, Conn.: Yale University Press, 1992). If *change* means change *of*, rather than *in*, the system then my opinion is that consensus movements, like all reform movements, are incapable of producing institutional change.

The no-growth movement includes a variety of grassroots movements usually identified with a handful of local residents who are leaders in a variety of campaigns and form a series of organizations with names like "Save Open Space" (SOS), "Friends of Mission Bay," or "Project Future." In some cases it appears that these organizations share members with the environmentalists. In Castleton the local Audubon Society is well represented in no-growth organizations. Thus, as Lou, the Habitat Protection Committee facilitator, noted, the no-growth and environmentalist movements are overlapping to some extent, at least in this one suburban city.

More important than the overlapping membership in local organizations is the existence of intermediate umbrella organizations composed of existing organizations that have local and national constituencies (see Aldon Morris, *The Origins of the Civil Rights Movement* [New York: Free Press, 1984], on importance of such organizations in the Civil Rights Movement). One such umbrella organization, Southern California Habitat Defenders, led by Steve, is able to bridge the gap to some extent between local and national organizations by including local Audubon Society chapters. This umbrella organization is at least indirectly involved in the NCCP negotiations at the state and regional level, where the Nature Conservancy is a leading actor, but, given its organization and interests, it is primarily focused on local negotiations to save large portions of threatened habitat. In the NCCP and local Habitat Conservation Plans in San Diego County and Orange County all of the major players are involved to some extent, but for the most part they are working at cross-purposes.

50. On the self-fulfilling prophecy, see Robert Merton, *Social Theory and Social Structure* (New York: Free Press, 1957). Local government is in varying degrees vulnerable to grassroots political challenges. See Doug McAdam, *Political Process and the Development of Black Insurgency, 1930–1970* (Chicago: University of Chicago Press,

1982); Sidney Tarrow, *Power in Movement;* Charles Tilly, *From Mobilization to Revolution* (Reading, Mass.: Addison-Wesley, 1978). This vulnerability creates opportunities for organized interests to gain new advantages or to fight for increased access to policy makers. The ability to take advantage of these opportunities is limited, however, not only by resources and organization, but also, at least indirectly, by interests (or goals) and tactics.

Aside from the conflicting interests and organizational and tactical problems within the coalition, the grassroots movements suffer from a conspiracy, or conflict, theory of land-use planning, which discourages attempts to negotiate on big-picture solutions. The fact that they don't trust local government makes it difficult for them to gain the privileges of membership, which come at the price of loyalty. This is, in part, why they tend to get preempted even when they have already been co-opted. On trust, see William A. Gamson, *Power and Discontent* (Homewood, Ill.: Dorsey Press, 1968), chapter 3. On loyalty, see Albert O. Hirschman, *Exit, Voice, and Loyalty* (Cambridge, Mass.: Harvard University Press, 1970).

Obviously both radicals and reactionaries might not be inclined to trust local government—or republican institutions more generally. Theoretically, however, the liberal environmentalist and conservative growth-control agenda could be accommodated within the progressive coalition promoting big-picture planning. Here it seems that local liberals and conservatives are effectively excluding themselves by uncritically accepting a conspiracy, or conflict, theory of local politics. The growth-machine perspective in particular offers deceptively simple but potentially dangerous ideological support. Defining the issue as growth implies that environmentalists and no-growth advocates share a common interest. In fact, each movement faces a similar but distinctive challenge.

Specifically, liberal environmentalists must choose between working within the system by joining the progressive coalition (as the Nature Conservancy has done) or fighting against the progressive coalition (as Sierra Club appears to be doing and as the Habitat Defenders clearly is doing). For the environmentalists, fighting against the system implies at least the possibility of a coalition with the radicals, which is, in my opinion, long overdue. For the no-growth advocates, the benefits of joining the progressive coalition come at the cost of redefining *no growth* as "growth control." The alternative, which seems to be the modal San Diego suburban strategy, is to join the reactionaries in fighting the government, the liberals, and the conservatives. If both no-growth and environmental interests followed their extremists and challenged the government and the progressive coalition, this would expand the intensity of the political challenge. Such expansion or escalation would further the possibilities for revolutionary challenges, given economic and political conditions that might facilitate political opportunities. See Tarrow, *Power in Movement*. Needless to say, this is the path the radicals would like to follow.

51. On the extent to which the class bias in neighborhood influence on local government is attributable to access rather than organization, see Graham and Hogan, "Social Class and Tactics."

Notes to Chapter 2

1. Donald Appleyard and Kevin Lynch, *Temporary Paradise? A Look at the Special Landscape of the San Diego Region* (a 1974 report to the City of San Diego, located in the Government Documents section of the University of California, San Diego, library), 28.

2. Challengers do not create political opportunities but can, if they are organized and prepared to defend their claims, expand opportunities and create opportunities for other challengers whose claims sustain the cycle of collective action and political challenge. Thus, as one student of collective action and social change has suggested, people "make history, but they do not make it just as they please" (Karl Marx, "The Eighteenth Brumaire of Louis Bonaparte," in *The Marx-Engels Reader*, 2d ed., ed. Robert C. Tucker [1850; reprint, New York: W. W. Norton & Co., 1978, 595). In "moments of madness" it appears that all things are possible (see Aristide R. Zolberg, "Moments of Madness," *Politics and Society* 2 [1972]: 183–207), but as opportunities decline at the end of the cycle, challengers can only expect "a residue of reform" (Sidney Tarrow, *Power in Movement: Social Movements, Collective Action, and Politics* [New York: Cambridge University Press, 1994], 186).

In keeping with this political-process perspective, I will argue that there was a cycle of political opportunity in the late 1960s and early 1970s that provided opportunities for challengers, particularly environmentalists, to affect public policy by influencing federal and state legislation, especially with regard to land use. There was also a cycle of political opportunity in the late 1970s that inspired grassroots political challenges that continued through the 1980s, inspiring comprehensive regional planning, which now seems to characterize the planning process, particularly in California. In the early 1990s political opportunities for grassroots challengers were much more limited as legal formalism yielded the benefits of overregulation. At that time the irony of popular participation was that grassroots efforts seemed to increase local government's dependence on developers. The extent to which these findings might be generalized beyond San Diego County in 1992 is considered in chapters 1 and 5 and might be debated for years to come.

3. "Taking" refers to the legal limits on regulation or development. If regulation effectively prohibits any reasonable use of property this constitutes a "taking." At the same time, when development results in the unintended death of a threatened or endangered species, this also constitutes a "taking." Whether the government is taking land or the property owner is taking a species is generally clear in context. On the "taking" issue, see William A. Fischel, *Regulatory Takings: Law, Economics, and Politics* (Cambridge, Mass.: Harvard University Press, 1995).

For a Great Society liberal perspective on the 1960s metropolitan versus 1970s postmodern separatist interests, see Zane L. Miller and Bruce Tucker, *Changing Plans for America's Inner Cities: Cincinnati's Over-the-Rhine and Twentieth-Century Urbanism* (Columbus: Ohio State University Press, 1998). For the early-twentieth-century Progressive vision, see Charles A. Beard, *Contemporary American History, 1877–1913* (New York: Macmillan, 1914). On the New Deal, see Lizabeth Cohen, *Making a New Deal: Industrial Workers in Chicago, 1919–1939* (New York: Cambridge University Press, 1990). On the New Federalist—or postmodern, Reagan-Thatcher—vision of privatization, see David Harvey, *The Condition of Postmodernity: An Enquiry into the Origins of Cultural Change* (Cambridge, Mass.: Blackwell, 1990), chapter 4. See also M. Gottdiener, "Recapturing the Center: A Semiotic Analysis of Shopping Malls," in *The City and the Sign: An Introduction to Urban Semiotics*, ed. M. Gottdiener and Alexandros Ph. Lagopoulos (New York: Columbia University Press, 1986); Jean Baudrillard, "Simulacra and Simulations: Disneyland," in *Social Theory: The Multicultural and Classic Readings*, ed. Charles Lemert (1988; reprint, Boulder, Colo.: Westview Press, 1993). On public funding, see Joseph R. Feagin, *Free Enterprise City: Houston in Political-Economic Perspective* (New Brunswick, N.J.: Rutgers University Press, 1988).

4. San Diego was called the unconventional city after it was turned down as the site of the 1972 Republican Party convention. Although being unconventional was and is to some extent a point of pride, efforts to redevelop downtown included plans for the new convention center. What I call Yuppie Heaven was planned as an alternative to the unconventional city. On the 1972 convention, see Raymond G. Starr, *San Diego: A Pictorial History* (Norfolk, Va.: Donning, 1986), 223; on San Diego's unconventional nature, see, for example, p. 239 of Starr's book for the "Over the Line" World Championship tournaments.

5. On smart growth, see chapter five. The Eagles album *Hotel California* includes the song "Life in the Fast Lane," which is presumably annoying by design. The whining guitar and the repetitive lyrics contribute to the overall aversion to the "beautiful" people of Los Angeles and of southern California in general.

6. On downtown nightlife, Harbor Island, Hotel Del Coronado, La Jolla, and Del Mar, see Richard Pourade, *History of San Diego,* vol. 7 (San Diego: Union-Tribune Publishing, 1977).

7. On the exposition in the park, see Pourade, *History of San Diego,* vol. 5 (1965) and 7 (1977):176; on Sea World, see 7:239–46.

8. Pourade, *History of San Diego,* 7:229; Starr, *San Diego: A Pictorial History,* 60–61, 219.

9. On the first freeway, see Pourade, *History of San Diego,* 7:84–85; see also Starr, *San Diego: A Pictorial History,* 207). On the streetcar closing, see Pourade, *History of San Diego,* 7:80. On the walking city, see Kenneth T. Jackson, *Crabgrass Frontier: The Suburbanization of the United States* (New York: Oxford University Press, 1985), 14–15.

10. The completion data for freeways and the opening dates for the shopping centers were provided by SANDAG. Updates are available from SANDAG's website: <www.sandag.cog.ca.us>. Data on population growth are from SANDAG and its predecessor, CPO. For the 1960s, see Comprehensive Planning Organization of the San Diego Region, "San Diego Region 1970 Census: Subregional Area Data Tables and Computer Maps" (unpublished 1972 report located in the Government Documents section of the University of California, San Diego, library). For the 1970s and 1980s, see San Diego Association of Governments (SANDAG), *Regional Housing Needs Statement: San Diego Region* (San Diego: Source Point, 1990). See also "Growth Control Plans and Trends," *San Diego Association of Governments (SANDAG) Association News* (spring/summer 1991). See also, Pourade, *History of San Diego,* 7:145–63. On the state-wide freeway expansion program as it impacted other coastal cities, notably Ventura and Santa Barbara, see Harvey Molotch, William Freudenberg, and Krista E. Paulsen, "History Repeats Itself, but How? City Character, Urban Tradition, and the Accomplishment of Place," *American Sociological Review* 65 (2000): 791–823.

11. See Pourade, *History of San Diego,* 7:145–51, on Mission Valley and 7:196–97 on other shopping centers. See also Starr, *San Diego: A Pictorial History,* 207–11.

12. Comprehensive Planning Organization of the San Diego Region, "Housing Needs in the San Diego Region (unpublished report located in the Government Documents section of the University of California, San Diego, library); Appleyard and Lynch, *Temporary Paradise?* 45.

13. See Daniel Boorstin, *The Americans: The National Experience* (New York: Vintage, 1965). On boosters and boosterism, see Carl Abbott, *Boosters and Businessmen: Popular Economic Thought and Urban Growth in the Antebellum Middle West* (Westport, Conn.: Greenwood Press, 1981). On railroad wars, see Hogan, *Class*

and Community in Frontier Colorado (Lawrence: University Press of Kansas), 146–50, 168–78, and 196–203.

14. Appleyard and Lynch, *Temporary Paradise?* 34.

15. William K. Reilly, ed., *The Use of Land: A Citizen's Policy Guide to Urban Growth. A Task Force Report Sponsored by the Rockefeller Brothers Fund* (New York: Thomas Y. Crowell, 1973), 1; the list of twelve members precedes table of contents.

16. Fred Bosselman and David Callies, *The Quiet Revolution in Land Use Control* (Washington, D.C.: U.S. Government Printing Office, 1972).

17. On "balance," see William K. Reilly, ed., *Use of Land,* 19. The second task force report was published as Gerald O. Barney, ed., *The Unfinished Agenda: The Citizen's Policy Guide to Environmental Issues; A Task Force Report Sponsored by the Rockefeller Brothers Fund* (New York: Thomas Y. Crowell, 1977). On the Progressive alliance, see Robert H. Wiebe, *Businessmen and Reform: A Study of the Progressive Movement* (Cambridge, Mass.: Harvard University Press, 1962; reprint, Chicago: Ivan R. Dee, 1989). On racism, progressivism, and first-wave feminism, see Aileen S. Kraditor, *The Ideas of the Woman Suffrage Movement, 1890–1920* (New York, Columbia University Press, 1965; reprint, New York: W. W. Norton, 1981), and Angela Y. Davis, *Women, Race, and Class* (New York: Random House, 1981).

18. Economic boom-and-bust cycles engender cycles of political opportunity. A boom facilitates the mobilization of challengers, who have slack resources in times of economic growth, and provides authorities with the resources to grant concessions or to preempt challengers by offering them new advantages. An economic depression, or bust, makes authorities vulnerable because they face increasing demands for action but lack the resources to act. Consequently, those who are able to mount successful challenges during the boom years tend to be co-opted, if possible, during the bust years. If that is successful, the new coalition works toward some creative solution to the crisis. On cycles of opportunity and challenge, see Tarrow, *Power in Movement,* 83–85. On crises and successful challenges, see chapter 8 of William A. Gamson, *The Strategy of Social Protest* (Chicago: Dorsey Press, 1975).

19. In volume 4 (1964) of Pourade, *History of San Diego,* see chapter 1, the map of San Diego in 1870 on p. 68, and the chronology for the years 1865–1898 on pp. 253–54. On Old Town, see Pourade, *History of San Diego,* 7:245–49.

20. Ernst C. Griffin, "San Diego's Population Patterns," in *San Diego: An Introduction to the Region, An Historical Geography of the Natural Environments and Human Development of San Diego County,* ed. Philip R. Pryde (Dubuque, Iowa: Kendall/Hunt, 1976), 62.

21. Richard Hogan, "Do Citizen Initiatives Affect Growth? The Case of Five San Diego Suburbs," in *Research in Community Sociology,* ed. Dan A. Chekki (New York: JAI Press, 1997); San Diego Association of Governments (SANDAG), *Association News* (spring/summer 1991).

22. Unless otherwise indicated, figures reported in this discussion are from the U.S. Census Bureau, *County and City Data Book* (Washington D.C.: U.S. Government Printing Office, 1949–1994).

23. These figures are from U.S. Census Bureau, "U.S.A. County Statistics," 1990, available on CD-ROM at HSSE Library, Purdue University.

24. On the importance of military spending in earlier years, see Abraham J. Shragge "Boosters and Bluejackets: The Civic Culture of Militarism in San Diego, California, 1900–1945" (Ph.D. diss., University of California, San Diego, 1998); for recent shifts, see U.S. Census Bureau, "U.S.A. County Statistics."

25. U.S. Census Bureau, *County and City Data Book,* 1994.

26. Harvey's characterization of the postmodern condition, in *Condition of Postmodernity*, provides a particularly useful approach to "the speculative frenzy of 1972–1989." See also Hogan, "Do Citizen Initiatives Affect Growth?" Most important for present purposes is the nature of the postmodern speculative crisis.

27. Kitty Calavita and Henry N. Pontell, "The Savings and Loan Crisis," in *Corporate and Governmental Deviance*, ed. M. David Erman and Richard J. Lundman (New York: Oxford University Press, 1992). "Paper entrepreneurialism" is from David Harvey, *The Condition of Postmodernity: An Enquiry into the Origins of Cultural Change* (Cambridge, Mass.: Blackwell, 1990).

28. Statistics reported in Hogan, "Do Citizen Initiatives Affect Growth?"

29. After Pete Wilson served as mayor of San Diego, he was elected to the U.S. Senate in 1982 and as governor of California in 1990. On the Reagan years, see Arthur M. Schlesinger Jr., *The Almanac of American History* (New York: G. P. Putnam's Sons, 1983), 610. On Pete Wilson, see Laura Ann Schiesl, "Problems in Paradise: Citizen Activism and Rapid Growth in San Diego, 1970–1990" (Senior honor's thesis, San Diego State University, Department of History, 1999). See also Anthony W. Corso, "San Diego: The Anti-City," in *Sunbelt Cities: Politics and Growth since World War II*, ed. Richard M. Bernard and Bradley R. Rice (Austin: University of Texas Press, 1983).

30. For the boomtowns of the 1960s, see Comprehensive Planning Organization of the San Diego Region, "San Diego Region 1970 Census." For the boomtowns of the 1970s and 1980s, see San Diego Association of Governments (SANDAG), *Regional Housing Needs Statement*, 1990.

31. Shragge, *Boosters and Bluejackets*.

32. On Earth Day and early environmental activism, see Harry Potter, "Precursors of Ecopopulism," paper presented at the American Sociological Association meeting, New York, 1996. On other events, see Schlesinger, *Almanac of American History*, 587–90. On environmental legislation, see Sherry Cable and Charles Cable, *Environmental Problems, Grassroots Solutions* (New York: St. Martin's Press, 1995).

33. On the endangered Species Act (ESA), see Cable and Cable, *Environmental Problems*; on Nixon, Vietnam, and the draft, see Schlesinger, *Almanac of American History*, 594.

34. On the California Coastal Act, see Paul Sabatier and Daniel Mazmamian, "Regulating Coastal Land Use in California, 1973–1975," *Policy Studies Journal* 11, no. 1 (1982): 88–102. The quote on correcting local zoning authorities is from p. 93; more generally, the authors equate the success of the California Coastal Commission with the denial of permits (93). From their perspective, the Coastal Act was intended to stop bad development. On the tax revolt of 1978, see Clarence Y. H. Lo, *Small Property versus Big Government: The Social Origins of the Property Tax Revolt* (Berkeley: University of California Press, 1990).

35. Hogan, "Do Citizen Initiatives Affect Growth?"

36. Michael H. Remy, Tina A. Thomas, and James G. Moose, *Guide to the California Environmental Quality Act (CEQA)* (Point Arena, Calif.: Solano Press, 1991), chapter 4. *Wild card* is the expression that my respondents used.

37. Andrew A. Smith, Margaret A. Moote, and Cecil R. Schwalbe, "The Endangered Species Act at Twenty: An Analytical Survey of Federal Endangered Species Protection," *Natural Resources Journal* 33 (1993): 1027–75, especially p. 1040; Steven L. Yaffee, "Lessons about Leadership from the History of the Spotted Owl Controversy," *Natural Resources Journal* 35, no. 2 (1995): 381–412, especially 382–84.

38. On the Habitat Conservation Plan (HCP), see Smith, Moote, and Schwalbe, "The Endangered Species Act at Twenty." On the listing of the gnatcatcher, see Bruce Babbitt,

"Protecting Diversity," *Nature Conservancy* 44, no. 1 (1994): 17–21. On the spotted owl, see Yaffee, "Lessons about Leadership," 401.

39. New-housing statistics from U.S. Census Bureau, "New Privately Owned Residential Construction Reports" (Series C-21) (Washington, D.C.: U.S. Government Printing Office, 1978–1994). Data since 1994 are not available in published reports but can be obtained by contacting the census bureau. The 1999 C-21 reports indicated economic recovery beginning in 1996. This was confirmed by reports from city planners in 1999.

40. City of Castleton, "Environmental Impact Report," 1986.

41. The general plan update in particular approached the ideal type that I call "the Carnival of public government" in *Class and Community in Frontier Colorado.*

42. On ideal location for successful growth-control campaigns, see Harvey Molotch, "The City as a Growth Machine," *American Journal of Sociology* 82 (1976): 309–32, especially p. 328. On these five cities, see Hogan, "Do Citizen Initiatives Affect Growth?"

43. This is much as Thomas K. Rudel, *Situations and Strategies in American Land-Use Planning* (New York: Cambridge University Press, 1989), would suggest.

44. On federal subsidies for development, see Feagin, *Free Enterprise City.* See volume 7 of Pourade on first freeways (pp. 84–87); on Mission Valley and other shopping centers, and Highways 80, 395, and 101 (pp. 145-151, 202–5); on demise of Electric Railroad Company (pp. 79–81); on eastern regional shopping centers (pp. 196–99); on freeway expansion in 1968 and goals for the 1970s (pp. 241–42).

45. Growth and growth control in these suburban cities are analyzed in Hogan, "Do Citizen Initiatives Affect Growth?" which presents data from the U.S. Census reports on population, housing, and constructions that are referenced in this discussion.

46. U.S. Census Bureau, *County and City Data Book,* 1949–1994, especially, 1950–1970, 1972, 1983, 1988.

47. On "free-market populism," see Harvey, *Condition of Postmodernity,* 77.

48. Frederick P. Stutz, "Communities and Towns of San Diego County," in *San Diego: An Introduction to the Region, An Historical Geography of the Natural Environments and Human Development of San Diego County,* ed. Philip R. Pryde (Dubuque, Iowa: Kendall/Hunt, 1976), 210.

49. Castleton, according to Harvey Molotch's criteria ("The City as a Growth Machine," 309–32), is most likely to effect growth control, so it is particularly interesting to see how grassroots political movements, including the no-growth movement, affected the housing boom in this suburban city. This case allows us to explore the local conditions that John R. Logan and Min Zhou allude to in their analysis of growth control using a national sample, "Do Suburban Growth Controls Control Growth? *American Sociological Review* 54 (1989): 461–71.

50. Castleton, "Draft Housing Element," 1991, citing the chamber of commerce.

51. There was a fourth, less troublesome, alteration. The city had changed the way that it measured building heights, which required the developers to petition for an amendment to their master plan so the proposed building heights would conform to the new measuring system. This problem was resolved without incident when the planning commission approved the amendment.

52. To the extent that the Coastal Act of 1972 was intended to promote public access to the coast, it was inclusionary. In practice, however, the Coastal Commission seems to be exclusionary in keeping unwanted land use off the coast. Particularly in southern California, the commissioners seem to be regulating local land use and excluding uses that local planning departments and city governments have approved. See Sabatier and

Mazmamian, "Regulating Coastal Land Use," and Richard G. Hildreth and Ralph W. Johnson, "CZM in California, Oregon, and Washington," *Natural Resources Journal* 25, no. 1 (1985): 103–65.

Notes to Chapter 3

1. On Ramapo, see John R. Logan and Min Zhou, "Do Suburban Growth Controls Control Growth? *American Sociological Review* 54 (1989): 461–71, especially p. 467. On Mount Laurel, New Jersey, see William A. Fischel, *Regulatory Takings: Law, Economics, and Politics* (Cambridge, Mass.: Harvard University Press, 1995), 336–41.

2. SANDAG is the organization that develops Regional Housing Needs Statements (RHNS) in compliance with state mandates. See San Diego Association of Governments (SANDAG), *Regional Housing Needs Statement: San Diego Region* (San Diego: Source Point, 1990). See also the spring/summer 1991 issue of SANDAG's *Association News.*

3. The quote is from Karl Marx, "Critique of the Gotha Program," in *The Marx-Engels Reader,* 2d edition, ed. Robert C. Tucker (1872; reprint, New York: W. W. Norton. 1978, 531). Fair share and regional share allocations are presented in SANDAG, *Regional Housing Needs Statement* (1990).

4. On the reactionary, exclusive interests of suburbanites, see Kenneth T. Jackson, *Crabgrass Frontier: The Suburbanization of the United States* (New York: Oxford University Press, 1985). The distinction between exclusive and inclusive interests and the significance of this conflict in community politics comes from Sidney Plotkin, *Keep Out: The Struggle for Land Use Control* (Berkeley: University of California Press, 1987). Research on which suburbs are most likely to oppose affordable housing or to impose growth control is reported in Todd Donovan and Max Neiman, "Community Social Status, Suburban Growth, and Local Government Restrictions on Residential Development," *Urban Affairs Quarterly* 28 (1992): 323–36, and Richard Hogan, "Do Citizen Initiatives Affect Growth? The Case of Five San Diego Suburbs," in *Research in Community Sociology,* ed. Dan A. Chekki (New York: JAI Press, 1997), 249–75.

5. SANDAG, *Regional Housing Needs Statement: San Diego Region,* 96.

6. Ibid., 3.

7. Ibid., 4–5.

8. Ibid., xviii; also, see p. 87, on "affordable" housing.

9. U.S. Census Bureau, *County and City Data Book* (Washington D.C.: U.S. Government Printing Office, 1983, 1994).

10. SANDAG, *Regional Housing Needs Statement: San Diego Region,* xix.

11. Ibid., 5.

12. Ibid., xviii, 12.

13. Ibid., xix, 12.

14. Ibid., 3, 103.

15. Comprehensive Planning Organization of the San Diego Region (CPOSD), "San Diego Region 1970 Census: Subregional Area Data Tables and Computer Maps (unpublished report located in the Government Documents section of the University of California, San Diego, library), 9.

16. See the following SANDAG reports: Housing Needs (Growth) Statement Summary, R-20, September 21, 1981; Regional Housing Needs Statement, R-36, November 16, 1981; Regional Housing Needs Statement, R-6, January 17, 1984;

Regional Housing Needs Statement (1985–1991), R-74, September 28, 1984; *Regional Housing Needs Statement: San Diego Region,* July 1990.

17. SANDAG, "Housing Needs (Growth) Statement," *Regional Housing Needs Statement,* 224.

18. SANDAG, "Housing Needs (Growth) Statement; *Regional Housing Needs Statement,* R-6; *Regional Housing Needs Statement,* 224–230.

19. SANDAG, *Regional Housing Needs Statement: San Diego Region.*

20. Ibid., 200–204.

21. Ibid., 103.

22. Hogan, "Do Citizen Initiatives Affect Growth?"

23. On the tax revolt of 1978, see Clarence Y. H. Lo, *Small Property versus Big Government: The Social Origins of the Property Tax Revolt* (Berkeley: University of California Press, 1990). On the fiscalization of planning, see William Fulton, *Guide to California Planning* (Point Arena, Calif.: Solano Press, 1991), 15–17.

24. Fulton, *Guide to California Planning,* 15–17.

25. William A. Fischel, in *Regulatory Takings,* blames the California courts for the inflated price of California real estate, the rise of growth control, the collapse of the building industry, and most of the problems associated with the 1972–1989 period. He denies that population growth, the citizen initiatives, and the tax revolt were responsible (232–48). He also rejects the notion of a speculative bubble because there was a sustained rise in housing prices, except during the recession of 1982 (244–45). Like most free-market conservatives, Fischel tends to ignore the larger structural conditions associated with cycles of boom and bust, but he does offer an important corrective to liberal conspiracy theories of the growth machine by focusing attention on the state as a semi-autonomous actor.

26. McCutchen, Doyle, Brown & Enersen, in "Shaping Future Development in a Slow-Growth Era: A McCutchen Land Use Seminar" (San Francisco: McCutchen, Doyle, Brown & Enersen, 1989), 19–20, cite the appellate court decision, *Buena Vista Gardens Apartments Association* v. *City of San Diego Planning Department* (175 Cal. App. 3d 289 [1985]). Housing and population figures are from SANDAG, *Regional Housing Needs Statement: San Diego Region,* 56.

27. SANDAG, *Regional Housing Needs Statement: San Diego Region,* 56.

28. See Fischel, *Regulatory Takings.*

29. On Hahn and the development of Mission Valley and Horton Plaza, see Raymond G. Starr, *San Diego: A Pictorial History* (Norfolk, Va.: Donning, 1986), 209, 231; Richard Pourade, *History of San Diego,* 7 vols. (San Diego: Union-Tribune Publishing Co., 1960–1977), 7:226.

30. Donald Appleyard and Kevin Lynch, *Temporary Paradise? A Look at the Special Landscape of the San Diego Region* (A 1974 report to the City of San Diego, located in the Government Documents section of the University of California, San Diego, library), 22.

31. David Harvey, in *The Condition of Postmodernity: An Enquiry into the Origins of Cultural Change* (Cambridge, Mass.: Blackwell, 1990), 77, uses these terms to describe the postmodern suburban shopping mall.

32. David Harvey, in *The Condition of Postmodernity,* uses *postmodern* to refer to a stage of late republican capitalism beginning in about 1972. My use of the word follows his.

33. M. Gottdiener, *The Social Production of Urban Space* (Austin: University of Texas Press, 1985), and "Recapturing the Center: A Semiotic Analysis of Shopping Malls," in

The City and The Sign: An Introduction to Urban Semiotics, ed. M. Gottdiener and Alexandros Ph. Lagopoulos (New York: Columbia University Press, 1986).

34. Richard Hogan, "Do Citizen Initiatives Affect Growth?" 252.

35. For details on growth and growth control in these suburban cities, see Hogan, "Do Citizen Initiatives Affect Growth?"; for statistics on population and housing, see U.S. Census Bureau, *County and City Data Book,* 1983, 1994, and SANDAG, Regional Housing Needs Statement.

36. See Hogan, "Do Citizen Initiatives Affect Growth?"

37. U.S. Census Bureau, *County and City Data Book,* 1970, 1977, 1983, 1994.

38. SANDAG, "Housing Needs (Growth) Statement Summary (R-20), Regional Housing Needs Statement (R-6), and *Regional Housing Needs Statement: San Diego Region;* Castleton, "Housing Element," 1985.

39. Introduction to Castleton's 1985 housing element.

40. Castleton's 1992 growth management plan (brochure available at the Castleton City Hall).

41. U.S. Census Bureau, "Housing Authorized by Building Permits and Public Contracts" (Series C-40) (Washington, D.C.: U.S. Government Printing Office), 1986, 1992.

42. SANDAG's 1984 Regional Housing Needs Statement had recommended assistance to over 500 households.

43. SANDAG, *Regional Housing Needs Statement: San Diego Region,* xviii–xvix.

44. Report of Castleton's Ad Hoc Committee, 1991.

45. Ibid.

46. Ibid.

47. Castleton affordable housing workshop minutes, 1992.

Notes to Chapter 4

1. On public ownership of the coast, see Donald Appleyard and Kevin Lynch, *Temporary Paradise? A Look at the Special Landscape of the San Diego Region* (a 1974 report to the City of San Diego, located in the Government Documents section of the University of California, San Diego, library), 41.

2. Class, status, and party interests are discussed in chapter 1. On diversity within the environmentalist movement, see Riley E. Dunlap and Angela G. Mertig, eds., *American Environmentalism: The U.S. Environmental Movement, 1970–1990* (Philadelphia: Taylor & Francis, 1992). Bankers and politicians served on the Rockefeller Brothers Fund citizen task force described in chapter 2. See William K. Reilly, ed., *The Use of Land: A Citizen's Policy Guide to Urban Growth: A Task Force Report Sponsored by the Rockefeller Brothers Fund* (New York: Thomas Y. Crowell, 1973). A list of the twelve task force members precedes table of contents. The second task force report is in Gerald O. Barney, ed., *The Unfinished Agenda: The Citizen's Policy Guide to Environmental Issues, a Task Force Report Sponsored by the Rockefellers Brothers Fund* (New York: Thomas Y. Crowell, 1977). This second task force included representatives of the major environmentalist organizations. On "good" and "bad" unions see Melvyn Dubofsky, *The State and Labor in Modern America* (Chapel Hill: University of North Carolina Press, 1994), and *We Shall Be All: A History of the Industrial Workers of the World,* 2d ed. (Urbana: University of Illinois Press, 1988).

3. Michael Allan Wolf, "Accommodating Tensions in the Coastal Zone: An Introduction and Overview," *Natural Resources Journal* 25 (January 1985): 7–19. For a discussion of NEPA, CEQA, and EIRs, see chapter 1; for references, see notes 12 and

45 of that chapter. The Clean Water Act of 1970 and its revision in 1972 are discussed in Odom Fanning, *Man and His Environment: Citizen Action* (New York: Harper & Row, 1975), 81. On the ESA, see Andrew A. Smith, Margaret A. Moote, and Cecil R. Schwalbe, "The Endangered Species Act at Twenty: An Analytical Survey of Federal Endangered Species Protection," *Natural Resources Journal* 33 (1993): 1027–75.

4. The legal formalism of the coastal commission hearings can be extremely frustrating for the person who is trying to accomplish something that appears to be relatively simple and harmless. A real estate professional from Laguna Beach, a coastal community north of San Diego County, experienced this frustration when trying to help an elderly neighbor get a permit to repair his stairway from his hillside house to the beach. The fact that the old man had been there long before the Coastal Act was passed and that all he wanted to do was to repair an existing structure was irrelevant. The permit was denied.

During a break, the real estate professional complained about the bureaucracy and the insensitivity of the commission, contrasting it with a planning board "back home" (in a border state): as he told the story, he had given the planning board back home the same kind of dog-and-pony show that he had just offered the commission. Then the chair of the board, looking somewhat bewildered by all the fuss, had said, "Well hell, it's your property," and the permit had been granted.

5. An example of the invasion of La Jolla is that of the Marine Street beach. Marine Street is a dead-end street in a residential district at the southern end of La Jolla. At the end of the street is a stairway descending to a beach that became popular among body surfers because of the large waves. In the 1990s Marine Street was still the beach for bad boys and wearers of thong bikinis; it was a stage for adolescent excess performed as public spectacle. Thus it was distinguished from the more sedate family-entertainment destination of La Jolla Shores and the private retreat of Blacks Beach.

6. At a California Coastal Commission meeting in February 1992 a speaker addressed the commissioners about the need to replace the berm that had been removed from the mouth of one of the local lagoons. The berm was removed to reduce the risk of flooding on Old Highway 101. The speaker argued that the berm should be replaced to protect habitat and the appearance of the lagoon. The city did not see this as an emergency matter, but the applicant was concerned that the rainy season might be over, so the lagoon might be moving into its swamp phase.

7. Quoted, with revisions, from the local Castleton newspaper.

8. State of California, *The Resources Agency of California Annual Report* (Sacramento: Secretary for Resources, January 1992).

9. Smith, Moote, and Schwalbe, "Endangered Species Act at Twenty." On the gnatcatcher listing, see Bruce Babbitt, "Protecting Biodiversity," *Nature Conservancy* 44, no. 1 (1994): 17–21; on the spotted owl, see Steven L. Yaffee, "Lessons about Leadership from the History of the Spotted Owl Controversy," *Natural Resources Journal* 35, no. 2 (1995): 381–412, especially p. 401.

10. State of California, "NCCP Special Report No. 1" (Sacramento: Secretary for Resources, February 1992), 2.

11. Yaffee, "Lessons about Leadership"; State of California, "NCCP Special Report No. 1"; Babbitt, "Protecting Biodiversity."

12. State of California, Assembly Bill 2172 [The Kelley Bill, establishing the NCCP]. (Sacramento: Legislative Council, March 1991).

13. State of California, "Memorandum of Understanding by and between the California Department of Fish and Game and the United States Fish and Wildlife Service Regarding Coastal Sage Scrub Natural Community Conservation Planning in Southern California," (Sacramento: Secretary for Resources, December 1991).

14. William Fulton, "Species Talks Drag: No Interim Controls in Place Yet," *California Planning and Development Report* 7, no. 3 (March 1992): 1.

15. On free riders, see Mancur Olson, *The Logic of Collective Action* (Cambridge, Mass.: Harvard University Press, 1965).

16. Richard Hogan, *Class and Community in Frontier Colorado* (Lawrence: University Press of Kansas, 1990).

17. Thomas K. Rudel, *Situations and Strategies in American Land-Use Planning* (New York: Cambridge University Press, 1989).

18. Although not pertinent to habitat conservation, the other business of the city council meeting is enlightening, particularly in indicating how laws sometimes get in the way and can be a barrier to popular influence, if not participation. In this case the city was forced to permit an addition to a garage that had already been approved by the planning department, despite the protests of an angry group of neighbors brandishing a petition with over 150 signatures. Ultimately the city was legally bound to deny the petition.

[The mayor asks the planning director for a report.]

Director: We did receive the complaint and put a stop-work order on it. Our ordinance does allow this structure so we had to allow him to restart. We may need to change our ordinance, [but the] ordinance allows accessory buildings on the rear property line.

Mayor: Thus this meets standard. I could build a two-story structure on the edge of my property line?

Director: I have discussed this with the city attorney. This is not the intent of the law. We need to make a change.

Councilor L: We need to get a legal opinion.

Mayor: Can we stop the building?

Attorney: You can change the law for the future [but] that will not resolve this particular problem.

[Mayor apologizes to neighbors and explains that they can't do anything else.]

19. On the statute of limitations, see State of California, *State CEQA Guidelines* (Sacramento: Secretary for Resources, 1989), section (5) (A), p. 131.

20. One of the more interesting petitions came from La Jolla, where neighbors were protesting a building permit that would destroy "the last sand dune" in the neighborhood and "a Torrey pine" (the tree for which Torrey Pines State Reserve, farther north on the rocky cliffs overlooking ocean, is named). After listening to an attorney speak on behalf of the neighbors, the commissioners voted unanimously to uphold the city's decision to approve the permit, since there were no issues of beach access or preservation involved.

21. Although the federal government listed the gnatcatcher, it appears that even the listing was designed to accommodate the concerns of big-picture planners and enlightened developers. Bruce Babbitt explained that "to assist California's effort, the federal government last March listed the gnatcatcher as threatened, rather than endangered." The importance of this decision to accommodate the NCCP is the precedent it set.

Babbit asserted, "This is the first time in the history of the Endangered Species Act that we have listed a species and then stepped back to defer to the state's planning process" ("Protecting Biodiversity," p. 18). Whether this marks the beginning of a new era of federal-state cooperation remains to be seen.

Notes to Chapter 5

1. Census data and SANDAG reports for population and housing were used to compare growth in five San Diego County suburban cities. See chapter three and Richard Hogan, "Do Citizen Initiatives Affect Growth? The Case of Five San Diego Suburbs," in *Research in Community Sociology,* ed. Dan A. Chekki (New York: JAI Press, 1997), pp. 249–75, for details on sources used in that analysis. Here the data for the population and housing growth of the five cities is broadly similar for the years 1992 to 1999. Unfortunately, the primary source of data for comparative purposes—U.S. Census Bureau, "Housing Authorized by Building Permits and Public Contracts" (Series C-40) (Washington, D.C.: U.S. Government Printing Office, 1968–1995)—is no longer published. The information is supposed to be available on the Internet or on CD-ROM, but I was able to get these data from the census bureau in 1999 only via telephone. Thus I obtained projected housing unit approvals for 1998, as well as updated figures for 1995–1997, via telephone. These figures, along with figures from SANDAG ("Preliminary 2020 Cities/Counties Forecast—Technical Update," Board of Directors Agenda Report 99-2-7 [San Diego, 1999]), tend to confirm the reports of city and SANDAG officials I interviewed in 1999.

2. The tendency to accommodate, if not facilitate, the efforts of reactionaries is perhaps, as Karl Marx suggests, a short-term response to a lack of class hegemony or state capacity ("The Eighteenth Brumaire of Louis Bonaparte," in *The Marx-Engels Reader,* 2d edition, ed. Robert C. Tucker [1850; reprint, New York: W. W. Norton, 1978]). In this regard, the initial big-picture planning coalition of 1992 attempted to accommodate local environmentalists and no-growth interests, particularly in the NCCP, to bolster the position of the liberal environmentalist social-movement organizations, especially the Nature Conservancy. By 1999 the Nature Conservancy and other big environmentalist groups were able to use the threat of radical (Earth First!) or reactionary (no-growth) opposition to pressure conservatives within the smart-growth coalition. At that point, however, the local environmentalist and no-growth interests were no longer being accommodated. They were no longer necessary because the liberal environmentalists were part of the governing coalition.

In some ways this is like the French industrial bourgeoisie of 1848, which used the proletariat to fight the Orleanist finance aristocracy. Once the industrial bourgeoisie was incorporated into the governing coalition, the Party of Order purged the radicals and ultimately had to rely on the reactionary Bonapartist peasant-bourgeois governing coalition to prevent the revolution from getting out of hand. Perhaps there is a parallel in the environmentalism of the 1980s and 1990s.

3. In the summer of 2000 a coalition of environmentalists, labor activists, and others confronted the World Trade Organization at its meeting in Seattle, Washington. This was a major confrontation, especially compared to the relative acquiescence of the left in the face of bipartisan support for NAFTA and other international agreements that were opposed by left-leaning, if not entirely radical, labor and environmentalist interests. The Seattle demonstrations suggest the possibility of a New Left coalition that encompasses the more radical elements of the various new social movements (e.g., environmentalist, new labor, race, gender, peace, and antinuclear). On new social movements, see Alberto

Melucci, "The New Social Movements: A Theoretical Approach," *Social Science Information* 19 (1980): 199–226.

4. The U.S. Small Business Administration, Office of Advocacy, report "Developing High-Technology Communities: San Diego" (Reston, Va.: Innovation Associates, 2000), comes with a disclaimer: "The statements, findings, conclusions, and recommendations are those of the authors and do not necessarily reflect the views of the U.S. Small Business Administration." Nevertheless, the report clearly represents the booster interest of the petite bourgeoisie. Quote is from p. xiii of the executive summary.

As we have already seen, Yuppie Heaven offers low-paying service-sector jobs in business and health care in lieu of living-wage employment in manufacturing. The workers in Yuppie Heaven cannot afford to rent, much less buy, the upscale housing that was being built in 1999. Yes, there have been some entrepreneurial capitalists and workers making large profits or earning high wages, but even theirs are not reliable earnings. If we move into another cycle of unregulated growth, with the second coming of the Bush regime we can expect another boom-and-bust cycle. Perhaps we will even witness another round of corporate-capitalist plunder, as the bankers steal the money before the pyramid scheme collapses as it did in 1989.

Perhaps after we win the war on terrorism we will return to the Contract with America. My prediction, however, is that George W. Bush, like his father before him, will win the battle but lose the war. He will be another one-term president. Barring a miraculous economic recovery before 2004, all the Democrats will need to do is find someone who can remember the Clinton slogan, "It's the economy, stupid."

5. Pete Wilson, Ronald Reagan, and their entourage of free-market deregulators are thus viewed as major actors in blunting the effects of environmental regulation. See Andrew Szasz, *EcoPopulism: Toxic Waste and the Movement for Environmental Justice* (Minneapolis: University of Minnesota Press, 1994), especially chapters 2, 5–7, and for summary chapter 8, pp. 137–39.

6. Donald Appleyard and Kevin Lynch, *Temporary Paradise? A Look at the Special Landscape of the San Diego Region* (a 1974 report to the City of San Diego, located in the Government Documents section of the University of California, San Diego, library).

7. Greg Hise and William Deverell, *Eden by Design: The 1930 Olmsted-Bartholomew Plan for the Los Angeles Region* (Berkeley: University of California Press, 2000).

8. In "Hotel California" the Eagles sang, "You can check out anytime you like, but you can never leave." Obviously, this is very different from the "Please come back again" Disneyland model.

9. Alexis de Tocqueville, *Democracy in America,* edited and abridged by Richard D. Heffner (New York: Mentor, 1956), 192–93.

10. See Laurie Graham and Richard Hogan, "Social Class and Tactics: Neighborhood Opposition to Group Homes," *Sociological Quarterly* 31, no. 4 (1990): 513–29. On racial and class discrimination in locating unwanted facilities, see Robert D. Bullard, *Dumping in Dixie: Race, Class, and Environmental Quality* (Boulder, Colo.: Westview Press, 1990). On the importance of neighborhood organization in opposition, see Richard Hogan, "Community Opposition to Group Homes," *Social Science Quarterly* 67 (1986): 442–49. See also Robert Dilger, *Neighborhood and Politics: Residential Community Associations in American Governance* (New York: New York University Press, 1992).

11. William Shakespeare, *Hamlet*, in *The Riverside Shakespeare* (Boston: Houghton Mifflin, 1974), 1160.

Here one might argue that there is a need to educate the general public not about the complex, abstract philosophy that determines the true interests of classes and the possible expressions of utopian imaginations, but about the concrete differences between extant political attitudes and interests. If nothing else, I hope that the discussion in chapter 1, with the model borrowed from my freshman political science instructor, might help in this effort.

12. On Houston and other free-market cities, see Joseph R. Feagin, *Free Enterprise City: Houston in Political-Economic Perspective* (New Brunswick, N.J.: Rutgers University Press, 1988).

13. Marx, in "Eighteenth Brumaire," analyzed the role of radicals and reactionaries in the intraclass struggles of the bourgeoisie. Liberals and conservatives became allied in the aftermath of the French Revolution in what Marx called "The Party of Order" (602). In France from 1789 to 1851 the progressives needed the reactionaries (and needed Napoleon I and Napoleon III) to protect them from the radicals. Marx notes that the peasants imposed limits on the revolution, implying that they were the reactionary force (607–11), but the *lumpenproletariat* of the Society of December 10 (615) was equally reactionary—or simply corrupted—in supporting the empire.

Marxists have tended to focus on the false consciousness of the peasants or on their lack of organization as a class for itself. Charles Tilly, in *The Vendee* (1964; reprint, Cambridge, Mass.: Harvard University Press, 1976), represents the revisionists, arguing that peasants constituted multiple classes and defended various interests, much as American farmers in the past three centuries have done.

The critical issue for our theoretical purposes, and for Marxist praxis more generally, is how to break the liberal-conservative coalition and turn the liberals, if not the conservatives, against the reactionaries. Joining forces with reactionaries, as in the Stalin-Hitler nonaggression pact, is—hopefully we all agree on this one—strategically and theoretically problematic. Why? Simply stated, it is suicidal. Instead of undermining the liberal-conservative coalition, joining with reactionaries reinforces the progressive attack on foreign, un-American influences, including fascism and communism. Historically the nonaggression pact fed the collective ignorance, fueled by the mass media and established parties, that legitimated the use of the term *radical* in association with everything "evil" and foreign. Thus *radical* refers to nationalism of every flavor; totalitarianism (whatever that means as an ideology that is distinguishable from nationalism); and even fundamentalism of the non-Christian, particularly Muslim, persuasion. This creates a rather difficult problem for the Marxist who wishes to claim radicalism while eschewing religious fundamentalism and nationalism. See Roger Keeran, *The Communist Party and the Auto Workers' Unions* (1980; reprint, New York: International Publishers, 1986).

14. British and U.S. planning are compared to each other in David Fasenfest, ed., *Community Economic Development: Policy Formation in the U.S. and the U.K.* (New York: Macmillan, 1993). Jon C. Teaford, in *City and Suburb: The Political Fragmentation of Metropolitan America, 1850–1970* (Baltimore, MD.: Johns Hopkins University Press, 1979), offers the British planning system as an alternative to the fragmentation of the U.S. system. Roger V. Gould, in *Insurgent Identities: Class, Community, and Protest in Paris from 1848 to the Commune* (Chicago: University of Chicago Press, 1995), describes urban planning in Paris from 1852 to 1870 in chapter 3.

15. Major state-centered planning revolutions that were not democratic also required the effective mobilization of a grassroots constituency, specifically shopkeepers in Hitler's Germany and peasants in Napoleon's France. Here I am focusing on the social-democratic path, but the problem is similar on the fascist path. The elitism of the professionals clashes with both the democratic sentiments of the socialists and the authoritarian sentiments of the fascists. That does not mean that socialists and fascists are the same, but simply that they have a similar love-hate relationship with professional planners, and with the intelligentsia in general.

16. See Judith Corbett, "The Ahwahnee Principles: Toward More Livable Communities," 2001, available, along with other such papers, at <www.lgc.org/freep-ub/land_use/articles/ahwahnee_article.html>. See also <www.walkable.org>.

Proponents of the Walkable Cities movement, like the Owenites and other communal-ists of the nineteenth century, face the challenge of attempting to live in a potentially hostile environment. Unless they are able to subsist more or less autonomously, it is not clear that they will be able to exist at all, except as relatively insulated professional com-munities in college towns like Davis, California. On communes and the problem of self-sufficiency and relations with the outside world across the "semi-permeable boundary," see Richard Hogan, "The Frontier as Social Control," *Theory and Society* 14 (1985): 35–51.

John R. Logan and Harvey Molotch, in *Urban Fortunes: The Political Economy of Place* (Berkeley: University of California Press, 1987), focus on the conflict between "use values" and "exchange values," which represent the interests of residents and investors, respectively. Karl Marx, in chapter 1 of *Capital: A Critique of Political Economy,* 3 vols. (New York: International Publishers, 1967), describes the alienation of use and exchange values in capitalist, as opposed to artisanal, petty commodity trade.

For Marx, the critical problem was that labor value no longer corresponded to use value, as each had become subservient to exchange value. The alienation, or estrange-ment, of labor was the source of conflicts and contradictions. The root of the trouble was the alienation of nature and the human, which was rooted in production and repro-duction, rather than the alienation of use and exchange, which was rooted in commerce, or trade. Thus the progressive and left-leaning liberals, including socialists, have stood Marxist economics on its head.

Percival Goodman and Paul Goodman, in *Communitas: Means of Livelihood and Ways of Life* (New York: Vintage, 1960), offer a different version of the form-fits-function argument and propose alternative forms that serve different functions. The Goodmans' neofunctionalist perspective is decidedly progressive. Ultimately their alternative visions of community combine socialist or social-democratic systems of government-sponsored sub-sistence with capitalist or free enterprise systems of production for gracious living. It is not clear, however, how public and the private economies could coexist in their social-demo-cratic, subsistence-plus community (chapter 7). Their regional autonomy model (chapter 6) is much closer to what I propose, but their model seems to accommodate the free mar-ket in commodities and policies.

It is also curious that the Goodmans do not consider public education an essential sub-sistence requirement (201). For them, the university is either a showcase for consumer goods (in the consumer city of chapter 5) or a technical training and engineering center (in the regionally autonomous production city of chapter 6). Despite these quibbles, howev-er, the Goodmans' is a most thoughtful and thought-provoking exploration of alternative visions that even with the passage of time is still worth considering. Like the walkable-cities literature, the Goodmans' work offers a much more detailed and empirically ground-ed vision of what is possible than I have attempted to provide here.

On urban ecology, see W. Parker Frisbie and John D. Kasarda, "Spatial Processes," in *Handbook of Sociology,* ed. Neil J. Smelser (Beverly Hills, Calif.: Sage, 1988), 629–66.

17. On the various types of cities (walking, rail, automobile), see Jackson, *Crabgrass Frontier: The Suburbanization of the United States* (New York: Oxford University Press, 1985).

18. Charlotte Perkins Gilman, *Herland: A Lost Feminist Utopian Novel by Charlotte Perkins Gilman, with an Introduction by Ann J. Jane* (New York: Pantheon Books, 1979).

19. Goodman and Goodman, in *Communitas,* use circles to designate the commercial center and the university. They use hexagons for their more life-centered community. This eliminates the problem of wasteland outside the circles, which may or may not be a problem.

Notes to Appendix A

1. Howard S. Becker, *Outsiders* (New York: Free Press, 1963).

2. On doing nonparticipant observation, see William Foote Whyte, *Street Corner Society: The Social Structure of an Italian Slum* (1943; reprint, Chicago: University of Chicago Press, 1981), Appendix A.

3. After one of these meetings Doug even invited me to lunch, Dutch treat, where he vented his frustration with the problems of accommodating environmental interests in state-level big-picture planning. This conversation was in some ways more informative than our interview. Unfortunately, I did not feel comfortable recording notes until after lunch. As soon as Doug got in his car, however, I starting writing furiously, sitting in my car in the parking lot of the restaurant. I learned this note-taking technique from sociologist James Jackson, who once told me in a personal conversation how he took notes when studying African American barroom behavior.

4. It is interesting in this regard to contrast the developer organization with the regional environmental organization. First, since I was honest with the environmental organization leader, I was granted multiple interviews and was put on the mailing list for a nominal fee to cover mailing costs (I had insisted that I could pay for the newsletter but could not join the organization). The developer was willing to put me on the mailing list at first, but the cost would be substantial—over $100 per year. Then it was decided that I could receive only public-information material. Finally it was determined that filtering the mailings was too much trouble. The association returned my check and dropped me from the mailing list.

5. See, for example, Richard Hogan, "Do Citizen Initiatives Affect Growth? The Case of Five San Diego Suburbs," in *Research in Community Sociology,* ed. Dan A. Chekki (New York: JAI Press, 1997), pp. 249–75.

6. Many of my contacts have read my article "Do Citizen Initiatives Affect Growth?" Thus far none have challenged the facts, but several have challenged the interpretation.

Works Cited

Abbott, Andrew. *The System of Professions: An Essay on the Division of Expert Labor.* Chicago: University of Chicago Press, 1988.

Abbott, Carl. *Boosters and Businessmen: Popular Economic Thought and Urban Growth in the Antebellum Middle West.* Westport, Conn.: Greenwood Press, 1981.

———. *The Metropolitan Frontier: Cities in the Modern American West.* Tucson: University of Arizona Press, 1993.

———. *The New Urban America: Growth and Politics in Sunbelt Cities.* Chapel Hill: University of North Carolina Press, 1987.

———. *Urban America in the Modern Age: 1920 to the Present.* Arlington Heights, Ill.: Harlan Davidson, 1987.

Anderson, Kevin. "Marx on Suicide in the Context of His Other Writings on Alienation and Gender." In *Marx on Suicide,* ed. Kevin Anderson and Eric A. Plaut. Evanston, Ill.: Northwestern University Press, 1999.

Appleyard, Donald, and Kevin Lynch. *Temporary Paradise? A Look at the Special Landscape of the San Diego Region.* A 1974 report to the City of San Diego, located in the Government Documents section of the University of California, San Diego, library.

Babbitt, Bruce. "Protecting Biodiversity." *Nature Conservancy* 44, no. 1 (1994): 17–21.

Bachrach, Peter, and Morton S. Baratz. "Two Faces of Power." *American Political Science Review* 56 (December 1962): 947–52.

Barney, Gerald O., ed. *The Unfinished Agenda: The Citizen's Policy Guide to Environmental Issues, a Task Force Report Sponsored by the Rockefeller Brothers Fund.* New York: Thomas Y. Crowell, 1977.

Baudrillard, Jean. "Simulacra and Simulations: Disneyland." In *Social Theory: The Multicultural and Classical Readings,* ed. Charles Lemert. 1988. Reprint, Boulder, Colo.: Westview Press, 1993.

Beard, Charles A. *Contemporary American History, 1877–1913.* New York: Macmillan, 1914.

Becker, Howard S. *Outsiders.* New York: Free Press, 1963.

Blumer, Martin. *The Chicago School of Sociology: Institutionalization, Diversity, and the Rise of Sociological Research.* Chicago: University of Chicago Press, 1984.

Bogue, Allan. "Social Theory and the Pioneer." *Agricultural History* 34 (1960): 21–34.

Boorstin, Daniel. *The Americans: The National Experience.* New York: Vintage, 1965.

Bosselman, Fred, and David Callies. *The Quiet Revolution in Land Use Control.* Washington, D.C.: U.S. Government Printing Office, 1972.

Bullard, Robert D. *Dumping in Dixie: Race, Class, and Environmental Quality.* Boulder, Colo.: Westview Press, 1990.

———, ed. *Confronting Environmental Racism: Voices from the Grassroots.* Boston: South End Press, 1993.

Burnham, Daniel, and Edward H. Bennett. *Plan of Chicago.* Chicago: Commercial Club, 1908.

Cable, Sherry, and Charles Cable. *Environmental Problems, Grassroots Solutions.* New York: St. Martin's Press, 1995.

Calavita, Kitty, and Henry N. Pontell. "The Savings and Loan Crisis." In *Corporate and Governmental Deviance*, ed. M. David Erman and Richard J. Lundman. New York: Oxford University Press, 1992.

Calavita, Nico. "Growth Machines and Ballot Box Planning: The San Diego Case." *Journal of Urban Affairs* 14, no. 1 (1992): 1–24.

California, State of. Assembly Bill 2172 (the Kelley Bill, establishing the NCCP). Sacramento: Legislative Council, March 1991.

———. *The California EIR Monitor* 14, no. 4. Sacramento: Secretary for Resources, 1988.

———. "Memorandum of Understanding by and between the California Department of Fish and Game and the United States Fish and Wildlife Service Regarding Coastal Sage Scrub Natural Community Conservation Planning in Southern California." Sacramento: Secretary for Resources, December 1991.

———. "Natural Community Conservation Plan Draft Process Guidelines." Sacramento: Secretary for Resources, April 1992.

———. "NCCP Special Report, No. 1." Sacramento: Secretary for Resources, February 1992.

———. *The Resources Agency of California Annual Report*. Sacramento: Secretary for Resources, January 1992.

———. *State CEQA Guidelines*. Sacramento: Secretary for Resources, 1989.

Capek, Stella M., and John I. Gilderbloom. *Community versus Commodity: Tenants and the American City*. Albany: State University of New York Press, 1992.

Castells, Manuel. *The City and the Grassroots: A Cross-Cultural Theory of Urban Social Movements*. Berkeley: University of California Press, 1983.

———. *The Informational City: Information, Technology, Economic Restructuring, and the Urban-Regional Process*. Oxford: Basil Blackwell, 1989.

Clark, Christopher. *The Roots of Rural Capitalism: Western Massachusetts, 1780–1860*. Ithaca, N.Y.: Cornell University Press, 1990.

Cohen, Lizabeth. *Making a New Deal: Industrial Workers in Chicago, 1919–1939*. New York: Cambridge University Press, 1990.

Cohn, Sam, and Carol Conell. "Learning from Other People's Actions: Environmental Variation and Diffusion in French Coal Mining Strikes, 1890–1935." *American Journal of Sociology* 101 (1995): 366–403.

Comprehensive Planning Organization of the San Diego Region. "Housing Needs in the San Diego Region." Unpublished report located in the Government Documents section of the University of California, San Diego, library, December 1972.

———. "San Diego Region 1970 Census: Subregional Area Data Tables and Computer Maps." Unpublished report located in the Government Documents section of the University of California, San Diego, library, 1972.

Corbett, Judith. "The Ahwahnee Principles: Toward More Livable Communities." 2001. Available, along with other such papers, at <www.lgc.org/freepub/land_use/articles/ahwahnee_article.html>. 2001

Corso, Anthony W. "San Diego: The Anti-City." In *Sunbelt Cities: Politics and Growth since World War II*, ed. Richard M. Bernard and Bradley R. Rice. Austin: University of Texas Press, 1983.

Dahl, Robert A. *Who Governs?* New Haven, Conn.: Yale University Press, 1961.

Davis, Angela Y. *Women, Race, and Class*. New York: Random House, 1981.

Davis, Mike. *City of Quartz: Excavating the Future in Los Angeles*. New York: Verso, 1990.

Dear, M. J., and S. M. Taylor. *Not on Our Street*. London: Pion, 1982.

Dilger, Robert. *Neighborhood and Politics: Residential Community Associations in American Governance*. New York: New York University Press, 1992.

Domhoff, G. William. *Who Rules America Now?* Englewood Cliffs, N.J.: Prentice Hall, 1983.

Donovan, Todd, and Max Neiman. "Community Social Status, Suburban Growth, and Local Government Restrictions on Residential Development." *Urban Affairs Quarterly* 28 (1992): 323–36.

Dubofsky, Melvyn. *The State and Labor in Modern America.* Chapel Hill: University of North Carolina Press, 1994.

———. *We Shall Be All: A History of the Industrial Workers of the World,* 2d ed. Urbana: University of Illinois Press, 1988.

Dunlap, Riley E., and Angela G. Mertig, eds. *American Environmentalism: The U.S. Environmental Movement, 1970–1990.* Philadelphia: Taylor & Francis, 1992.

Durkheim, Emile. *The Division of Labor in Society.* 1893. Reprint, New York: Free Press, 1933.

Engels, Frederick. *Socialism: Utopian and Scientific, with the Essay on the Mark,* trans. Edward Averling. New York: International Publishers, 1985.

Epstein, Barbara. *Political Protest and Cultural Revolution: Nonviolent Direct Action in the 1970s and 1980s.* Berkeley: University of California Press, 1991.

Fanning, Odom. *Man and His Environment: Citizen Action.* New York: Harper & Row, 1975.

Fasenfest, David, ed., *Community Economic Development: Policy Formation in the U.S. and the U.K.* New York: Macmillan, 1993.

Feagin, Joseph R. *Free Enterprise City: Houston in Political-Economic Perspective.* New Brunswick, N.J.: Rutgers University Press, 1988.

Fields, A. Belden. "The Revolution Betrayed: The French Student Revolt of May–June 1968." In *Students Revolt,* ed. Seymour Martin Lipset and Philip G. Altbach. Boston: Beacon Press, 1970.

Fischel, William A. *Regulatory Takings: Law, Economics, and Politics.* Cambridge, Mass.: Harvard University Press, 1995.

Foster, John Bellamy. "Marx's Theory of Metabolic Rift: Classical Foundations for Environmental Sociology." *American Journal of Sociology* 105 (1999): 366–405.

Frisbie, W. Parker, and John D. Kasarda. "Spatial Processes." Pp. 629–66 in *Handbook of Sociology,* ed. Neil J. Smelser. Beverly Hills, Calif.: Sage, 1988.

Fulton, William. *Guide to California Planning.* Point Arena, Calif.: Solano Press, 1991.

———. "Species Talks Drag: No Interim Controls in Place Yet." *California Planning and Development Report* 7, no. 3 (March 1992): 1, 9.

Gamson, William A. *Power and Discontent.* Homewood, Ill.: Dorsey Press, 1968.

———. *The Strategy of Social Protest.* Chicago: Dorsey Press, 1975.

———. *Talking Politics.* New York: Cambridge University Press, 1992.

Gamson, William A., and Andre Modigliani. "Media Discourse and Public Opinion on Nuclear Power." *American Journal of Sociology* 95 (1989): 1–37.

Gilman, Charlotte Perkins. *Herland: A Lost Feminist Utopian Novel by Charlotte Perkins Gilman, with an Introduction by Ann J. Lane.* New York: Pantheon Books, 1979.

———. *The Home: Its Work and Influence.* New York: McClure, Phillips & Co., 1903.

———. *Women and Economics: A Study of the Economic Relation between Men and Women as a Factor in Social Evolution.* Boston: Small, Maynard & Co., 1900.

Goodman, Percival, and Paul Goodman. *Communitas: Means of Livelihood and Ways of Life.* New York: Vintage, 1960.

Gottdiener, Mark. "Recapturing the Center: A Semiotic Analysis of Shopping Malls." In *The City and the Sign: An Introduction to Urban Semiotics,* ed. Mark Gottdiener and Alexandros Ph. Lagopoulos. New York: Columbia University Press, 1986.

———. *The Social Production of Urban Space*. Austin: University of Texas Press, 1985.

Gould, Roger V. *Insurgent Identities: Class, Community, and Protest in Paris from 1848 to the Commune*. Chicago: University of Chicago Press, 1995.

Graham, Laurie, and Richard Hogan. "Social Class and Tactics: Neighborhood Opposition to Group Homes." *Sociological Quarterly* 31, no. 4 (1990): 513–29.

Griffin, Ernst C. "San Diego's Population Patterns." In *San Diego: An Introduction to the Region, An Historical Geography of the Natural Environments and Human Development of San Diego County*, ed. Philip R. Pryde. Dubuque, Iowa: Kendall/Hunt, 1976.

Haar, Charles M., and Jerome S. Kayden, eds. *Zoning and the American Dream: Promises Still to Keep*. Chicago: Planners Press, 1989.

Habermas, Jürgen. *Legitimation Crisis*. Boston: Beacon Press, 1975.

———. *Lifeworld and System: A Critique of Functionalist Reason*, trans. Thomas McCarthy. Vol. 2 of *The Theory of Communicative Action*. Boston: Beacon Press, 1987.

Harvey, David. *The Condition of Postmodernity: An Enquiry into the Origins of Cultural Change*. Cambridge, Mass.: Blackwell, 1990.

———. "Labor, Capital, and Class Struggle around the Built Environment." *Politics and Society* 6 (1976): 265–95.

Hildreth, Richard G., and Ralph W. Johnson. "CZM in California, Oregon, and Washington." *Natural Resources Journal* 25, no. 1 (1985): 103–65.

Hirschman, Albert O. *Exit, Voice, and Loyalty*. Cambridge, Mass.: Harvard University Press, 1970.

Hise, Greg, and William Deverell. *Eden by Design: The 1930 Olmsted-Bartholomew Plan for the Los Angeles Region*. Berkeley: University of California Press, 2000.

Hogan, Richard. *Class and Community in Frontier Colorado*. Lawrence: University Press of Kansas, 1990.

———. "Community Opposition to Group Homes." *Social Science Quarterly* 67 (1986): 442–49.

———. "Do Citizen Initiatives Affect Growth? The Case of Five San Diego Suburbs." in *Research in Community Sociology*, ed. Dan A. Chekki, 249–75. New York: JAI Press, 1997.

———. "The Frontier as Social Control." *Theory and Society* 14 (1985): 35–51.

———. "Residential Segregation in Monterrey County." University of California, Santa Cruz, unpublished undergraduate paper, 1973.

Jackson, Kenneth T. *Crabgrass Frontier: The Suburbanization of the United States*. New York: Oxford University Press, 1985.

Joppke, Christian. "Social Movements during Cycles of Issue Attention: The Decline of Anti- Nuclear Energy Movements in West Germany and the USA." *British Journal of Sociology* 42 (1991): 43–60.

Keeran, Roger. *The Communist Party and the Auto Workers' Unions*. 1980. Reprint, New York: International Publishers, 1986.

Kling, Rob, Spencer Olin, and Mark Poster, eds. *Postmodern California: The Transformation of Orange County since World War II*. Berkeley: University of California Press, 1991.

Kornhauser, William. *The Politics of Mass Society*. New York: Free Press, 1959.

Kraditor, Aileen S. *The Ideas of the Woman Suffrage Movement, 1890–1920*. New York: Columbia University Press, 1965. Reprint, New York: W. W. Norton, 1981.

Kulikoff, Allan. "The Transition to Capitalism in Rural America." *William and Mary Quarterly*, 3d series, 46 (January 1989): 120–44.

Kwartler, Michael. "Legislating Aesthetics: The Role of Zoning in Designing Cities." In *Zoning and the American Dream: Promises Still to Keep*, ed. Charles M. Haar and Jerome S. Kayden. Chicago: Planners Press, 1989.

LaDuke, Winona. "Foreword." In Al Gedicks, *The News Resource Wars: Native and Environmental Struggles against Multinational Corporations*. Boston: South End Press, 1993.

Lenin, V. I. *What Is to Be Done? Burning Questions of Our Movement*. Peking: Foreign Languages Press, 1975.

Lo, Clarence Y. H. *Small Property versus Big Government: The Social Origins of the Property Tax Revolt*. Berkeley: University of California Press, 1990.

Lofland, John. *Social Movement Organizations: Guide to Research on Insurgent Realities*. New York: Aldine de Gruyter, 1996.

Logan, John R., and Harvey Molotch. *Urban Fortunes: The Political Economy of Place*. Berkeley: University of California Press, 1987.

Logan, John R., and Min Zhou. "Do Suburban Growth Controls Control Growth?" *American Sociological Review* 54 (1989): 461–71.

Lotchin, Roger W. *Fortress California, 1910–1961: From Warfare to Welfare*. New York: Oxford University Press, 1992.

Marshall, Harvey. "White Flight to the Suburbs." *American Sociological Review* 44 (1979): 975–94.

Marx, Karl. *Capital: A Critique of Political Economy*. 3 vols. New York: International Publishers, 1967.

———. "Critique of the Gotha Program." In *The Marx-Engels Reader*, 2d edition, ed. Robert C. Tucker. 1872. Reprint, New York: W. W. Norton, 1978.

———. *The Economic and Philosophic Manuscripts of 1844*. New York: International Publishers, 1964.

———. "The Eighteenth Brumaire of Louis Bonaparte." In *The Marx-Engels Reader*, 2d edition, ed. Robert C. Tucker. 1850. Reprint, New York: W. W. Norton, 1978.

———. "Introduction to a Critique of Political Economy." In *The German Ideology*, ed. C. J. Arthur. New York: International Publishers, 1970.

Marx, Karl, and Frederick Engels. "The German Ideology," in *The German Ideology*, ed. C. J. Arthur. New York: International Publishers, 1970.

———. "Preface to the Russian Edition of 1882, Manifesto of the Communist Party." In *The Marx-Engels Reader*, 2d edition, ed. Robert C. Tucker. New York: W. W. Norton, 1978.

McAdam, Doug. "Gender As a Mediator of the Activist Experience: The Case of Freedom Summer." *American Journal of Sociology* 97 (1992): 1211–40.

———. *Political Process and the Development of Black Insurgency, 1930–1970*. Chicago: University of Chicago Press, 1982.

McCarthy, John D., and Mark Wolfson. "Consensus Movements, Conflict Movements, and the Cooptation of Civic and State Structures." In *Frontiers in Social Movement Theory*, ed. Aldon D. Morris and Carol McClurg Mueller. New Haven, Conn.: Yale University Press, 1992.

McCutchen, Doyle, Brown & Enersen. "Shaping Future Development in a Slow-Growth Era: A McCutchen Land Use Seminar." San Francisco: McCutchen, Doyle, Brown & Enersen, 1989.

Melucci, Alberto. "The New Social Movements: A Theoretical Approach." *Social Science Information* 19 (1980): 199–226.

Merton, Robert. *Social Theory and Social Structure*. New York: Free Press, 1957.

Miller, Zane L. "Pluralism, Chicago School Style: Louis Wirth, the Ghetto, the City, and

Integration." *Journal of Urban History* 18 (May 1992): 251–79.

Miller, Zane L., and Bruce Tucker. *Changing Plans for America's Inner Cities: Cincinnati's Over-the-Rhine and Twentieth-Century Urbanism.* Columbus: Ohio State University Press, 1998.

Mills, C. Wright. *The Power Elite.* New York: Oxford University Press, 1956.

Molotch, Harvey. "The City as a Growth Machine." *American Journal of Sociology* 82 (1976): 309–32.

Molotch, Harvey, William Freudenberg, and Krista E. Paulsen. "History Repeats Itself, but How? City Character, Urban Tradition, and the Accomplishment of Place." *American Sociological Review* 65 (2000): 791–823.

Molotch, Harvey, and John R. Logan. "Tensions in the Growth Machine: Overcoming Resistance to Value-Free Development." *Social Problems* 31 (1984): 483–99.

Morris, Aldon. *The Origins of the Civil Rights Movement.* New York: Free Press, 1984.

Morris, Aldon D., and Carol McClurg Mueller, eds. *Frontiers in Social Movement Theory.* New Haven, Conn.: Yale University Press, 1992.

Nolen, John. *San Diego: A Comprehensive Plan for Its Improvement.* Boston: George H. Ellis and Company, 1908. Cited in Abraham J. Shragge, "Boosters and Bluejackets: The Civic Culture of Militarism in San Diego, California, 1900–1945." Ph.D. diss., University of California, San Diego, 1998.

O'Connor, James. *Accumulation Crisis.* New York: Basil Blackwell, 1984.

Olson, Mancur. *The Logic of Collective Action.* Cambridge, Mass.: Harvard University Press, 1965.

Olson, Todd G., and Dennis M. Moser. "The Habitat Transaction Method of Conservation Planning, Land Acquisition, and Funding." Unpublished discussion draft, May 27, 1992.

Pfeffer, Max J., and Mark B. Lapping. "Farmland Preservation, Development Rights, and the Theory of the Growth Machine: The Views of Planners." *Journal of Rural Studies* 10, no. 3 (1994): 233–48.

Plotkin, Sidney. *Keep Out: The Struggle for Land Use Control.* Berkeley: University of California Press, 1987.

Popper, Frank J. "When the Development is a LULU." *Re:Sources* (spring/summer 1981): 14–15.

Potter, Harry. "Precursors of Ecopopulism." Paper presented at the American Sociological Association meeting, New York, 1996.

Pourade, Richard. *History of San Diego.* 7 vols. San Diego: Union-Tribune Publishing, 1960–1977.

Pryde, Phillip R., ed. *San Diego: An Introduction to the Region, An Historical Geography of the Natural Environments and Human Development of San Diego County.* Dubuque, Iowa: Kendall/Hunt, 1976.

Reilly, William K., ed. *The Use of Land: A Citizen's Policy Guide to Urban Growth: A Task Force Report Sponsored by the Rockefeller Brothers Fund.* New York: Thomas Y. Crowell, 1973.

Remy, Michael H., Tina A. Thomas, and James G. Moose. *Guide to the California Environmental Quality Act (CEQA).* Point Arena, Calif.: Solano Press, 1991.

Reps, John W. *The Making of Urban America: A History of City Planning in the United States.* Princeton, N.J.: Princeton University Press, 1965.

Rudel, Thomas K. *Situations and Strategies in American Land-Use Planning.* New York: Cambridge University Press, 1989.

Ruth, Thomas. "Lectures in California Politics." Unpublished course lectures, Grossmont Community College, El Cajon, Calif., 1970.

Sabatier, Paul, and Daniel Mazmamian. "Regulating Coastal Land Use in California, 1973–1975." *Policy Studies Journal* 11, no. 1 (1982): 88–102.

San Diego Association of Governments (SANDAG). "Housing Needs (Growth) Statement Summary," Agenda Report R-20. San Diego, September 21, 1981.

———. "Preliminary 2020 Cities/Counties Forecast—Technical Update," Board of Directors Agenda Report 99-2-7. San Diego, 1999.

———. "Protecting Region's Quality of Life Is Growth Strategy Aim." *Association News* (spring/summer 1991).

———. Regional Housing Needs Statement, Agenda Report R-36. San Diego, November 16, 1981.

———. Regional Housing Needs Statement, Agenda Report R-6. San Diego, January 17, 1984.

———. *Regional Housing Needs Statement: San Diego Region.* San Diego: Source Point, 1990.

Schiesl, Laura Ann. "Problems in Paradise: Citizen Activism and Rapid Growth in San Diego, 1970–1990." Senior honor's thesis, San Diego State University, Department of History, 1999.

Schlesinger, Arthur M., Jr. *The Almanac of American History.* New York: G. P. Putnam's Sons, 1983.

Schwartz, Michael. *Radical Protest and Social Structure: The Southern Farmers' Alliance and Cotton Tenancy, 1880–1890.* New York: Academic Press, 1976. Reprint, Chicago: University of Chicago Press, 1988.

Schwartz, Michael, and Shuva Paul. "Resource Mobilization versus the Mobilization of People: Why Consensus Movements Cannot Be Instruments of Social Change." In *Frontiers in Social Movement Theory,* ed. Aldon D. Morris and Carol McClurg Mueller. New Haven, Conn.: Yale University Press, 1992.

Shakespeare, William. *Hamlet.* In *The Riverside Shakespeare.* Boston: Houghton Mifflin, 1974.

Shragge, Abraham, J. "Boosters and Bluejackets: The Civic Culture of Militarism in San Diego, California, 1900–1945." Ph.D. diss., University of California, San Diego, 1998.

———. "'A New Federal City': San Diego during World War II." *Pacific Historical Review* 63 (1994): 333–61.

Smiley, Jerome. *History of Denver.* Denver: Old Americana, 1901.

Smith, Andrew A., Margaret A. Moote, and Cecil R. Schwalbe. "The Endangered Species Act at Twenty: An Analytical Survey of Federal Endangered Species Protection." *Natural Resources Journal* 33 (1993): 1027–75.

Stahura, John. "Suburban Status Evolution/Persistence." *American Sociological Review* 44 (1979): 937–47.

Starr, Raymond G. *San Diego: A Pictorial History.* Norfolk, Va.: Donning, 1986.

Stutz, Frederick P. "Communities and Towns of San Diego County." In *San Diego: An Introduction to the Region, An Historical Geography of the Natural Environments and Human Development of San Diego County,* ed. Philip R. Pryde. Dubuque, Iowa: Kendall/Hunt, 1976.

Szasz, Andrew. *EcoPopulism: Toxic Waste and the Movement for Environmental Justice.* Minneapolis: University of Minnesota Press, 1994.

Targ, Harry. *Strategy of an Empire in Decline.* Minneapolis: MEP, 1986.

Tarrow, Sidney. *Power in Movement: Social Movements, Collective Action, and Politics.* New York: Cambridge University Press, 1994.

Taylor, Verta. "Social Movement Continuity: The Women's Movement in Abeyance." *American Sociological Review* 54 (1989): 761–75.

Teaford, Jon C. *City and Suburb: The Political Fragmentation of Metropolitan America, 1850–1970*. Baltimore, Md.: Johns Hopkins University Press, 1979.

———. *Post-Suburbia: Government and Politics in the Edge Cities*. Baltimore, Md.: Johns Hopkins University Press, 1997.

———. *The Unheralded Triumph: City Government in America, 1870–1900*. Baltimore, Md.: Johns Hopkins University Press, 1984.

Tilly, Charles. *The Contentious French: Four Centuries of Popular Struggle*. Cambridge, Mass.: Harvard University Press, 1986.

———. *From Mobilization to Revolution*. Reading, Mass.: Addison-Wesley, 1978.

———. *The Vendee*. 1964. Reprint, Cambridge, Mass.: Harvard University Press, 1976.

Tocqueville, Alexis de. *Democracy in America,* edited and abridged by Richard D. Heffner. New York: Mentor, 1956.

U.S. Census Bureau. *County and City Data Book*. Washington, D.C.: U.S. Government Printing Office, 1949–1994.

———. "Housing Authorized by Building Permits and Public Contracts" (Series C-40). Washington, D.C.: U.S. Government Printing Office, 1968–1995.

———. "New Privately Owned Residential Construction Reports" (Series C-21). Washington, D.C.: U.S. Government Printing Office, 1978–1994.

———. "U.S.A. County Statistics" (on CD-ROM). Washington, D.C.: U.S. Department of Commerce, 1990.

U.S. Small Business Administration, Office of Advocacy. "Developing High-Technology Communities: San Diego." Reston, Va.: Innovation Associates, 2000.

Van Hoy, Jerry. *Franchise Law Firms and the Transformation of Personal Legal Services* Westport, Conn.: Quorum, 1997.

Weber, Max. *Economy and Society: An Outline of Interpretive Sociology,* ed. Guenther Roth and Claus Wittich. 1956. Reprint, Berkeley: University of California Press, 1978.

———. *The Protestant Ethic and the Spirit of Capitalism*. 1958. Reprint, New York: Charles Scribner's Sons, 1976.

Whyte, William Foote. *Street Corner Society: The Social Structure of an Italian Slum*. 1943. Reprint, Chicago: University of Chicago Press, 1981.

Wiebe, Robert H. *Businessmen and Reform: A Study of the Progressive Movement*. Cambridge, Mass.: Harvard University Press, 1962. Reprint, Chicago: Ivan R. Dee, 1989.

Williams, Robert A., Jr. "Euclid's Lochnerian Legacy." In *Zoning and the American Dream: Promises Still to Keep,* ed. Charles M. Haar and Jerome S. Kayden. Chicago: Planners Press, 1989.

Williams, Vernon J., Jr. *From a Caste to a Minority: Changing Attitudes of American Sociologists toward Afro-Americans, 1896–1945*. New York: Greenwood, 1989.

Wolf, Michael Allan. "Accommodating Tensions in the Coastal Zone: An Introduction and Overview." *Natural Resources Journal* 25 (January 1985): 7–19.

Wolman, Harold. "Cross-National Comparisons of Urban Economic Programmes: Is Policy Transfer Possible?" In *Community Economic Development: Policy Formation in the U.S. and U.K.,* ed. David Fasenfest. New York: Macmillan, 1993.

Yaffee, Steven L. "Lessons about Leadership from the History of the Spotted Owl Controversy." *Natural Resources Journal* 35, no. 2 (1995): 381–412.

Zolberg, Aristide R. "Moments of Madness." *Politics and Society* 2 (1972): 183–207.

Index

Plague of Strangers: Social Groups and the Origins of City Services in Cincinnati, 1819–1870
Alan I. Marcus

Visions of Place: The City, Neighborhoods, Suburbs, and Cincinnati's Clifton, 1850–2000
Zane L. Miller

Boss Cox's Cincinnati: Urban Politics in the Progressive Era
Zane L. Miller

Changing Plans for America's Inner Cities: Cincinnati's Over-the-Rhine and Twentieth-Century Urbanism
Zane L. Miller and Bruce Tucker

Polish Immigrants and Industrial Chicago: Workers on the South Side, 1880–1922
Dominic A. Pacyga

The Rise of the City, 1878–1898
Arthur Meier Schlesinger

The New York Approach: Robert Moses, Urban Liberals, and Redevelopment of the Inner City
Joel Schwartz

Designing Modern America: The Regional Planning Association and Its Members
Edward K. Spann

Hopedale: From Commune to Company Town, 1840–1920
Edward K. Spann

Visions of Eden: Environmentalism, Urban Planning, and City Building in St. Petersburg, Florida, 1900–1995
R. Bruce Stephenson

Welcome to Heights High: The Crippling Politics of Restructuring America's Public Schools
Diana Tittle

Washing "The Great Unwashed": Public Baths in Urban America, 1840–1920
Marilyn Thornton Williams